200 Devotionals from the Hebrew Bible

200 Devotionals from the Hebrew Bible

Hélène M. Dallaire

RESOURCE *Publications* • Eugene, Oregon

200 DEVOTIONALS FROM THE HEBREW BIBLE

Copyright © 2020 Hélène M. Dallaire. All rights reserved. Except for brief quotations in critical publications or reviews, no part of this book may be reproduced in any manner without prior written permission from the publisher. Write: Permissions, Wipf and Stock Publishers, 199 W. 8th Ave., Suite 3, Eugene, OR 97401.

Resource Publications
An Imprint of Wipf and Stock Publishers
199 W. 8th Ave., Suite 3
Eugene, OR 97401

www.wipfandstock.com

PAPERBACK ISBN: 978-1-62564-432-9
HARDCOVER ISBN: 978-1-4982-8546-9
EBOOK ISBN: 978-1-7252-4898-4

Manufactured in the U.S.A.   05/27/20

Preface

O THAT SEMINARIANS AND scholars would continue to enjoy the Hebrew Bible after their initial language training. For most students, biblical languages—Hebrew, Aramaic, Greek—become tools of exegesis for teaching and preaching only. But for some, the Hebrew Bible continues to feed their soul with nuggets of wisdom often absent in modern English translations. The precious treasures revealed in the Hebrew Scriptures serve as building blocks for personal theology. In the words of Heinrich Bitzer,

> The more a theologian detaches himself from the basic Hebrew and Greek text of Holy Scriptures, the more he detaches himself from the source of real theology! And real theology is the foundation of a fruitful and blessed ministry.[1]

Indeed, personal theology—one based on Scripture (hopefully in the original languages), one that forms the foundation of faith in God—comes first. Only after a solid foundation is established can one teach and preach a message that reflects the character and nature of God.

It has always been my desire to see students enjoy the richness of Hebrew for more than academic purposes. For this reason, I decided to ask students from some of my Advanced Hebrew Exegesis class to study the Hebrew text for devotional purposes. With this in mind, I designed the following exercise and asked students to:

1. Choose *a verse or two* from the Hebrew Bible (different book for each devotional)
2. *Translate* the verse(s)
3. Comment on the *biblical context* in which the passage appears
4. Provide a brief note on *life application*
5. Suggest *New Testament passages* for supplementary reading
6. Analyze the *verbs* in the Hebrew text
7. Write a *prayer* based on the theme of the devotional

---

1. Heinrich Bitzer, ed., *Light on the Path* (Grand Rapids: Baker, 1969), 1:10.

I have been deeply enriched by the students' thoughtful examination of Hebrew passages and by their rich comments. For the purpose of this book, I have removed the parsing of the Hebrew verbs and replaced it with a brief prayer and space for readers to write their own personal reflections. I encourage those who delve into this devotional to read the entire context and go beyond the verse(s) highlighted in the devotional.

I wish to thank all the contributors for their thorough reflections on the texts, and for sharing their theological discoveries and personal experiences with the readers. I am convinced that these devotionals will bless all who read them and will provide an opportunity for readers to appreciate these passages through a fresh lens.

Hélène M. Dallaire, PhD
Earl S. Kalland Professor of
Old Testament and Semitic Languages
Denver Seminary

Contributors

Hélène Dallaire, Ph.D.   *Earl S. Kalland Professor of Old Testament and Semitic Languages, author and editor*

Anna Barnett	MA/OT	Megan Joranstaad	MA/OT
Brandon Benziger	MA/OT	Alisha Keim	MA/OT
Amy Borjas	MA/OT	Christopher Kendrick	MA/OT
Shawn Bowen	MA/OT	Bryan Lee	MA/OT
Brandon Brackett	MDiv/MJ	Ryan Le	MA/OT
Micah Brewster	MA/OT	Jonathan LeJeune	MDiv
Deirdre Brouer	MA/OT	Amy McConnell	MA/OT
Linda Brown	MA/OT	Michelle McCorkle	MA/OT
Adrian Clifton	MA/OT	Peggy McIntyre	MA/OT &NT
Kaila Coon	MA/OT	Chris Montgomery	MA/OT
Stephanie Cooper	MA/OT	Denise Morris	MA/OT
Eliot Corwin	MA/OT	Nancy Nelson	MA/OT
Megan Crandall	MDiv/MJ	Meredith Newmaker	MA/OT
Julie Dykes	MA/OT & NT	Jeffrey R. Oetter	MA/OT
Steven Faulkner	MA/OT	Renee Overstreet	MA/OT
Robert Flood	MDiv	Don Prismon	MDiv
Ryan Florer-Smith	MA/OT & NT	Matthew Proctor	MDiv
Kevin Foth	MA/OT	Kelly Parker	MA/OT
Steve Franka	Non-degree	Nathan Scherrer	MA/OT
Steve Griffin	MA/OT	Darlene Seal	MA/NT
Saikrishna Gomatam	MA/NT	Bong Shin Bae	MA/OT
Kaylee Gosselin	MA/OT	Siobhan Siu	MA/OT
Jonathan Groce	MA/OT	Jacki Soister	MA/OT
Kendra Hendrick	MA/OT	Eli Spector	MA/OT
Laure Hittle	MA/OT	J. Ed Tomlinson	Non-degree
Matthew Hollomon	MA/OT	Kayla White	MA/OT
Andrew Jones	MA/CS		

Genesis 1:3

וַיֹּאמֶר אֱלֹהִים יְהִי אוֹר וַיְהִי־אוֹר׃

And God said, "Let light be!" And light was.

Biblical Context

IN THE FIRST PART of the creation story of Genesis 1, we find God in the midst of his creation, commanding order out of the chaos. What is intriguing in this verse and in the following verses is the jussive use of the verb הָיָה "to be." God could order the chaos to obey without using an imperative. Instead, God willed each act of creation to be, and by his authority, it obeyed. Even more intriguing is the lack of central location for the light. Modern translations add the word *there* to smooth out the English. But inserting *there* positions the light and makes a theological statement. As sun, moon, and stars do not yet appear in the narrative, this seems to be a declaration that the light which God created existed in ways unknowable to humankind. It continues to exist in ways that are beyond our modern scientific view of light. Now we know that light exists both as a wave and as substance. In the ancient Near East, it came from a god. In ancient Israel, it existed. From creation's beginning, where there was no darkness, light existed. And mankind cannot even hide in the shadows of darkness; according to Psalm 139, "even the darkness is not too dark for you to see, and the night is as bright as day; darkness and light are the same to you" (v. 12; NET).

Life Application

By inserting *there* in "Let there be light," modern translations make the theological statement that the light was in one specific location for one purpose. I hated the darkness growing up. I thought there were monsters under my bed and that they were most active at nighttime when the light was away. But God calls us to walk in lightened locations, where the word already exists, and also in darkened locations, where mavericks seek out the lost and bring them to salvation. Jesus spoke incredible words of encouragement in John 8:12 by telling us that we will never walk without the Light. "Then Jesus spoke out again, 'I am the light of the world. The one who follows me will never walk in darkness, but will have the light of life'" (NET). How would we live differently if we remembered that Jesus gives us light when we walk in darkness? Would we choose to leave the darkness for a known fortress of light or would we continue forward into that darkness knowing we have Light and are lights for Him?

NT Scriptures

John 8:12

Prayer

O Light of the World, your light permeates the chaos of life around us. Even in our darkest times, help us to remember that we carry your light. As we shine, help us to declare the Light, which You are, for all the world to see. O Light, please let light shine in our lives!

Personal Notes and Prayers

Genesis 1:26–27

וַיֹּאמֶר אֱלֹהִים נַעֲשֶׂה אָדָם בְּצַלְמֵנוּ כִּדְמוּתֵנוּ וְיִרְדּוּ בִדְגַת הַיָּם
וּבְעוֹף הַשָּׁמַיִם וּבַבְּהֵמָה וּבְכָל־הָאָרֶץ וּבְכָל־הָרֶמֶשׂ
הָרֹמֵשׂ עַל־הָאָרֶץ: וַיִּבְרָא אֱלֹהִים אֶת־הָאָדָם בְּצַלְמוֹ בְּצֶלֶם אֱלֹהִים
בָּרָא אֹתוֹ זָכָר וּנְקֵבָה בָּרָא אֹתָם:

God said, "Let us make mankind in our image and according to our likeness. Let them rule over the fish of the sea, the birds of the heavens, the livestock, all the land and every creeping thing that creeps on the earth. So God created mankind in his image, in the image of God he created him, male and female he created them."

Biblical Context

GOD FINISHED CREATING THE world in six days. He brought order out of chaos and created life in all its splendor and diversity. The final act of creation described in this passage differs from earlier acts. God declares that this last created being would be made in the image and likeness of God himself. The Hebrew word צֶלֶם is translated "image." The word is rarely used and its origins are uncertain, possibly from an Arabic word that means "to cut" or a word found in both Akkadian and Arabic that means "to become dark." Thus, scholars have posited a variety of meanings: physical resemblance, dualistic nature, representative of the divine. Here it is set in parallel to דְמוּת, a word that clearly means "to be like," an indication that, at least here, the two words round out the idea that mankind was made by God and for God, in some manner as a representative on the created earth of the divine being in uncreation.

Life Application

When people ask me about verses demonstrating God's great love, these two verses always come to mind. Jesus said that the greatest love a human can show is to die for friends and to love enemies. But here, at the very beginning of time, God manifests his love. Out of a motivation that is beyond human understanding, without a need to be met or a void to be filled, God chose to create humankind to be a reflection of himself. Even knowing that this created being would find it very hard to love in return. He would disobey, reject, forget, and revile his own creator. He would spurn the love offered to him by the very source of his existence. Even knowing that in the end, the disobedience and broken relationship would require a sacrifice that our human minds can only barely begin to fathom; even knowing that God himself would have to suffer and die in exchange for the privilege of creating and loving this being created in his image; even knowing the immense cost and pain, God chose to create humankind. Knowing the cost, *he did it anyway*. In John 13:34–35, Jesus commands his disciples to love as he had loved, a command that, when obeyed, reveals God to the world. Let us love as God has loved us. Let us count the cost, and then love anyway.

NT Scriptures

John 15:12–17; 1 John 4:7–12

Prayer

O LORD, what an amazing example of love you have displayed, giving your own life for us—your created beings—knowing full well that we would not appreciate your sacrifice, and fail to reflect in the world who you really are. Have mercy on us and teach us to love as you love us.

Personal Notes and Prayers

Genesis 1:27

וַיִּבְרָא אֱלֹהִים אֶת־הָאָדָם בְּצַלְמוֹ בְּצֶלֶם אֱלֹהִים בָּרָא אֹתוֹ זָכָר וּנְקֵבָה בָּרָא אֹתָם:

So God created humankind in his image. In the image of God, he created him. Male and female he created them.

Biblical Context

BEFORE RESTING FROM HIS extraordinary creative acts, God forms mankind in his own image and his own likeness. Scholars have noted a parallel between this creation narrative and the image of gods in ancient Near Eastern cultures. It was believed that a god came to "rest" and inhabited its temple only after an image or likeness of that god was placed at the center of the cultic area. The temple was not functional without this likeness in its proper place, as it represented the god's authority and power. Was the creation account in Genesis meant to convey the counter-cultural idea that the temple of Israel's God is, in fact, all of creation? Further, is humankind the very representation of God's authority, power and likeness in all of creation? It is possible that the biblical creation narrative implied that creation could not function as intended without us—the beings God created in his own image.

Life Application

What would the impact on our day-to-day life be if we were to internalize the truths contained in Genesis 1:27? When we pass someone on a sidewalk, when we are stuck in traffic, when we are told that we are about to lose our job? What if we were to recognize in those moments that the person into whose eyes we are staring embodies the image of the God of all creation? In reality, each person we see, whether in passing or at length, is intended to be an ambassador for God and creation literally cannot function as intended without him or her. How quick we might be to extend grace, to refrain from judging and criticizing if we were to recognize the image of God in those around us? How much more compassionate would we be in our efforts to evangelize? How increasingly motivated we might be to meet the need of the poor, the hurting and the downtrodden.

NT Scriptures

2 Corinthians 3:18

Prayer

O LORD, your image is everywhere around us, in our brothers and sisters, in our friends and acquaintances, and even in our enemies. Help us recognize your presence in this world. Help us remind one another that you are in us, and desire to be reflected through us every day of our lives. O Holy Spirit, please remind us of these truths.

Personal Notes and Prayers

Genesis 5:24

וַיִּתְהַלֵּךְ חֲנוֹךְ אֶת־הָאֱלֹהִים וְאֵינֶנּוּ כִּי־לָקַח אֹתוֹ אֱלֹהִים׃

*Enoch walked [intimately] with God,
and then he was not, for God took him.*

Biblical Context

IMMEDIATELY BEFORE THE FLOOD narrative, the reader encounters a seemingly unimportant character named Enoch, who is said to have *walked* (וַיִּתְהַלֵּךְ) *with God* until God took him (presumably) into heaven (vv. 22, 24). During this time, life expectancy ranged from 800 to 1,000 years. Enoch lived on earth for a relatively short period of time—only 365 years—before he was taken from the earth. The verb הָלַךְ ("to walk") appears here in the Hithpael as it does in Genesis 3:8, where Adam and Eve hear the voice of God in the Garden of Eden. In these two texts, the Hithpael indicates a motion to-and-fro and here-and-there, a habitual action and a consistency in behavior. In the Garden of Eden (3:8), the voice of God could be heard coming from all directions at the same time. In our passage (5:24), the verb implies that Enoch *walked with God* habitually and consistently wherever he went, moving about here-and-there in the presence of the LORD for his entire life. According to the writer of Hebrews, Enoch—who is mentioned only in passing in the Old Testament—was a man of faith who pleased God, believed in him and sought him all the days of his life (Heb 11:5; cf. Sir 44:16). And for this reason, God noticed him and took him. The only other biblical character who is taken into heaven without experiencing death is Elijah (2 Kgs 2:1–14). In the case of Elijah, there are several chapters devoted to his life while only four verses are attributed to Enoch. Nonetheless, both men were considered righteous and had an intimate relationship with God.

Life Application

The story of these two men testifies that God notices those who *walk with him* habitually, who seek him and believe in him, no matter how long they have lived on the earth. God is looking for people who are unswerving in their commitment to him, who *walk with him* with consistency and steadfastness, and model an unshakable relationship with him. The world in which we live bombards us with temptations to deviate from the path and to compromise in our *walk with God*. God calls us to be single-minded and to establish him as the center of our lives as we journey through life.

NT Scriptures

Hebrews 11:5; Jude 14

Prayer

O LORD, as your eyes are on the sparrow so are your eyes on us, watching us, keeping us, noticing us and guiding us. All things are open and naked before you. You know our thoughts and our deeds. And you reward us according to our commitment to you. Help us be consistent in our walk with you. Help us keep you as the apple of our eyes.

Personal Notes and Prayers

Genesis 11:4

וַיֹּאמְרוּ הָבָה נִבְנֶה־לָּנוּ עִיר וּמִגְדָּל וְרֹאשׁוֹ בַשָּׁמַיִם וְנַעֲשֶׂה־לָּנוּ שֵׁם פֶּן־נָפוּץ עַל־פְּנֵי כָל־הָאָרֶץ׃

Then they said, "Come, let us build for ourselves a city and a tower with its top in the heavens, so we may make a name for ourselves. Otherwise, we will be scattered upon the face of all the earth."

Biblical Context

THE ACCOUNT OF THE tower of Babel (Gen 11:1–9) follows immediately after the flood narrative (Gen 6–9). As the story reveals, the motivation of the builders was selfish. Their aim was to build a tower *for themselves*, so *they* could make a name for *themselves*. At that time, the people spoke one language and their common speech gave them unlimited ability to accomplish great things. Unfortunately, their motivation for building a city and a tower displayed a high level of arrogance towards God. The building plan was about *them* and had not received divine approval. One wonders why Noah's descendants would turn away from God so quickly after God had judged them harshly for their arrogance and wickedness. The answer is clear—man is sinful, selfish, prideful, and definitely forgetful.

Life Application

How quickly we forget God, the Creator of heaven and earth. After I became a Christian, I was committed to God and sought after him with every fiber of my being. However, over the years, my commitment to him waned. Feeling over confident and pursuing my own selfish ambitions, I left God in the dust and chased after other gods. Consequently, I experienced difficult times, and only then did I cry out to God for help and begged him to deliver me from my troubles. I cannot count the number of times I convinced myself to do something even though I knew I should not do it. I have often fallen into the trap of selfishness and pride, and pursued the evil desires prompted by my sinful nature. The account of the tower of Babel reminds me of my foolishness as a human, to think that I can reach the lofty places of God in my own feeble strength. No matter how strong we think we are, we are all in desperate need of God's love, mercy, grace, forgiveness, strength and compassion. We need to humble ourselves before God every day lest we pursue lofty goals out of arrogance and pride, and invite judgment into our lives.

NT Scriptures

John 15:5; Philippians 2:3; Colossians 3:17

Prayer

O LORD, how quickly we forget that You are the Creator of heaven and earth, that you are seated on the throne, that you are in control of all things and that you love us with an everlasting love. LORD, help us humble ourselves before you every day of our short lives on earth.

Personal Notes and Prayers

Genesis 11:4–5

וַיֹּאמְרוּ הָבָה נִבְנֶה־לָּנוּ עִיר וּמִגְדָּל וְרֹאשׁוֹ בַשָּׁמַיִם וְנַעֲשֶׂה־לָּנוּ שֵׁם פֶּן־נָפוּץ עַל־פְּנֵי כָל־הָאָרֶץ׃

וַיֵּרֶד יְהוָֹה לִרְאֹת אֶת־הָעִיר וְאֶת־הַמִּגְדָּל אֲשֶׁר בָּנוּ בְּנֵי הָאָדָם׃

Then they said, "Come, let us build for ourselves a city and a tower whose top is in the heavens. Let us make for ourselves a name, lest we be scattered over the face of the whole earth." But YHWH came down to see the city and the tower that the sons of man had built.

Biblical Context

THESE EARLY HUMANS ARRIVED on the plains of Shinar, commonly understood as Sumer of Mesopotamia. Those who arrived in this region quickly learned about the lack of natural stone for building material. Thus, the text explains the development of oven-fired brick and bitumen-based mortar that matches archeological findings of this kind in Mesopotamia. The labor and cost of building in these new methods lends to a specific understanding of what this "city" and "tower" were to these settlers. The municipal function of these cities meant that the buildings within were primarily public complexes while the average citizen lived outside of the city. Most important in the city was the central temple, often associated with its patron deity. While the Hebrew reads a generic word for tower (מִגְדָּל), often used to describe defensive fortresses in Israelite cities, the city in our passage is not Israelite but Mesopotamian. In this century the most prominent structure in Mesopotamian cities is the ziggurat—a stepped tower commonly described in ANE literature as having its "head in the heavens" and often found adjacent to the city temple. At its top, the gateway of heaven welcomed the gods to rest and afterwards, travel conveniently down the steps and into the city's temple. Moreover, the Akkadian equivalent of the Hebrew understands the title "Babel" as "the gate of god." Because the function of the ziggurat brought easy travel for the gods, it was deemed holy as it was rarely if ever approached by people.

Instead, the god's presence in the city's temple brought prosperity and protection for all the members of the region. In this way, we may recognize that the tower of Babel served not to gain humans access to the heavens but to bring gods down into their midst.

Life Application

How often do we find ourselves attempting to set heaven on earth in our own lives? In the age after the great flood, the sons of Noah attempt to restore a quasi-garden of Eden by building a full temple complex. Why? The story is motivated by fear, the fear of being scattered throughout the earth. Yet the character of God differs from the gods of the ANE in that He is not tied to any one place, but intends to be present with all peoples across the earth (Gen 9:7). God looks on their work and sees how capable they are at accomplishing what they want (i.e., control of their own destinies) their own "name." Certainly we can sympathize with the desire for security, unity, and the fear of prior mistakes. But to manipulate God's presence to provide for our own interests ignores his intent for our lives and may very well bring us to the very end we were trying to avoid.

NT Scriptures

Matthew 23:12; Luke 18:14; James 4:6

Prayer

Living God, give to me, or take from me. Let me henceforth no longer desire health or life except to spend it on you and in you. Take, LORD, and receive all my liberty, memory, understanding, will, and all I possess. To you I return it. All is yours, dispose of it wholly according to your will. Give me grace, for your will is sufficient for me. Amen.

Personal Notes and Prayers

Genesis 11:31

וַיִּקַּח תֶּרַח אֶת־אַבְרָם בְּנוֹ וְאֶת־לוֹט בֶּן־הָרָן בֶּן־בְּנוֹ וְאֵת שָׂרַי כַּלָּתוֹ
אֵשֶׁת אַבְרָם בְּנוֹ וַיֵּצְאוּ אִתָּם מֵאוּר כַּשְׂדִּים לָלֶכֶת אַרְצָה כְּנַעַן
וַיָּבֹאוּ עַד־חָרָן וַיֵּשְׁבוּ שָׁם׃

Terah took his son Abram, Lot the son of Haran, his son's son, and Sarai his daughter-in-law, the wife of his son Abram. They set out from Ur of the Chaldeans to go to the land of Canaan. When they came to Haran, they settled there.

Biblical Context

BIBLE READERS ARE FAMILIAR with the call of Abram and his willingness to leave his country in obedience to the LORD (Gen 12:1–9). A detail tucked away in the preceding chapter reveals that Abram's father, Terah, had left Ur of the Chaldeans and was headed for Canaan with his family when he decided to stop in Haran. Although we are not told why he did so, we can speculate that Terah may have heard a call from the LORD similar to that of Abram before leaving Ur. It is also possible that Terah left Ur without receiving a divine call and headed for Canaan simply to provide a better life for his family. But how would he have known that Canaan was a better place without divine revelation? According to the story, Terah dies in Haran, the place where Abram eventually receives his call. In reality, Abram continues a journey originally begun by his father, a journey that would bring him to the very land God promised to give to him and to his descendants. In the covenant ceremony in Genesis 15:7, Abram is directly connected with Ur of the Chaldeans (not Haran). This information may confirm that Terah is the one who originally received the call to find the Promised Land, a call that was eventually fulfilled by Abram.

Life Application

Terah no doubt cared for his children very much and wanted nothing but the best for them. I know that as a parent I want my children to be where God wants them to be, to be more intimate with God than I am, and to go further with Him than I ever could. Perhaps if I set them on the right path (as Terah did for Abram), they will continue to follow the voice of God and fulfill his call in ways that are beyond anything I can imagine. For this I pray.

NT Scriptures

Ephesians 6:1–4

Prayer

O LORD, you orchestrate the journey of our lives. Your Word is a lamp for our feet and light on our path. Help us follow you as you enlighten every step of the way. Help us journey through life with you until your will is done, to your glory and honor. May we incite others to join us as we journey towards the heavenly Promised Land.

Personal Notes and Prayers

Genesis 15:1

אַחַ֣ר ׀ הַדְּבָרִ֣ים הָאֵ֗לֶּה הָיָ֤ה דְבַר־יְהוָה֙ אֶל־אַבְרָ֔ם בַּֽמַּחֲזֶ֖ה לֵאמֹ֑ר
אַל־תִּירָ֣א אַבְרָ֗ם אָנֹכִי֙ מָגֵ֣ן לָ֔ךְ שְׂכָרְךָ֖ הַרְבֵּ֥ה מְאֹֽד׃

After these things, the word of the LORD came to Abram in a vision saying "Do not fear Abram, I am a shield to you, your exceedingly great reward."

Biblical Context

THE STORY OF ABRAM starts with a divine calling in which God tells Abram to go to a new land He will show him. God promises to Abram that in this new land, he will bless him with riches and descendants. In Genesis 13:13–17, God shows Abram the Promised Land. During a conflict between rulers from the region of Sodom and Gomorrah, Abram's nephew Lot is taken captive. Abram comes to the rescue and frees Lot and the other detainees from captivity. Before heading back, the king of Sodom offers Abram some of the loot from the battle. Abram refuses to take anything, because he did not want anyone to be able to say that they—his enemies—had made him rich. Following this event, God reassures Abram that He is his reward.

Life Application

Why did Abram pass on all the treasures offered to him by the ruler? It would have been appropriate for him to take some of the plunder since he had helped defeat the kings who captured his nephew. The king of Sodom's gratitude was well intended since Abram was the one who had saved him and his people from captivity. Surely an offer like this from a grateful king was a reasonable reward for his labors! But Abram had no use for the king of Sodom's riches. When God called Abram, he promised to enrich him. God had shown Abram the land he had promised him. The question should be, "How could Abram take Sodom's riches?" God confirms his commitment to Abram in even more intimate language here when He states, "*I am your exceedingly great reward.*" What would we do in Abram's position? What are the things that God has promised us? Do we trust that God is for us, and able to do what He said or do we need to rely on human resources? Do we try to help God (as if He needed it)?! If our God needs help to accomplish what He has promised us, then he is not God. I am not saying that God does not help us through others. I am trying to put a check in our spirits so that we do not replace "faith" with our "force of will." What we need is a renewed vision of our God! What better reward is there to our faith than God's profession to us, "*I am your exceedingly great reward*"?

NT Scriptures

Hebrews 11:24–27

Prayer

O LORD, help us be completely dependent on you. How easy it is for us to accept the strategies of the world and to rely on human efforts. Forgive us for compromising and seeking to supplement our faith with the tangible things of this world. You are well able to fulfill your will in our lives, without our help. We love you and thank you for your faithfulness to us, even when we are unfaithful.

Personal Notes and Prayers

Genesis 15:8

וַיֹּאמַר אֲדֹנָי יֱהֹוִה בַּמָּה אֵדַע כִּי אִירָשֶׁנָּה׃

Then he [Abram] said, "O Sovereign LORD how will I know that I will possess it?"

Biblical Context

VERSE 8 FALLS ON the heels of one of the most famous Scriptures in the Bible: "*Abram believed the LORD and he credited it to him as righteousness*" (Gen 15:6 NIV). YHWH had promised an heir to Abram but no offspring had yet come from his loins. Somehow God's reassuring words lead Abram to believe in his promises (15:4–5). As such, Abram is credited with righteousness. Abram eventually becomes the father of all who would believe in the promises of God, no matter how unbelievable they really are (Rom 4:1–24). In Genesis 15:7, YHWH makes another promise to Abram regarding his plan to give him and his descendants the land of Canaan (see Gen 12:1). And yet, the man who was considered righteous because of his faith asks for some reassurance that YHWH will really fulfill his promise. God responds by establishing a covenant with him through the shedding of the blood of a heifer, a she-goat, a ram, a turtledove and a young pigeon (Gen 15:9–21).

Life Application

John 3:16 promises eternal life to everyone who believes in the Son of God. Hebrews 11:6 states that it is impossible to please God without faith. But what does it mean to believe and have faith? What does it mean to have the assurance of things hoped for and the confidence of things unseen (Heb 11:1)? It appears from Genesis 15:8 that faith can be kind of fickle. The great Abraham had his doubts, desired some assurance, and could believe God in one area of life and still have some uncertainties present in his soul in other areas. If the great patriarch of the faith still needed God's reassurance at times (even at times of great faith—Gen

15:6), it is understandable that we too need to come back to God and to his Word from time to time to seek reassurance. The Psalms are littered with people who struggled with doubt (see Pss 13; 73). There are times when God seems to be far off and aloof. At other times, God's Word seems to remain unfulfilled. Rather than wallow in our doubts, let us be like Abraham. Seek God! Ask Him for reassurance! Return to his Word for comfort! Bow before YHWH in surrender! And always remember that even the greatest people of the faith have had their own moments of confusion and doubt. They too have needed a sign.

NT Scriptures

Mark 1:15; John 3:16; Romans 4:5; Hebrews 11:1, 6

Prayer

O LORD, we thank you for the gift of faith. We thank you for remaining faithful to us even when we are faithless. Thank you for forgiving us when we doubt. We ask you to reassure our hearts daily through your Word and by your Spirit.

Personal Notes and Prayers

Genesis 16:13

וַתִּקְרָא שֵׁם־יְהוָה הַדֹּבֵר אֵלֶיהָ אַתָּה אֵל רֳאִי כִּי אָמְרָה הֲגַם הֲלֹם
רָאִיתִי אַחֲרֵי רֹאִי:

Then she called on the name of the LORD, the one who was speaking to her, "You are the God who sees me," for she said, "Am I even here after having seeing the one who sees me?"

Biblical Context

COMMENTATORS HAVE NOTICED THE complete shock in Hagar's observation and question. As a lowly servant in a foreign land running away from her mistress, she had no expectation of a personal encounter with the angel of the LORD. God had long ago promised that he would make Hagar's master, Abraham, into a great nation but after years of infertility his wife, Sarah, had lost hope that she would be part of this promise. When Sarah decided to give Hagar to Abram to build the family God promised, Hagar likely had little choice but to go along. After Hagar conceived, however, she relished her new status and became contemptuous of her mistress. She was not prepared when Sarah fought back. Hagar became so miserable that she decided to run away. It was near a spring in the desert that the angel of the LORD found Hagar. To her surprise he commanded her to return to Sarah and submit to her. However, she now had new knowledge, not only was she was to be the mother of more descendants than she could count but she knew that the God of the universe noticed her. Overwhelmed, she named him "El Roi," or "the God who sees me."

Life Application

God revealed himself to Hagar in a special and unexpected way. For Hagar the encounter was so profound that she had to give God a name that could capture the experience. According to the Scripture, this new knowledge would help her to face Sarah again. However, the striking nature of Hagar's statement makes the situation with Sarah and Abraham seem almost insignificant by comparison. For Hagar now knows that there is a God who sees her, and has profoundly altered her perception of God and her own life. Even we can learn from Hagar's dramatic experience, for the same God who revealed himself to her in her time of need wishes to reveal himself to us.

NT Scriptures

Luke 12:6–7; John 4:7–26; Acts 17:26–28

Prayer

O LORD, you are there when life treats us well and you are there in our times of need. Thank you for coming to us and speaking with us when we need you. As you comforted Hagar and gave her hope in the desert, so you comfort us and encourage us to go on with you in the path that you set forth for us. Thank you for pouring your grace on us and for accompanying us every step of the way.

Personal Notes and Prayers

Genesis 19:22

מַהֵר הִמָּלֵט שָׁמָּה כִּי לֹא אוּכַל לַעֲשׂוֹת דָּבָר עַד־בֹּאֲךָ שָׁמָּה עַל־כֵּן קָרָא שֵׁם־הָעִיר צוֹעַר:

Escape there quickly! Because I am not able
to do anything until you arrive there.

Biblical Context

WHEN THE MEN OF Sodom surrounded Lot's house in order to have sex with the angelic messengers whom Lot had invited home, the angels pulled Lot into the house, shut the door and struck the men outside with blindness. Then they told Lot to get out of the city with everyone who belonged to him because they were going to destroy the city. As morning approached, the angels began to rush Lot. However, Lot hesitated so again, the angels grabbed him and his wife and daughters and led them safely out of the city, urging them to flee for their lives. When the angels ordered him to flee to the mountains, Lot protested and asked to flee to a small town nearby. The angels not only spared Lot's life, but granted his request. However, there was a restraint on the angel to act until Lot reached it. When Lot reached the town, the LORD then rained burning sulfur on Sodom and Gomorrah. the LORD chose not to act until Lot had left behind everything that was familiar to him—friends, relatives, belongings, home, neighborhood. One wonders what was racing through Lot's mind as he debated whether he should stay or go. Leaving his past behind was difficult and the unknown ahead of him was not very appealing. Yet, with a serious nudge by the messengers of the LORD, Lot obeyed and found refuge in Zohar, a nearby town. The rain of burning sulfur was held back until Lot had obeyed the LORD's instructions. In other words, God waited for Lot to move before he executed judgment on the cities of Sodom and Gomorrah.

Life Application

Should we conclude from this story that sometimes God chooses to wait for us before executing judgment on the evils of this world? Indeed, he does. God will go to great lengths to protect us from harm. Because of his great compassion for us (19:16), he will even take us by the hand when we hesitate—as he did with Lot and his family—and lead us to a safe place. Scripture tells us to "wait on the LORD" but do we ever consider that God is often "waiting for us" to obey him before manifesting his judgment in this world. His mercies are great towards us!

NT Scriptures

Philippians 3:7–15

Prayer

O LORD, how slow we are to listen to your voice and to obey your instructions. Have mercy on us. Help us LORD take your hand and walk with you without hesitation. You have set a path before us and you lead us to safety day after day. Help us understand your patience and longsuffering, your love and mercy toward us. What a blessed people we are to know you and to follow you all the days of our lives.

Personal Notes and Prayers

Genesis 22:12

וַיֹּ֗אמֶר אַל־תִּשְׁלַ֤ח יָֽדְךָ֙ אֶל־הַנַּ֔עַר וְאַל־תַּ֥עַשׂ ל֖וֹ מְא֑וּמָה כִּ֣י ׀ עַתָּ֣ה
יָדַ֗עְתִּי כִּֽי־יְרֵ֤א אֱלֹהִים֙ אַ֔תָּה
וְלֹ֥א חָשַׂ֛כְתָּ אֶת־בִּנְךָ֥ אֶת־יְחִידְךָ֖ מִמֶּֽנִּי׃

*Then he said, "Do not stretch out your hand against the
boy, and do not do anything to him. For now, I know that
you fear God, for you have not withheld
from me your son, your only son.*

Biblical Context

TWENTY-FIVE YEARS AFTER GOD had promised to make Abraham into a great nation (Gen 12), fourteen years after God had promised him offspring as numerous as the stars in the heavens (Gen 15), and less than a year after God had promised that his wife Sarah, nearly ninety years old at the time, would bear him a son (Gen 17), God finally came through on his promise. Isaac's birth (Gen 21) had been long awaited indeed. And now God was testing him by asking him to sacrifice his son, his only son, whom he loved! Yet, without a word of protest, Abraham set out to do just that. After a three-day journey, they arrive at the place of sacrifice. Yet, far from hopeless, Abraham exhibits signs of faith, telling his servants that both he and the boy will return (v. 5), and telling Isaac that the LORD himself would provide the sacrifice (v. 8). At the climax of the scene, right as Abraham is about to slay his son, the angel of the LORD intervenes with the above speech. Abraham has passed the test. He will get to keep his son, knowing that he has placed God first in his heart.

Life Application

How often do the good things that God promises and gives to us become more important to us than Him? Family, an effective ministry, and many other good things can quickly become idols in our hearts that compete with our affection for God. While we may not receive tests so vividly dramatic as Abraham's, the challenge remains the same for all of us: Are we willing to place on the altar what is most precious to us, to know that we fear God above all else? Are we willing to say, "Not my will, but yours be done"?

NT Scriptures

Luke 22:42; Hebrews 11:17–19

Prayer

O LORD, you ask one thing from us—that we honor you and place you at the highest place in our lives. You desire our love, our worship, our obedience and our willingness to follow you without holding anything back. The distractions of this world and the temptations to compromise are ever before us. Help us LORD walk in your paths with commitment, energy, faith, compassion and sacrifice. Help us not turn to the right or to the left. Help us keep our eyes on you and follow you wherever you lead, even to the difficult altar of sacrifice. We are yours, O LORD. We belong to you. Here we are, take us and use us for your glory and for the furthering of your Kingdom. In Jesus's name.

Personal Notes and Prayers

Genesis 22:12

וַיֹּאמֶר אַל־תִּשְׁלַח יָדְךָ אֶל־הַנַּעַר וְאַל־תַּעַשׂ לוֹ מְאוּמָה כִּי עַתָּה
יָדַעְתִּי כִּי־יְרֵא אֱלֹהִים אַתָּה
וְלֹא חָשַׂכְתָּ אֶת־בִּנְךָ אֶת־יְחִידְךָ מִמֶּנִּי:

*And then He said, "Do not stretch out your hand against
the boy and do not do anything to him, for now,
I know that you fear God, for you did not
withhold your son, your only one, from me.*

Biblical Context

ABRAHAM AND SARAH HAD waited many years for the son that God had promised them. Then God told Abraham to offer to the LORD his son as a burnt offering. While it obviously pained him to do so, Abraham obeyed. It would be a gross understatement to say Abraham did not want to obey, or that it was difficult for him to do so. But Abraham did obey. As he held the knife over his head in preparation for killing the son he loved, God stopped him and provided a ram to be the sacrifice instead. In the end, Abraham did not have to sacrifice his son, but he had proved to the LORD that he was willing.

Life Application

Because we live under a different system than that of Abraham, we will never be asked to sacrifice one of our children to the LORD. We will, however, be asked to do things that are difficult, or that we do not want to do. Perhaps someone encouraged you to apply for a job for which you think you are not sufficiently qualified. Perhaps you are being asked to lead a ministry for which you do not feel qualified or work in an area of ministry that causes you fear. There are times when, after obedience in pursuing the opportunity, albeit reluctantly, the door closes. A sense of peace washes over you when you realize God is pleased with your obedience and you are relieved that you do not have to engage in the tasks you were not looking forward to doing. It may be the case that God did not want you to fulfill the position, but He wanted you to be willing to go wherever He sends you. Obedience is the expression of faith in God.

NT Scriptures

Luke 22:42

Prayer

O LORD, thank you for providing examples of faith for us. Thank you for Abraham's willingness to listen and follow-through, even when the task seemed desperately difficult and costly. Thank you LORD for seeing our faith and for honoring our attempts to obey you. We trust you. We depend on you. We know you will never ask us to do things that will not benefit your kingdom. Although much of it is a mystery to us, you see the larger picture and you have a purpose for all things. LORD, help us to trust your voice and to obey your instructions without holding anything back.

Personal Notes and Prayers

Genesis 24:58

וַיִּקְרְאוּ לְרִבְקָה וַיֹּאמְרוּ אֵלֶיהָ הֲתֵלְכִי עִם־הָאִישׁ הַזֶּה וַתֹּאמֶר אֵלֵךְ׃

They called to Rebekah and said to her, "Will you go with this man?" And she said, "I will go."

Biblical Context

IN GENESIS 24, ABRAHAM asks his servant to go to his homeland to find a suitable wife for his son, Isaac. So, the servant takes gifts for the family of the woman and goes on his way. He asks the LORD to prosper his journey and to show him who is to become Isaac's wife. The LORD leads him to Rebekah, a woman who is drawing water at the communal well. Almost certain that she is "the right woman," the servant goes to Rebekah's home and shares the purpose of his visit with the family patriarch. Although Rebekah and her family did not know YHWH, it was not unusual in this culture for individuals to believe that their lives were determined by the gods. Rebekah's family would have assumed that YHWH was a local deity from the region of Canaan. It probably impressed them that this man knew of their family and spoke highly of their relative Abraham. Or maybe the nice bride price had something to do with their willingness to give Rebekah to this stranger. But regardless of their considerations, the choice was left up to Rebekah. They called her and said, "*Will you go with this man?*" And while it is not indicated in the text, I believe there was here a dramatic pause. We are not privy to Rebekah's facial expressions nor to all the questions that were likely bombarding her mind—"Who is this Isaac?" Will he love me? Will he even be nice to me? Maybe he is violent—even abusive. Or maybe he is terribly romantic! Does he have other wives already? Will they like me? Is he handsome? And what of this land—will I have a nice home? Will I ever see my family again?" Regardless of the thoughts that ran through her mind, Rebekah chose to take part in the adventure. She took the way of faith and said "*I will go.*"

Life Application

Along life's journey, we are asked to make important decisions that could change the course of our lives (and possibly that of others also) in drastic ways. In those moments, our minds race with worthy and important questions. Although we may feel unsure and vulnerable, what matters most is that our choices be made with great care and reflect the will of God. If someone were to read the story of our lives in 3,000 years, would they learn that we responded by saying, *"I will go"* or would they be privy to the consequences of our refusal to follow the path God set before us?

NT Scriptures

Matthew 17:20; John 14:1; Romans 10:11

Prayer

O LORD, thank you for the surprises of life and for the wisdom to recognize them as gifts from you. We ask for your leading and discernment as we seek to do your will. Guide us LORD!

Personal Notes and Prayers

Genesis 26:4–5

וְהִרְבֵּיתִ֤י אֶֽת־זַרְעֲךָ֙ כְּכוֹכְבֵ֣י הַשָּׁמַ֔יִם וְנָתַתִּ֣י לְזַרְעֲךָ֔ אֵ֥ת כָּל־הָאֲרָצֹ֖ת הָאֵ֑ל וְהִתְבָּרֲכ֣וּ בְזַרְעֲךָ֔ כֹּ֖ל גּוֹיֵ֥י הָאָֽרֶץ׃

עֵ֕קֶב אֲשֶׁר־שָׁמַ֥ע אַבְרָהָ֖ם בְּקֹלִ֑י וַיִּשְׁמֹר֙ מִשְׁמַרְתִּ֔י מִצְוֺתַ֖י חֻקּוֹתַ֥י וְתוֹרֹתָֽי׃

I will multiply your seed like the stars of the sky and I will give to your descendants all these lands. And in your seed all the nations of the earth will be blessed, because Abraham obeyed my voice and kept my requirements, my commands, my regulations and my laws.

Biblical Context

IN THIS PASSAGE, THE promises made to Abraham are reiterated to his son Isaac. The restatement of these covenant promises is intended to confirm that God would surely fulfill his promises to future generations and that none of his promises would be forgotten. God was proud of Abraham and boasted to his son about his faithfulness, noting that he had kept the divine commands and walked in the ways of the LORD. It was important for God to assure Isaac that he was indeed a part of the fulfillment of the divine promises before he would encounter king Abimelech in Gerar. In the manner in which his father had kept God's commands, Isaac was expected to continue the legacy and obey as Abraham had obeyed.

Life Application

God really does want to reward those who are seeking him. In the Hebrew Bible, God often praises people for deeds they have done. The New Testament explicitly states that Christ did not die on a cross so that we could live however we want. While the law may no longer be required, that does not mean that nothing is required of us. Long *before* the Law was given, Abraham followed everything God required of him.

NT Scriptures

Romans 4:2; James 2:23–24

Prayer

O LORD, you have called us to a life of obedience. Help us listen to your instructions and obey without delay or hesitation, as your Holy Spirit leads us into your perfect will. Give us the strength and courage to obey in every situation. We want to serve you with all our hearts, as Jesus served you completely. May our will be submitted to you and may our words, thoughts, and actions be pleasing to you.

Personal Notes and Prayers

Genesis 32:29

וַיֹּאמֶר לֹא יַעֲקֹב יֵאָמֵר עוֹד שִׁמְךָ כִּי אִם־יִשְׂרָאֵל כִּי־שָׂרִיתָ עִם־אֱלֹהִים וְעִם־אֲנָשִׁים וַתּוּכָל:

Then he said, "Your name will not be called Jacob anymore, but rather Israel, for you have persisted with God and with men, and you have prevailed."

Biblical Context

THE NAME YAAKOV (JACOB) comes from a Hebrew word that signifies "circumventing, assailing insidiously (deceptively), overreaching." Yaakov is known for his deceptive acquisition of Esau's birthright and for receiving the blessing reserved for the firstborn. Yaakov is also reputed for working persistently for Laban for a period of fourteen years in order to acquire his beloved Rachel. Twenty years had passed since Yaakov had fled his home, where God had first revealed himself to him. The day before crossing back into his homeland and reuniting with his estranged brother, Yaakov questions God's promises and prepares for the worst, ready to encounter the wrestling match of his life against his brother (32:7–21). Yaakov was good at overcoming the odds, even in a wrestling match with God (32:22–31). Although Yaakov had not always persisted honorably, he never gave up. Even after suffering a crippling blow administered by God himself, he stayed engaged in full contact with God, determined not to give up on his blessing and favor. Surprisingly, not only did God allow Yaakov to wrestle with him, but he also allowed Yaakov to overcome him. However, in doing so He renamed him "Israel" meaning "God persists." God's persistence (even though it seemed as if He had lost the fight) brought forth a new identity for Jacob, the man who brought forth the royal line of Judah through whom came the Savior of the world—Yeshua.

Life Application

God does not give up on us, his people, even when it seems that He has abandoned us and that our ways seem to prevail over his ways. He does not persist with us and for us in the way we expect. At times, He blesses us with debilitating afflictions and bruises our limbs. We limp along and wonder why we suffer pain. But God is at our side, holding us steady and leading us along the way. He knows the purpose of all things. Like Yaakov, we must persist with him, continue the journey with him, and trust that he will one day reveal the reason for the injuries of life.

NT Scriptures

Romans 5:1–5; Philippians 1:3–6; Revelation 2:17; 22:1–4

Prayer

O LORD, thank you for knowing us by name and for dealing with us personally. Thank you for engaging us deeply and for allowing us to wrestle with you. Thank you for allowing us to meet with you face to face and to open our hearts to you in times of need.

Personal Notes and Prayers

Genesis 32:30

וַיִּשְׁאַל יַעֲקֹב וַיֹּאמֶר הַגִּידָה־נָּא שְׁמֶךָ וַיֹּאמֶר לָמָּה זֶּה תִּשְׁאַל לִשְׁמִי וַיְבָרֶךְ אֹתוֹ שָׁם׃

Then Jacob asked, "Please tell me your name!"
But he responded, "Why is this, that you ask my name?"
And he blessed him there.

Biblical Context

JACOB WAITS ALONE IN preparation for his meeting with his brother, Esau. As he waits, a man appears, and they (mysteriously) wrestle until daybreak. As Jacob is about to emerge victorious, the visitor simply touches Jacob's thigh, dislocating it. Despite this injury, Jacob retains his hold upon this man, who finally demands that Jacob release him. Jacob responds that he will not let the man go until he blesses Jacob. The man decides to bless Jacob by renaming him "Israel," one who strives with God and men and prevails. Yet, the man's identity is still a mystery, so Jacob then dares to ask, "Please tell me your name!" But the man refuses, answering simply, "Why is this, that you ask my name?"

Life Application

When I think of this text, I am immediately drawn to its mystery. It displays a stubborn, almost adamant refusal to make the significance of these events clear to the reader. Why do Jacob and the man wrestle? Who is this man, after all, and why does he refuse to reveal his name? Is he the same man as the messenger of Judges 13:18, that refused to reveal his name to Samson's father, explaining that it was simply "too wonderous" for him to reveal? Yet this text, with all its unexplained events, is a solid reminder for me that not all of God's actions are going to be explained. Nor is God obligated to explain them. I recall Job's answer to God's divine challenge: "I have declared that which I did not understand. Things too wonderful for me, which I did not know" (Job 42:3b). I must allow God to refuse to reveal. Of course, Jacob still dared to ask the question, "Tell me your name!" and God does not rebuke him for this. He (or his messenger) simply refuses to answer. May I continue to engage and encounter God, but may I also accept when He refuses me on account of the wonder that I could not begin to comprehend.

NT Scriptures

Matthew 10:41; Ephesians 1:15–19

Prayer

O LORD, thank you for revealing yourself to us. Thank you for choosing the means by which you do so, the timing of the revelation and the measure by which you show us who you are. We are so aware that we now see you in part, through a glass darkly, but that one day, we will see you in all of your glory. Help us be patient! Help us have faith when we wonder who you really are. Thank you for allowing us to wrestle with you, as Jacob did you your messenger—the LORD.

Personal Notes and Prayers

Genesis 37:10

וַיְסַפֵּ֣ר אֶל־אָבִיו֮ וְאֶל־אֶחָיו֒ וַיִּגְעַר־בּ֣וֹ אָבִ֔יו וַיֹּ֣אמֶר ל֔וֹ מָ֛ה הַחֲל֥וֹם הַזֶּ֖ה אֲשֶׁ֣ר חָלָ֑מְתָּ
הֲב֣וֹא נָב֗וֹא אֲנִי֙ וְאִמְּךָ֣ וְאַחֶ֔יךָ לְהִשְׁתַּחֲוֺ֥ת לְךָ֖ אָֽרְצָה׃

He recounted to his father and his mother. Then his father rebuked him, saying to him "What is this dream which you dreamed? Shall we really go, I and your mother and your brothers, to prostrate ourselves to you to the ground?

Biblical Context

AFTER SHARING AN AMAZING dream with his brothers, Joseph is ostracized, mocked and even hated. Unable to contain his excitement at a second dream, Joseph goes to his father and his brothers and recounts the dream in which he sees the sun, the moon, and 11 stars bowing down to him. His father Jacob—the patriarch of the family—is understandably unimpressed by his teenage son's dream where he, his wife, and his sons would bow down to Joseph. *"Shall we really go to prostrate ourselves before you?"* asks Jacob. The use of the infinite absolute in the phrase הֲבוֹא נָבוֹא indicates just how taken back Jacob probably was at Joseph's dream. The notion that a father, the patriarch of a large extended family, would bow down before one of his youngest sons, would have been absurd in the Ancient Near East. The initial exchange is almost comical, "Me? Bow to you? I am the patriarch of the household and you're still an unmarried boy. My word is law and you do what I say, when I say it. This stuff may work on your brothers, but do not start that nonsense on me, son." Shortly thereafter, Joseph is thrust into his journey to Egypt through an unfortunate series of events.

Life Application

How often we look at ourselves and wonder how we compare to the people mentioned in the Bible? We ask ourselves if we can be like Noah,

Enoch, Moses, Isaiah, Mary and others. Can we be like these heroes of the faith? Maybe we can, and maybe we cannot. One person we can be like is Joseph. The youthful Joseph is no role model. But over the years, we see him transformed from a brash, ostracized youth to a Vizier of Egypt who, led by the Spirit of God, deliverers many people from certain death. No matter what our personal stories may be, we can look to the elder Joseph who, through many trials and hardships, grows from being a naïve young man into becoming a role model of personal growth and faith to us all.

NT Scriptures

1 Timothy 4:12–16; Hebrews 11:22

Prayer

O LORD, thank you for guiding us along the way and for transforming us from babes in Christ to mature believers who can serve you and others. Help us be grateful for your faithfulness towards us as we grow from innocence and naivety to wisdom and maturity. Thank you for keeping watch over us as we learn the precious lessons of life.

Personal Notes and Prayers

Genesis 38:1–26

Do not leave your credit card in the hands of a prostitute!

Biblical Context

WHILE MARRIED TO TAMAR, Judah's sons Er and Onan die. Grieving over his loss, Judah withholds his third son Shelah from his daughter-in-law, thinking he would at least keep his last heir alive. Judah may have thought that Tamar was cursed and caused his sons to die but the narrative tells us otherwise. Er *"was wicked in the eyes of the LORD so the LORD put him to death"* (Gen 38:7) and *"what he [Onan] did was wicked in the eyes of the LORD so the LORD put him to death"* (38:10). Er and Onan brought about their own demise. Humiliated and sorrowful, Tamar returns to her father's house as a widow. Many years later, she finds out that Judah, who withheld Shelah from her, is coming to a nearby town. She dresses as a street prostitute, covers herself and tricks Judah into pledging some of his personal belongings for a later payment. He gives her his most precious treasures: his seal (*credit card*), his cord (*driver's license*) and his staff (*passport*). Three months later, Tamar is pregnant and accused of prostitution. She is brought before Judah who quickly condemns her to death (thinking he would finally get rid of her completely). But to Judah's surprise, Tamar produces the evidence he left behind months earlier and turns the tables on him. Ashamed, Judah falls to his knees, repents and declares Tamar more righteous than he. Pregnant with twins, Tamar gives birth to Zerah and Perez who later appears in the genealogy of Jesus (Matt 1:3; Luke 3:33).

Life Application

Dead sons, spilled seed, lies, prostitution, manipulation, and yet God fulfills his redemptive plan and prepares the way for the *Lion of the tribe of Judah* (Rev 5:5). The moral of the story—*Do not leave your credit card in the hands of a prostitute . . .* but if you do, pray God forgives you and uses it to fulfill his greater purposes. Your credit card will show up somewhere in the least expected places at the least expected times! Indeed, pray it does so you can repent and ask God to use your entire life—the good, the bad, and the ugly—for his glory.

NT Scriptures

Romans 4:7–8; 5:8–19

Prayer

O LORD, thank you for being merciful to us when we sin, lie, manipulate and pretend to be innocent. Thank you for bringing our sins to light so we can repent and return to you with all our hearts. We thank you for your wonderful gifts of mercy and grace.

Personal Notes and Prayers

Genesis 45:8a

וְעַתָּ֗ה לֹֽא־אַתֶּ֞ם שְׁלַחְתֶּ֤ם אֹתִי֙ הֵ֔נָּה כִּ֖י הָאֱלֹהִ֑ים
Now, it is not you who sent me here, but it is God!

Biblical Context

JOSEPH'S BROTHERS WENT THROUGH a roller coaster of emotions when they realized that Joseph was standing before them. The events of Genesis 37 flashed before their eyes. They remembered hating Joseph to the point of selling him to traveling merchants. Now, the tables were turned and Joseph had the upper hand. Realizing their plight, fear gripped their hearts and confusion set in. They felt deep guilt for their actions of long ago, and then, the blame game began to unfold. Who would take the responsibility for the events of the past? Joseph, a man chosen by God to save his people during a time of severe famine, turned away from unforgiveness, forsook the opportunity to retaliate, and chose not to hold a grudge against those who had hurt him deeply. He was able to do so only because he recognized that God had orchestrated the events of his life. He could have been bitter and taken advantage of the situation, but motivated by the love of God, Joseph had compassion on his brothers and extended grace to them. For years, Joseph had yearned for the moment when he could be reunited with his family. Finally, it had come!

Life Application

As human beings, we see events from an earthly standpoint, generally oblivious to God's plan and involvement in our situations. Long before Joseph revealed himself to his brothers, he had recognized that God's hand was in what seemed to most, unfortunate circumstances and the regrettable outcome of sibling rivalry. When the opportune moment arose, Joseph revealed what he had pondered in his heart during his years in Egypt—God had a plan and a purpose for each person's life, a design that no human mind can fully grasp. God is to be trusted! Only He can bring his design to past.

NT Scriptures

Matthew 6:12–15; Luke 6:27–36

Prayer

O LORD, please give me grace to forgive those who treat me with contempt. Help me see them through your eyes. As Joseph waited for a long long time before extending the right hand of fellowship to his brothers, help me be patient in waiting. To you be the glory forever and ever.

Personal Notes and Prayers

Genesis 49:10

לֹא־יָסוּר שֵׁבֶט מִיהוּדָה וּמְחֹקֵק מִבֵּין רַגְלָיו עַד כִּי־יָבֹא שִׁילֹה וְלוֹ יִקְּהַת עַמִּים:

The scepter will not depart from Judah and the commander's staff from between his feet until the one to whom it belongs comes and to him (will be) the obedience of the nations.

Biblical Context

SELLING A BROTHER INTO slavery, lying to his father and hiring a prostitute who turns out to be his daughter-in-law; these are just a few of the infamous acts of Jacob's fourth son, Judah. He certainly was not the worst of Jacob's offspring, but he was not the child that every father dreamt of having. Nevertheless, at the end of his life, Jacob pronounced a blessing on Judah and foretold that from his offspring would come a Ruler, whose scepter would never depart from Judah. Although Jacob pronounced this blessing, he was speaking words with far greater significance than he could ever imagine. On a much deeper level, God was foretelling his plan for cosmic redemption. Through Jacob, God was revealing that One would come and restore order to a world in chaos. No ruler in all of human history has been worthy to receive the obedience of all nations. But through this unexceptional character Judah, God would bring forth the most remarkable Ruler, the One to whom every knee would bow and every tongue confess that He is "King of kings and LORD of LORDs" (1 Tim 6:15).

Life Application

It would have been interesting to see how Judah processed this blessing as he was standing in a foreign country, under the rule of his little brother (whom he sold as a slave), watching his father die, with two sons dead because they were evil, and two sons by his daughter-in-law. How ironic that God would choose Judah and his tainted history to carry the family line through which God would send the Messiah. God's plan is not always easily discernable. How is He working? Who is He working through? But one thing is very clear, He is working toward restoration and redemption; restoration of a fallen creation and redemption of a sinful human race, and He is doing this in unexpected ways and places. Although God's methods and instruments are somewhat unpredictable, He has revealed the One through whom He has and will accomplish his perfect will, Jesus the Messiah.

NT Scriptures

Revelation 5:5

Prayer

O LORD, thank you for your redemptive plan and for your willingness to use us, simple creatures, as instruments in your hands. Throughout the ages, you have spoken, acted and done miraculous deeds through the lives of sinful men and women. How amazing that you would consider us worthy to be used by you to reveal your majesty on earth. Thank you.

Personal Notes and Prayers

Genesis 50:17

כֹּה־תֹאמְרוּ לְיוֹסֵף אָנָּא שָׂא נָא פֶּשַׁע אַחֶיךָ וְחַטָּאתָם כִּי־רָעָה
גְמָלוּךָ וְעַתָּה שָׂא נָא
לְפֶשַׁע עַבְדֵי אֱלֹהֵי אָבִיךָ וַיֵּבְךְּ יוֹסֵף בְּדַבְּרָם אֵלָיו׃

This say to Joseph, "Please forgive, I pray you, the transgression of your brothers and their sin, for they have done evil against you; and now please forgive the transgression of the servants of the God of your father." Joseph wept as they spoke to him.

Biblical Context

THIS VERSE REFERS TO Jacob's instructions to his sons regarding the forgiveness to be granted to them by Joseph. The story of Joseph is replete with favoritism, sibling rivalry, rejection, imprisonment, suffering, slavery, alienation from home, acquisition of power, the gaining of success, family reunions and even reconciliation. This is a story of a disturbed family. It explores the realities of a house torn apart by the quarrels of mothers, by a father's preferential treatment of a younger son, by that son's recognition of his own unique role and by the jealous rage of the older brothers towards their younger brother. As the story unfolds, it hints to the possibility of revenge. Yet, one of the major themes of the story is that of "redemption." This redemption can only come from forgiveness by the one transgressed. In this verse, the verb שָׂא from נָשָׂא whose basic meaning is "to lift" or "to carry" is used in an idiomatic expression that signifies "to forgive" someone (literally "lifting or carrying someone's sin"). It is noteworthy that נָשָׂא is also used in Scripture for bearing the penalty of sin (Ps 32:1; Job 7:21). Joseph's forgiveness is both redeeming for his brothers as well as self-redeeming. In this story, the "lifting of sin" allows for reconciliation, unity and wholeness in the fulfillment of Gods plan.

Life Application

In life, we are offended, maligned and abused. We harbor pain and feel that retaliation is the only way to bring justice on our assailants. Unforgiveness is an insidious toxin that poisons our soul and an impediment to the great and wonderful plan God has for our lives. How many times must we forgive? "Seventy-seven times," says Jesus (Matt 28:22). There is no other option provided in Scripture.

NT Scriptures

Matthew 6:14; Romans 4:7; Ephesians 4:32

Prayer

O LORD, teach us to forgive as you forgive. While hanging on the cross in excruciating pain, you did not think of yourself, but rather, you said to the Father, "Forgive them, for they do not know what they are doing" (Luke 23:34). You prayed that their lives would be changed and that they would find forgiveness from their horrific sin. Thank you for showing us the way to freedom from bondage through the forgiveness of sin.

Personal Notes and Prayers

Genesis 50:20

וְאַתֶּם חֲשַׁבְתֶּם עָלַי רָעָה אֱלֹהִים חֲשָׁבָהּ לְטֹבָה לְמַעַן עֲשֹׂה כַּיּוֹם הַזֶּה לְהַחֲיֹת עַם־רָב׃

You meant to harm me (but) God meant it for good in order that he might now keep many people alive.

Biblical Context

AFTER THE DEATH OF Jacob, his sons approach their brother Joseph out of fear that he might exact revenge for what they had done to him years earlier. In the climax of this narrative, Joseph makes an unexpected and amazing proclamation. To his brothers he says: "What you meant for evil, God meant for good." In spite of his brothers attempt to get rid of him, Joseph survives victimization, overcomes incarceration and rises to a place of authority no one could have imagined. His resilience and his trust in the God of Abraham, Isaac, and Jacob kept him on a journey of restoration and redemption. The book of Genesis closes with these important words, summarizing the failed plans of humanity in its endless pursuit of selfishness and exploitation, revealing the victorious and redeeming works of God who brings good things out of people's disastrous situations.

Life Application

Life can be messy, and a lot of it is because of choices made by individuals and/or organizations. The great thing about this passage is that God can make good out of bad situations. God redeems and restores in the direst circumstances. As one lyricist wrote, God makes "beautiful things out of the dust." As beautiful as this idea is, what comforts me more is the belief that there is hope in the midst of pain and heartache. As the saying goes, *"and this too shall pass."* What we might add, is this idea that God does not overlook our afflictions and sorrows, but in fact He is actively involved in redeeming all of the chaotic and damaging events of life. Bad stuff happens, that is inevitable; but a God who concerns himself with our hardships provides an amazing picture of hope.

NT Scriptures

John 9:1–5 (especially v. 3)

Prayer

O LORD, you are there in every situation—good, bad and ugly. All things are in your hands. Under your care, none of life is wasted. You give us hope when we are hopeless. You redeem us when we least expect it. You restore our lives when we do not deserve it. Thank you for taking such good care of us—for loving us, leading us, keeping us, and healing us. To you be all the glory.

Personal Notes and Prayers

Exodus 1:15, 17

וַיֹּאמֶר מֶלֶךְ מִצְרַיִם לַמְיַלְּדֹת הָעִבְרִיֹּת אֲשֶׁר שֵׁם הָאַחַת שִׁפְרָה וְשֵׁם הַשֵּׁנִית פּוּעָה:

וַתִּירֶאןָ הַמְיַלְּדֹת אֶת־הָאֱלֹהִים וְלֹא עָשׂוּ כַּאֲשֶׁר דִּבֶּר אֲלֵיהֶן מֶלֶךְ מִצְרָיִם

The king of Egypt said to the Hebrew midwives whose names were Shiphrah and Puah . . . The midwives feared God so they did not accomplish what the king of Egypt had said to them.

Biblical Context

THE HEBREW MIDWIVES FEARED God more than they feared the king of Egypt. However, it seems strange that the king of Egypt spoke directly to them. Even more strangely, neither the proper name of the king of Egypt nor the names of other male officials appear in chapter 1. Even in chapter 2 where the birth of Moses is described, the names of Moses's parents do not appear. In chapters 1 and 2, only the names of the midwives appear. Should any significance be given to the mention of those names or with those individuals that we should know them by name? Absolutely. Shiphrah and Puah feared God. "The name of the one is Shiphrah and the name of the other is Puah," this couplet is frequent in Exodus. "The one . . . and the other . . ." appears nine times in the instructions regarding the building of the ark of covenant (Exod 25–36). When I read the passage mentioned above, it was as if I could hear God calling the names of the two women who feared him. God honored Shiphrah and Puah—two precious individuals who would have never been known in history were it not for their faith in the living God—by calling them by name.

Life Application

"The *fear of the LORD* is the beginning of wisdom" (Pro 1:7) and "A woman who *fears the LORD* will be praised" (Pro 31:20). The book of Proverbs begins and ends with the "fear of the LORD." Fearing God should be the mark of the people of God. I often ask myself, "Who do I fear more? My boss? My colleagues?" Because people see me and know my ways, do I fear them more than I fear God? Because I cannot see God, do I fear him less or even ignore him? God calls those who fear him by name. "*Shiphrah! Puah!*" I want my name to be called by the LORD as the names of the midwives were called by the king. I pray I might be the person who fears God more than I fear anything else in this life.

NT Scriptures

Matthew 10:16–28 (especially v. 28)

Prayer

O LORD, the world may never know me by name, but you do. You call my name gently, speaking to me wonderful words of life. Thank you for calling Shiphrah and Puah by name, and for teaching me through their love for you. May I fear you like Shiphrah and honor you like Puah, even in difficult situations. Teach me to fear you, to fear your name and to honor you in all I do.

Personal Notes and Prayers

Exodus 3:5

וַיֹּאמֶר אַל־תִּקְרַב הֲלֹם שַׁל־נְעָלֶיךָ מֵעַל רַגְלֶיךָ כִּי הַמָּקוֹם אֲשֶׁר
אַתָּה עוֹמֵד עָלָיו אַדְמַת־קֹדֶשׁ הוּא:

Then (the LORD) said, "Do not come near here, remove your sandals from your feet! For the place on which you are standing is holy ground."

Biblical Context

AT AN INOPPORTUNE MOMENT, Moses kills an Egyptian who was beating a fellow Hebrew. But he was seen! So, fearing for his life, Moses escapes to Midian, a foreign country. Meanwhile, the Hebrews continue to be mistreated in Egypt, and God "remembers" his covenant with the people, and He sees their troubles. One particular day, as Moses is pasturing sheep in Midian, he sees a bush blazing with fire but miraculously, the bush itself is unharmed! As Moses heads over to investigate, God calls to him from the bush, and gives him the warning issued in Exodus 3:5. Immediately after this, God identifies himself to Moses as the "God of his father, the God of Abraham, Isaac, and Jacob." Ultimately, God issues Moses forth with a mission: Go to Pharaoh and bring God's people out of Egypt. The defining moment of Israelite history, the Exodus towards the Promised Land and out of slavery, begins with a call from God for reverence but also recognition. Recognition that the very place in which Moses stands, a simple pasture, is in fact sacred and holy.

Life Application

What initially drew me to this text was its uncanny similarity to Joshua 5:15, wherein the command to Joshua is almost identical to that given to Moses. Do these verses merely imply that the ground is holy in that moment because God himself is present there? Or, I wonder, was the ground on which Moses and Joshua walked always holy, but they were unable to recognize it? Passages like these make me stop and ponder on the sacredness of

God's presence. Though, as Hebrews 10:19–22 notes, I have full ability as a Christ-follower to enter the most holy place unafraid, there are times when I am reminded that I enter sacred spaces daily along the journey of life. I confess sin, I temper my arrogance, and I relinquish my ego so much more easily when I recall this principle: that sometimes the ground on which I walk has been prepared for an encounter with the Almighty.

NT Scriptures

Hebrews 10:19

Prayer

O LORD, you are holy and you invite us into your holy presence not because of our own merits, but simply because you want to fellowship with us. You love us and you provide a safe place for us to dwell with you. Show us the sacredness of your dwelling and the awesomeness of your presence. Forgive us for taking your presence for granted and for keeping you at arms length. Help us come near you with assurance that you will welcome us with open arms, gather us unto yourself and heal our wounds.

Personal Notes and Prayers

Exodus 3:7

וַיֹּאמֶר יְהוָה רָאֹה רָאִיתִי אֶת־עֳנִי עַמִּי אֲשֶׁר בְּמִצְרָיִם וְאֶת־צַעֲקָתָם
שָׁמַעְתִּי מִפְּנֵי נֹגְשָׂיו
כִּי יָדַעְתִּי אֶת־מַכְאֹבָיו׃

Then the LORD said, "I have clearly seen the affliction of my people who are in Egypt. Their outcry I have heard before the ones who oppress them. For I know their pain.

Biblical Context

THIS CONVERSATION BETWEEN THE LORD and Moses took place during the famous burning bush story. Here we find God calling Moses to lead the people of Israel out from under severe oppression in Egypt. God exhibited compassion for his people. Their cry had reached him and he could no longer allow them to suffer at the hands of the Egyptians. The time had come for God to intervene and respond to the cries of his people.

Life Application

As Christians, we can take enormous comfort in the fact that God knows our every need. He sees our affliction, hears our cry and understands our suffering. Although his timing may not always be our timing, God will not leave us to suffer through life alone. He sustains us and gives us the strength we need to go through life's challenges. When all else is failing around us, we can always put our hope in God. He sees, he hears, he knows. The verbs "to see" and "to know" (רָאָה and יָדַע) often imply more than just the physical acts of seeing and knowing. "To see" can have a more penetrating meaning: "to truly see the very heart of the matter, to understand it." Similarly, the verb "to know" often refers to "a more intimate knowledge, a full understanding that leads to compassion." How blessed we are to have a God who fully *sees* and *knows* our situations, desires, sufferings, struggles, heart cries, etc.

NT Scriptures

John 10:14–15; Romans 8:26–27

Prayer

O LORD, we thank you for seeing us and knowing us deeply. You saw us and knew us when we were woven together in our mother's womb (Ps 139:13–16) and never has there been a moment in our lives when you did not have complete knowledge of us. Help us understand your presence, your attention, your love and your willingness to reveal yourself to us every day of our lives. Thank you LORD.

Personal Notes and Prayers

Exodus 4:12-13

וְעַתָּ֖ה לֵ֑ךְ וְאָנֹכִי֙ אֶֽהְיֶ֣ה עִם־פִּ֔יךָ וְהוֹרֵיתִ֖יךָ אֲשֶׁ֥ר תְּדַבֵּֽר׃

וַיֹּ֖אמֶר בִּ֣י אֲדֹנָ֑י שְֽׁלַֽח־נָ֖א בְּיַד־תִּשְׁלָֽח׃

Now go, and I will be with your mouth and will teach what you must say. But he said, "O my LORD, please send someone else."

Biblical Context

MOSES IS ASKED BY God to speak on his behalf. Even after God reveals himself to him miraculously in a burning bush, assures him of his divine plan, confirms his identity, and answers his *"what if"* questions, Moses still allows his low self-esteem to get in the way of trusting God. He states, "I am not an eloquent man and am slow of mouth and tongue" (4:10). But God—who always has the final answer—challenges Moses with this rhetorical question, "Who gave man his mouth?" (4:11). In spite of God's reassuring words, Moses still wants to withdraw from the call and follow the easy and safe path. He does not hide his fear from God, and God does not hide his anger towards him. God is more intent on fashioning Moses as a great leader and a man of faith than allowing him to miss his calling.

Life Application

God does not want us to remain where we are. Our biggest fears and logical reasonings will not prevent God from taking us where He wants us to go. There is not a "someone else" who can fulfill the call on our lives. Our weaknesses and perceived inadequacies will not deter God from sending us where we least expect. Are we more determined to trust our own self perception rather than believe that God is able to accomplish his "seemingly impossible" will in us?

NT Scriptures

1 Corinthians 1:26—2:5; Hebrews 11:25–27

Prayer

O LORD, help us step out of our comfort zone and challenge us to follow you wholeheartedly. Forgive us LORD for attempting to withdraw from your call and stay nestled in our safe places. Help us trust you as you lead us into the unknown.

Personal Notes and Prayers

Exodus 4:31

וַיַּאֲמֵן הָעָם וַיִּשְׁמְעוּ כִּי־פָקַד יְהוָה אֶת־בְּנֵי יִשְׂרָאֵל וְכִי רָאָה אֶת־עָנְיָם וַיִּקְּדוּ וַיִּשְׁתַּחֲוּוּ׃

Then the people believed. When they heard that the LORD had paid attention to the children of Israel and had seen their afflictions, they bowed down and worshiped.

Biblical Context

IN THIS PASSAGE, MOSES arrived with the message that God had seen the suffering of the Israelites in Egypt. In order to convince the people of his legitimacy, God provided Moses with a series of miracles that would serve as evidence of God's involvement in this impending act of freedom. Not surprisingly, these signs had their intended consequence. The people believed the message and understood that God had seen their misery and was preparing to intervene on their behalf. Their final response was to bow down and worship. The signs God provided were not simply miracles to prove God's power. Rather, they represented God's concern toward his people. The miracles they saw, that Moses requested for this very purpose, were evidence that they were not alone. God cared about them. The signs garnered belief, leading to renewed understanding of God's care toward them, ultimately resulting in their worship.

Life Application

The relational nature of God's miracles in this passage present a fascinating dynamic for believers today. What is particularly intriguing is that God did not allow for their doubt. He provided a miracle in order to convince them of the legitimacy of Moses's message. The knowledge that God actively drew the Israelites to trust in him in this way should impact the way we approach the formation of our faith. Although miracles in general are rare today, the character of God revealed in this Scripture remains just as powerful. God desires individuals to believe in him, to understand his concern and to trust in his compassion toward them. As believers, we can trust that God is drawing us to a deeper understanding of his compassion. As we recognize this, we then follow the example of the Israelites and bow down and worship.

NT Scriptures

Mark 9:24; John 4:48; 5:38

Prayer

O LORD, you pursue us with your love, mercies, kindness and truth. You seek to get our attention with signs and wonders. Help us see how much you desire to free us from our yokes of slavery. For only then will we truly be thankful and bow down in worship to you.

Personal Notes and Prayers

Exodus 5:22-23

וַיָּשָׁב מֹשֶׁה אֶל־יְהוָה וַיֹּאמַר אֲדֹנָי לָמָה הֲרֵעֹתָה לָעָם הַזֶּה לָמָּה זֶּה שְׁלַחְתָּנִי:

וּמֵאָז בָּאתִי אֶל־פַּרְעֹה לְדַבֵּר בִּשְׁמֶךָ הֵרַע לָעָם הַזֶּה וְהַצֵּל לֹא־הִצַּלְתָּ אֶת־עַמֶּךָ:

Moses returned to the LORD and said, "LORD, why have you brought harm to this people? Is this why you sent me? Since I came to Pharaoh to speak in your name he has brought harm to this people and you have not rescued your people at all."

Biblical Context

IN MIDIAN, MOSES RELUCTANTLY agreed to be the harbinger of God and to intercede before Pharaoh for the deliverance of the Israelites from slavery. Not only did Pharaoh denied the request, but he maliciously increased the Hebrews's toils. Consequently, suffering escalated and the Hebrews began to arraign Moses (5:20–21). In the backlash, Moses despaired of God's intentions and used the same indicting rhetoric against God that he had previously used against Pharaoh—"Why have you brought harm to this people" (15), "Why have you brought trouble on this people?" (22). In this tension, the LORD not only reassures Moses but also reveals his character to him (Exod 6:1–8). The plan the LORD has for his people begins with liberating them from slavery. Second, their freedom is to serve as a foundation for a new covenant where He will be their God and they his people. Third, Israel will come to truly know the LORD as יְהוָה through a miraculous deliverance. God's purpose for this liberation is to fulfill his promises to the patriarchs and give his people the land of Canaan. At this time, land was a requirement for life, necessary for creating material resources, providing sustenance, and establishing identity. Thus, the LORD intended that his people live free, enjoying a life of righteousness and justice in a land of their own.

Life Application

Moses is amongst some of the most renowned characters of faith and obedience in the Scriptures. Yet his story serves as a reminder that life with God is not without travail. Even after the LORD affirms his intentions, Moses meets further opposition from the Hebrews (6:9), encounters difficulties in the desert (16:2), and is prevented from seeing the fulfillment of the promise of land (Deut 1:37). As we navigate life, we run up against circumstances of failure, discouragement and confusion. Shaken, we may ask of God, "What are you up to?" Yet I suspect that God is still up to much of the same. Certainly, this is what the gospel of Christ affirms as well: liberation (from sin), being a covenant people (as the children of God), intimacy (knowing God through Christ and the indwelling Spirit), and living a life fulfilled (the fruitful kingdom of God). Just as Moses's frustrations were not chastised, may we also honestly engage with our struggles as a part of God's story of redemption.

NT Scriptures

Romans 10:11; 1 Peter 2:6

Prayer

Living God, I surrender the parts of me that have yet to yield to you, that are resistant in shame, fear, disappointment, and hurt. I give you my life of self-determination and self-reliance. Expose every place in me that has yet to come home to you. Break every limit I have placed on who you are and what you can do. I ask for your forgiveness for the limitations I have placed on you. I ask that you make me good soil. Counsel me in my struggle, that my roots may grow deeper into the truth of your character and your story of redemption. Amen.

Personal Notes and Prayers

Exodus 12:23

וְעָבַר יְהוָה לִנְגֹּף אֶת־מִצְרַיִם וְרָאָה אֶת־הַדָּם עַל־הַמַּשְׁקוֹף וְעַל שְׁתֵּי הַמְּזוּזֹת

וּפָסַח יְהוָה עַל־הַפֶּתַח וְלֹא יִתֵּן הַמַּשְׁחִית לָבֹא אֶל־בָּתֵּיכֶם לִנְגֹּף׃

The LORD will pass over to smite the Egyptians. And when he sees the blood upon the lintel and upon the two doorposts, the LORD will pass over the door and he will not allow the destroyer to enter your houses to smite (you).

Biblical Context

IT IS THE NIGHT of the final plague in Egypt when the Israelites are finally going to be set free from Egyptians bondage. So far, Pharaoh hardened his heart but this last plague will leave him devastated. Exhausted and exasperated, he reluctantly allows the Israelites to leave Egypt. In this chapter, God gives specific instructions for the first Passover meal. The Israelites are to kill an unblemished lamb, place some of its blood on the doorposts of their houses, bake unleavened bread, roast the animal, eat it in a hurry and burn whatever is left over. Most importantly, they must take hyssop and spread the blood of the Passover lamb over the doors of their houses. the LORD is about to pass over Egypt. He will smite the firstborn in homes where doorposts and lintels are not painted with the blood of the lamb.

Life Application

Each year, we celebrate Easter and/or the Passover in remembrance of our deliverance from bondage. After suffering in Egypt for four hundred years, the LORD saved his people from their oppressor. It was a monumental night in the history of Israel, one that is still remembered over three thousand years later. God gave his people a tangible way to commemorate their freedom from bondage—a special meal comprised of lamb, herbs and unleavened bread. From this point on, every time they would eat this Passover meal (yearly), they would remember the mighty deeds of the LORD. This amazing freedom came at a cost—innocent blood was shed to protect God's people. As believers in Jesus, we know that the most precious blood—the blood of the Lamb of God—was shed for us. The Lamb who takes away the sins of the world gave his life for us and brought us freedom from the kingdom of darkness. As Israel remembers the blood spread on the doorposts and lintel of the houses, so we cover our lives with the blood of the Lamb who protects us from destruction. What a precious and costly gift we received from our LORD.

NT Scriptures

Matthew 26:20-30; 1 Corinthians 5:7-8

Prayer

O LORD—Lamb of God whose blood was shed for us—you suffered and died that we might be set free from bondage. May we learn to suffer with grace, to sacrifice our lives for the sake of others and to carry our cross in the power of your Spirit. Help us lay down our lives as you laid yours down for us.

Personal Notes and Prayers

Exodus 12:48

וְכִי־יָג֨וּר אִתְּךָ֜ גֵּ֗ר וְעָ֣שָׂה פֶסַח֮ לַיהוָה֒ הִמּ֧וֹל ל֣וֹ כָל־זָכָ֗ר וְאָז֙ יִקְרַ֣ב
לַעֲשֹׂת֔וֹ וְהָיָ֖ה כְּאֶזְרַ֣ח הָאָ֑רֶץ
וְכָל־עָרֵ֖ל לֹא־יֹ֥אכַל בּֽוֹ׃

If a foreigner sojourns with you and would keep the Passover to the LORD, let all his males be circumcised and then he shall draw near to keep it, and he shall be as a native of the land. But all who are uncircumcised shall not eat of it.

Biblical Context

IN THIS PASSAGE, THE Israelites receive instructions regarding the institution of the Passover—what to eat, how to prepare the meal, and even what to wear while eating it. For Israel, the Passover serves as a core element of her identity and reminds her of God's love, protection and provision for his people, expressed with a mighty hand and outstretched arm (Deut 5:15). The passage also infers that God loves the foreigner—the non-Israelite—who elects to believe in the God of Abraham, Isaac and Jacob and follows Israel in her journey. the LORD tells Moses and Aaron that the foreigners travelling with them are allowed to eat the Passover with the rest of the community. Though they are not descendants of Abraham, they are invited to share in Abraham's covenantal blessings. The LORD requires that those traveling with Israel be circumcised as a sign of their faithfulness to the covenant. Afterwards, the foreigners are to be treated as natives!

Life Application

While Israel is a testimony to the LORD's love for his people, the message of the Bible is that God's love is offered to all. Just as the foreigner was welcome to the Passover meal, so the Gentile is welcome to the cross of Christ and receives the benefits of his love. Following God requires commitment, sacrifice and obedience. All who follow the God of Abraham,

Isaac and Jacob, whether Jew or Gentiles—are held to the same standards of holiness and devotion to God. God will bless all whose heart is wholly surrendered to Him.

NT Scriptures

Matthew 19:21–30; Luke 14:28

Prayer

O LORD, you invited us to serve you, follow you and love you with complete surrender. Help us be fully committed to your call and obey you wherever you lead us. Help us decrease so that you may increase in us. As you have delivered the children of Israel from bondage, so you have delivered us from darkness and brought us into the light. Circumcise our hearts anew that we may serve you even more fully in days to come.

Personal Notes and Prayers

Exodus 14:13–14, 27b

וַיֹּאמֶר מֹשֶׁה אֶל־הָעָם אַל־תִּירָאוּ הִתְיַצְּבוּ וּרְאוּ אֶת־יְשׁוּעַת יְהוָה
אֲשֶׁר־יַעֲשֶׂה לָכֶם הַיּוֹם
כִּי אֲשֶׁר רְאִיתֶם אֶת־מִצְרַיִם הַיּוֹם לֹא תֹסִיפוּ לִרְאֹתָם עוֹד עַד־
עוֹלָם: . . .
יְהוָה יִלָּחֵם לָכֶם וְאַתֶּם תַּחֲרִישׁוּן: וַיְנַעֵר יְהוָה אֶת־מִצְרַיִם בְּתוֹךְ
הַיָּם:

Moses said to the people: "Do not fear! Stand and see the
salvation of the LORD, which He will do for you today;
for as you have seen the Egyptians today, you will not see
them anymore, forever. the LORD will fight for you if you
will be still." And the LORD violently shook
the Egyptians in the midst of the sea.

Biblical Context

AFTER YEARS OF CAPTIVITY in Egypt, the Israelites are finally freed, leaving not as common beggars, but with their hands full with Egyptian wealth (Exod 12:35–36). Now at the edge of the Sea of Reeds, the Israelites see the Egyptian army hemming them in to kill or re-enslave them. The panic they feel is natural but the answer they receive from Moses eventually proves to be foundational for Israel. Moses's words are simple: "The LORD will fight for you." This simple statement may not have meant much to Israel at this point since this generation had not yet experienced I AM as the supreme God of heaven and earth. the LORD had orchestrated this event in order to save his covenant people and to make his glory known to all ("The Egyptians will know that I am the LORD" [14:4]). After the crossing, God destroys the army by "violently shaking" the Egyptians in the sea, ensuring that none would survive. It is interesting to note that the author chose a verb in the Piel stem to describe the LORD's activity of "violently shaking" the enemies of Israel, something that gets lost in most English translations—"The LORD swept them" (TNIV); "The LORD overthrew them" (NASB/ESV/KJV).

Life Application

Indeed, the LORD fights for us. How often we rush into situations with our swords drawn and our shields raised only to make an absolute mess of things? Perhaps we respond out of panic, loss of control, or a need for justice. Had the Israelites ignored Moses's instructions and engaged the Egyptians in battle, the narrative could have had an entirely different ending, resulting in death and re-enslavement. As the story reveals, God showed the Israelites that they did not even have to lift a finger. the LORD did all the work—He called, separated, confused the enemy and completely destroyed them. Our feeble attempts at solving our own problems seem so small and insignificant compared to this kind of power. Remember that *"the LORD will fight for you!"* Let him!

NT Scriptures

Romans 12:19–21; Revelation 19:11–16

Prayer

O LORD, you are so much greater, powerful, faithful, generous and merciful than what our minds can comprehend. Help us let go of our own ways and help us trust in yours.

Personal Notes and Prayers

Exodus 15:3

יְהוָה אִישׁ מִלְחָמָה יְהוָה שְׁמוֹ׃

The LORD is a man of war. The LORD is his name.

Biblical Context

THROUGH A MIRACULOUS EVENT, Moses and the nation of Israel leave Egypt and watch Pharaoh's army drown in the swirling waters of the Sea of Reeds. Unbeknownst to Israel, this event would become a defining moment for the nation, and in some respects, for Israelite religion. Through this miracle, Israel learned that God would not only provide for them; the miracle of the Exodus confirmed that God who would fight for them, protect them, perform miracles on their behalf and free them from the harshest of bondage. During this period, Egypt was one of the most powerful countries in the world, and Pharaoh's army was also one of the best in warfare. Yet, God did not hesitate or break a sweat in his dealing with them. The Hebrews saw a God who was not only all powerful, but who was willing to perform amazing deeds on their behalf.

Life Application

God loves to meet the needs of his people. When Noah needed a God to trust in, God was trustworthy. When Moses did not know what to say, God was a voice for him. When David needed a God to talk to, God listened. When the Israelites needed rescuing, God was a man of War. But when it comes right down to it, God is Almighty, limitless in power, abundant in love, generous in lovingkindness and always ready to do exceeding, abundantly, above all we can as or think.

NT Scriptures

Matthew 3:11–12; Ephesians 3:20–21

Prayer

O LORD, thank you for your amazing display of love towards us. You fight for us; you sustain us in battle; you teach us true warfare and you graciously bring us to victory. Help us depend on you during our trials and tribulations. Help us call on you in times of trouble. Remind us of who you are when the enemy comes against us to tempts us, distract us, discourage us and cause us to fall. Thank you for being there always!

Personal Notes and Prayers

Exodus 19:5–6a

וְעַתָּ֗ה אִם־שָׁמ֤וֹעַ תִּשְׁמְעוּ֙ בְּקֹלִ֔י וּשְׁמַרְתֶּ֖ם אֶת־בְּרִיתִ֑י וִהְיִ֨יתֶם לִ֤י
סְגֻלָּה֙ מִכָּל־הָ֣עַמִּ֔ים כִּי־לִ֖י כָּל־הָאָֽרֶץ׃

וְאַתֶּ֧ם תִּהְיוּ־לִ֛י מַמְלֶ֥כֶת כֹּהֲנִ֖ים וְג֣וֹי קָד֑וֹשׁ

*And now, if you will indeed hear my voice and keep my
covenant, then you will be to me a treasured possession
from among all the peoples, for all the earth belongs to me.
But you yourselves will be to me a kingdom
of priests and a holy nation.*

Biblical Context

IN THE THIRD MONTH after the Israelites left Egypt, the LORD spoke to Moses on Mount Sinai and commanded him to relay these words (vv.5–6a) to the Israelites. In the previous verse, the LORD recounts how he defeated the Egyptians, rescued them out of bondage, and brought them to himself "on eagles's wings" (v.4). Then, he declares to Israel that she was chosen to be a kingdom of priests and a holy nation, a people whose very existence was to testify of the love of God for all humanity. Thus, Israel was called to serve as a *mediator* (a kingdom of priests to represent the LORD) and as a *model* (holy, set apart, distinct from the nations) before the nations of the world. Fulfilling this call would require complete obedience, faithfulness and commitment to God's covenant. Nothing less.

Life Application

Israel was required to obey and keep God's covenant in order to fulfill the purpose for which she was called—to bless all the nations of the world. Israel was not to keep the law in order to earn "salvation" from God. God had already redeemed them. As Christians who have been redeemed by God's grace, by his Son's death and resurrection, we obey God not to earn his favor, but to fulfill the purpose for which he designed us. And this purpose is the same purpose for which he called

Abraham and his descendants—to bless all the nations of the world. As Christians, we are called to live consecrated lives, holy and set apart from the world for the sake of the world. Our light, which comes from God, is meant to shine before all people in order that they may know our Father in heaven (Matt 5:16).

NT Scriptures

Matthew 5:14–16; 1 Peter 2:4–5, 9–10

Prayer

O LORD, we thank you for the free gift of salvation. We are humbled by your love and by your call on our sinful lives. It is truly beyond human comprehension. You faithfully work in us and through us to reveal your glory on the earth and you eagerly use us for the sake of the lost and for the sake of your Kingdom. Have your own way in us today and as long as we are on this earth.

Personal Notes and Prayers

Exodus 19:6

וְאַתֶּם תִּהְיוּ־לִי מַמְלֶכֶת כֹּהֲנִים וְגוֹי קָדוֹשׁ אֵלֶּה הַדְּבָרִים אֲשֶׁר
תְּדַבֵּר אֶל־בְּנֵי יִשְׂרָאֵל׃

*"And you shall be to me a kingdom of priests and a holy
nation." These are the words that you shall
speak to the children of Israel.*

Biblical Context

THREE MONTHS AFTER GOD brings Israel out of Egypt and defeats the Egyptian army, the Israelites arrive at Mt. Horeb in the Sinai. While the people gather at the foot of the mountain, Moses ascends the peak by himself to speak with God. God promises the Israelites (through Moses) that he will make them into "a kingdom of priests and a holy nation," if they agree to hear his voice and keep his covenant (laid out in chapter 20). Ethical distinctiveness, or holiness, was part of God's plan for Israel from the very beginning when he first called Abram and promised to make him into a great nation through which all the nations of the earth would be blessed (Gen 12:1–3). Abram and his descendants were to "keep the way of the LORD by doing righteousness and justice" (Gen 18:19); holy living is precisely what Israel was elected for, and blessing the nations as a priest blesses his people is the intended end result.

Life Application

This verse represents a biblical call to mission for the people of God and it presents a strong challenge for how we should live as Christians. If we are to fulfill the purpose of our lives as believers in Jesus and successfully bless the nations and the people around us, we must live ethically distinct lives. The Decalogue presents a summary of what that distinctiveness looks like, and our faith in the LORD should affect every aspect (spiritual/religious, but also social, political, economic, etc.) of our existence. In addition, we are called to live as priests—that is, as intermediaries between the people around us and God. That involves cultivating relationships with them so we might communicate God's truth to them effectively, but it also means interceding on their behalf.

NT Scriptures

Acts 13:47; Romans 12:1–2; Galatians 3:14

Prayer

O LORD, what a privilege it is to be called "priests of the LORD" to intercede for people and to minister life, healing, peace and joy. Thank you for granting us this privilege and for giving us this heavy responsibility. Help us be faithful to bring the lost into your kingdom and to nurture those who have chosen to follow you. Help us be living sacrifices so that, through our love, we may cover a multitude of sins. LORD, have your way in us and through us this day.

Personal Notes and Prayers

Exodus 20:20

וַיֹּ֨אמֶר מֹשֶׁ֤ה אֶל־הָעָם֙ אַל־תִּירָ֔אוּ כִּ֗י לְבַֽעֲבוּר֙ נַסּ֣וֹת אֶתְכֶ֔ם בָּ֖א הָאֱלֹהִ֑ים

וּבַעֲב֗וּר תִּהְיֶ֧ה יִרְאָת֛וֹ עַל־פְּנֵיכֶ֖ם לְבִלְתִּ֥י תֶחֱטָֽאוּ׃

Then Moses said to the people, "Do not be afraid. For God came in order to test you and in order that his fear (awe) be before you, so that you do not sin."

Biblical Context

MOUNT SINAI WAS NOT the first place where Israel was commanded not to fear. Not long before crossing the Sea of Reeds, the Israelites thought they were as good as dead. Pursued by Pharaoh and his army, they cried out and blamed Moses for putting them in this pickle! Unmoved by their emotional address, Moses responds: "Do not fear!" (אַל־תִּירָאוּ; Exod 14:13). How could this be? Certainly, Pharaoh's army was something to be feared, and so was the trumpet blast accompanied by smoke and lighting at the mountain. Surely, no one could fault the people for such a human reaction. In our passage, the command to not fear is followed by two occurrences of בַּעֲבוּר ("in order that" indicating purpose for the command). First, it was God's intention to test the Israelites. The verb נַסּוֹת "testing" carries the idea of "proving." In this case, God wanted to prove to Israel that YHWH was indeed the most powerful God. The second בַּעֲבוּר ("in order that") precedes the statement that "fear, awe, respect" is to be reserved for YHWH alone. God's intention was not to illicit fear or dread of physical harm, but rather, it was to generate fear and respect towards the very One who controlled the terrifying elements.

Life Application

Many are the thing that produce terror in this world, both through human actions and through natural phenomena (e.g., terrorism, wars, earthquakes, floods) and on a smaller scale, illness, anxiety, rejection, job-loss, to name a few. To live fearlessly seems an impossible venture these days. Fearlessness is an expression of a transformed way of life, one that is dependent on YHWH. Fearlessness arises not out of our own human competence, for we can do little to prevent real disasters from occurring. Rather, it comes from our knowledge of the supremacy of God over all things, and from the fear (awe, respect) of the one who has dominion over all objects of terror. It must produce in us a desire to serve the Creator in holiness, steadfastness and resolve.

NT Scriptures

Matthew 10:16–28; Mark 4:35–41

Prayer

O LORD, the ground on which we stand is shaking and unstable. Help us keep our eyes on you at all times, especially when trials come in like floods. Help us trust you when persecution, suffering, illness and rejection rise up against us. Make us fearless in the face of our enemies. Make us steadfast, unmovable and always abounding in the work of the LORD.

Personal Notes and Prayers

Exodus 31:12-13

וַיֹּאמֶר יְהוָה אֶל־מֹשֶׁה לֵּאמֹר׃ וְאַתָּה דַּבֵּר אֶל־בְּנֵי יִשְׂרָאֵל לֵאמֹר
אַךְ אֶת־שַׁבְּתֹתַי תִּשְׁמֹרוּ
כִּי אוֹת הִוא בֵּינִי וּבֵינֵיכֶם לְדֹרֹתֵיכֶם לָדַעַת כִּי אֲנִי יְהוָה מְקַדִּשְׁכֶם׃

The LORD said to Moses, "You, speak to the sons of Israel saying, 'Only, keep my Sabbaths, for it is a sign between me and you throughout your generations, so that you may know that I am the LORD who sanctifies you.'"

Biblical Context

THE THEME OF SABBATH permeates Scripture from the beginning of the Torah to the end of the New Testament. As God exists throughout times so does the Sabbath. God's instructions to observe the Sabbath appear in the Ten Commandments (Exod 20:8-11; Deut 5:12-15) and at the conclusion of the divine revelation of Torah to Moses on Mount Sinai (Exod 31:12-17). This discourse between God and Moses (Exod 19-31) begins on the mountain where God gives the Ten Commandments and prescribes ethical, moral, and social laws. This portion of Scripture is known as the Sinai Covenant. The Sabbath pericope in Exodus 31:12-17 forms an inclusio as it revisits the theme of Sabbath in Exodus 20:8-11. In a way, this commandment is unique in that it is to be a "sign" between God and his people forever. None of the other commandments are identified as such. The Sabbath is a feature that sets God's people apart, and it is remains so throughout all times.

Life Application

Often we try to take things into our own hands. Especially in the Western world, we seek to make ourselves better by working harder, being the best, and never stopping. Yet, God himself calls us to stop, cease from our labor, rest from work. He insists that we take time to remember Him and what he has done for us. Just as the Israelites remember on the Sabbath how God rested on the seventh day (Exod 20:8–11) and brought them up out of Egypt with "a mighty hand and an outstretched arm" (Deut 5:12–15), today we remember that God sent his son Jesus to redeem us and reconcile us to himself. Weekly, we cease from our work and remember that we are being sanctified, not by what we do or by how hard we work, but by the redemptive work of Yeshua the Messiah.

NT Scriptures

Luke 23:50–56; Acts 13:42–44; 16:13–14; 17:2–4; Hebrews 4:1–13

Prayer

O LORD, we thank you for the institution of Shabbat, for the opportunity to cease from our labor and reflect on your awesome deeds. On that special day, open our eyes that we may see your majesty and teach our hearts to love you with abandon. Fill our minds and hearts with your thoughts and help us release the cares of this world into your hands.

Personal Notes and Prayers

Exodus 33:15–16

וַיֹּ֖אמֶר אֵלָ֑יו אִם־אֵ֤ין פָּנֶ֙יךָ֙ הֹלְכִ֔ים אַֽל־תַּעֲלֵ֖נוּ מִזֶּֽה: וּבַמֶּ֣ה ׀ יִוָּדַ֣ע
אֵפ֗וֹא כִּֽי־מָצָ֨אתִי חֵ֤ן בְּעֵינֶ֙יךָ֙
אֲנִ֣י וְעַמֶּ֔ךָ הֲל֖וֹא בְּלֶכְתְּךָ֣ עִמָּ֑נוּ וְנִפְלֵ֙ינוּ֙ אֲנִ֣י וְעַמְּךָ֔ מִכָּ֨ל־הָעָ֔ם אֲשֶׁ֖ר
עַל־פְּנֵ֥י הָאֲדָמָֽה:

Then (Moses) said to him (the LORD), "If your Presence does not go with us, do not send us up from this place. Indeed, how then will anyone know that I have found favor in your eyes, I and your people, unless you go with us? How else will I and your people be distinguished from all the people who are upon the face of the earth?

Biblical Context

AFTER THE GOLDEN CALF incident at Mt Sinai, the LORD tells Moses that He *will not dwell* in the midst of his people during their journey to the Promised Land, but will instead send an angel before them (Exod 33:1–6). Shortly thereafter, Moses enters the Tent of Meeting and intercedes face-to-face before the LORD on behalf of Israel, knowing full well that without the presence of God in the midst of the community, the people would surely be doomed. Moses pleads with God to reveal His ways so that he may know Him and find favor in his sight. Moved by Moses's petition, God responds mercifully with the following words: "My presence *will go* with you and I will give you rest." These are the words of reassurance and comfort Moses had longed for. Meanwhile, as the people noticed a pillar of cloud standing at the entrance of the Tent of Meeting (i.e., the place of the manifestation of the presence of God), they stood up and worshiped with repentant hearts at the door of their own tents.

Life Application

Like Moses, we must consider what would become of us if the LORD's presence failed to accompany us on the journey of life. Today, the LORD's presence does not escort us in a pillar of fire or cloud, rather, God is ever present with us in the person of the Holy Spirit. Several times in Scripture, God promised that "He would *never* leave us nor forsake us" (Deut 31:6–8; Josh 1:5; 1 Kgs 8:57). The Holy Spirit who indwells us teaches us to walk in the ways of the LORD and helps us fulfill his will in our lives.

NT Scriptures

John 16:7–15; Galatians 5:22–26; Hebrews 13:5; 1 John 3:19–24

Prayer

O LORD, we would be completely helpless without your presence in our lives. Already you have done so much to change our hearts and minds to conform to your will. Increase your presence in our lives and help us be sensitive to the leading of your Holy Spirit. Have your own way in us LORD, have your own way in us.

Personal Notes and Prayers

Exodus 33:17

וַיֹּאמֶר יְהוָה אֶל־מֹשֶׁה גַּם אֶת־הַדָּבָר הַזֶּה אֲשֶׁר דִּבַּרְתָּ אֶעֱשֶׂה כִּי־מָצָאתָ חֵן בְּעֵינַי וָאֵדָעֲךָ בְּשֵׁם:

The LORD said to Moses: "I will do this very thing that you have asked; for you have found favor in my sight, and I know you by name."

Biblical Context

MOSES COMES DOWN FROM Mt. Sinai with two stone tablets engraved with the Laws of the LORD and witnesses the "great sin" of Israel—the creation and worship of a golden calf. In anger, Moses sends the tablets crashing to the ground. Subsequently, the Israelites repent but Moses must go back to the LORD to plead for mercy on their behalf. The camp is cleansed by a plague, but the LORD declares that they will not receive the benefit of his presence "among them." So, in yet another plea for this "stiff-necked people," Moses appeals to the LORD by drawing upon his own reputation: "You have said 'I know you by name, and you have found favor in my sight.'" And the LORD replies not with a curse upon Israel, but with a promise: "My Presence will go with you, and I will give you rest." Does Moses respond with thanks and worship, or even with a sigh of relief? No, instead he questions the LORD! As if the LORD had not spoken at all, Moses asks Him not to send them out into the wilderness without his protection and presence. Does the LORD's wrath finally come? Amazingly, verse 17 tells us that the LORD answers yet again with grace and patience, repeating not only his promise to his people, but also his favor toward Moses.

Life Application

Moses spoke to the LORD "face to face, as a man speaks to his friend" (33:11). Oh, to be like Moses . . . to be a friend of God! And yet I am; for Jesus said: "I have called you friends" (John 15:15). Oh, to find favor in

God's sight . . . yet I do: "In the time of favor I answered you" (Isa 49:8). And to have Him know me by name! So, He does; for Jesus "calls his own sheep by name and leads them out" (John 10:3b). But also, like Moses, I often respond in my humanity . . . with fear and need for reassurance. Moses heard from the LORD, and yet he questioned. I do the same, wondering whether the LORD is or will be with me, even after He has already promised to be so. Yet He responds with love, so that even in my times of doubting or demanding, I am in his favor, He still knows me by name, and his presence and rest go with me.

NT Scriptures

John 10:3b

Prayer

O LORD, how great is your mercy towards. We deserve wrath and you extend mercy; death and you give us life. Grant that we may live in the shadow of your love and extend grace, mercy and love to all who live in this broken world. Thank you for loving us with an everlasting love.

Personal Notes and Prayers

Exodus 34:1

וַיֹּאמֶר יְהוָה אֶל־מֹשֶׁה פְּסָל־לְךָ שְׁנֵי־לֻחֹת אֲבָנִים כָּרִאשֹׁנִים
וְכָתַבְתִּי עַל־הַלֻּחֹת אֶת־הַדְּבָרִים אֲשֶׁר הָיוּ עַל־הַלֻּחֹת הָרִאשֹׁנִים
אֲשֶׁר שִׁבַּרְתָּ׃

*Then the LORD said to Moses: Carve two
stone tablets like the first ones!*

Biblical Context

ENRAGED AT THE SIGHT of the Israelites worshipping and dancing before a golden calf, Moses took the tablets of stones that contained the Ten Commandments, and threw them on the ground at the foot of the Mt Sinai (Exod 32:19). After witnessing idolatry and debauchery from the very people whom God had recently delivered from horrendous bondage, Moses was unable to contain his fury. He destroyed the precious tablets of the covenant, cremated the golden calf, and challenged the Israelites to repent of their evil deeds. Shortly thereafter, God called Moses back into his presence and gave him an opportunity to vent his frustrations and to intercede on the behalf of those who had transgressed. Although God was not pleased with the behavior of the Israelites, He was not about to give up on them. He instructed Moses to carve a second set of tablets and inscribe the commandments He had given to him during his previous excursion to the top of Mt Sinai. While fasting for forty days and forty nights, Moses wrote the Ten Commandments on the new tablets (34:27–28).

Life Application

Out of anger, we break things, people, and ourselves. Out of anger, we lose control and mar the image of God in us and in others. Yet God, who excels in restoring and healing what is broken, is always ready to provide a second chance. God commanded Moses to carve a new set of tablets like the first ones, with the purpose of redeeming what was lost and with the intention to restore what was near and dear to his heart. "*Like the first ones!*" God had formed the first tablets and written on them with his own fingers. In Exodus 34, Moses carves and God restores what was broken. Once again, Moses becomes the hand of God and a divine instrument of reconciliation. Even leaders can count on second chances!

NT Scriptures

James 1:19–20

Prayer

Thank you LORD for never giving up on us when we are angry and sin, when we take matters in our own hands and mess things up. Thank you for teaching us to react the way you react and to be redemptive in dealing with every situation. To you be the glory.

Personal Notes and Prayers

Leviticus 16:30

כִּי־בַיּוֹם הַזֶּה יְכַפֵּר עֲלֵיכֶם לְטַהֵר אֶתְכֶם מִכֹּל חַטֹּאתֵיכֶם לִפְנֵי יְהוָה תִּטְהָרוּ׃

Because on this day, he will make atonement for you to purify you, before the LORD you will be cleansed from all your sins.

Biblical Context

THE BOOK OF LEVITICUS contrasts vividly the clean from the unclean. The unclean was intolerable before God and could not remain in his presence. Unfortunately, the people of Israel had a knack for making themselves unclean with ungodly practices and rebellion against God. Knowing their propensity to sin, in his grace and mercy, the LORD made a way for his people to be purified from their sins. Throughout the year, people would come to God's holy place and present sacrifices and offerings and in a sense, leave their guilt and sin at his sanctuary. Moreover, on the Day of Atonement (which only happened once a year), the High priest would undergo an extensive ritual of cleansing and offering of sacrifices to purify the sanctuary, himself and the people for the sins of the previous year. The end result was that sin was removed from the camp and once again the people were considered clean before God.

Life Application

The Day of Atonement foreshadowed a much greater sacrifice that was to be made by Jesus Christ, the Son of God. The Day of Atonement cleansed the people for that year while Christ's sacrifice provided cleansing and forgiveness of sin for people once for all, as Hebrews 10:1–10 teaches. God in his infinite mercy has provided more than just a yearly sacrifice. Through Jesus Christ our sins have been cleansed for all eternity, the ultimate atonement has been made and no more sacrifices are necessary. Not only did He cleanse us from our sins, He was the sacrifice who made atonement for us. Because of his work on the cross we too are cleansed and welcome into the presence of God freely to fellowship with Him and worship Him.

NT Scriptures

Romans 3:25–26; Hebrews 10:1–14; 1 John 1:6–10; 2:1–2; 4:9–10

Prayer

O LORD, how amazing is your love for us, that you would become our atoning sacrifice once and for all. We were once separated from you and you came willingly to reconcile us to you. We were afar off and now, thanks to your shed blood, we have been brought near. We have open access to your throne of grace and can now come into your presence with grateful hearts and reverence. Receive our praise, our thanks, our adoration O LORD.

Personal Notes and Prayers

Leviticus 20:7

וְהִתְקַדִּשְׁתֶּ֕ם וִהְיִיתֶ֖ם קְדֹשִׁ֑ים כִּ֛י אֲנִ֥י יְהוָ֖ה אֱלֹהֵיכֶֽם:

*Consecrate yourselves and you will become holy,
because I am the LORD your God.*

Biblical Context

THE BOOK OF THE Law contains the terms by which the Israelites were to live righteously before God. In order for the people to live as such, their sins had to be removed or hidden through the sacrificial system and through the yearly ritual of the High Priest on the day of atonement. In addition to God providing the means of atonement for sin, the Israelites were to consecrate themselves before coming into the presence of God. Nestled in a list of serious offences (i.e., offering children to Molech, consulting with mediums and soothsayers, committing adultery with father's wife) is the command to consecrate oneself and be holy. The reason given is that the LORD was their God, and since the LORD was holy, the Israelites should seek to be holy. They were required to engage actively in the cleansing process by sanctifying themselves and offering themselves to God. This practice of sanctification ensured that the Israelites dedicated time on a regular basis to reflecting on the holiness of God.

Life Application

The Mosaic Law provided a guide for living in right relationship with God. But no matter how well the people followed the Law or became ceremonially clean before God, they still could not get rid of sin on their own. Sin could only be cover temporarily. Jesus was sent by the Father to be the ultimate cleanser of sin for all mankind. In the Hebrew Bible, God required that the Israelites sanctify themselves and be clean in order to come before Him. Now that Jesus Christ has come to save us and sanctify us, we can all come before God freely. As Paul told the Corinthians, as we come into the presence of God and behold his glory, "we are being transformed into the same image from one degree of glory to another" by the power of the Holy Spirit (ESV 2 Cor 3:18).

NT Scriptures

Hebrews 9:13–14; 1 John 3:3

Prayer

O LORD, how we yearn to be free from sin. Purify us with your blood and cleanse us O LORD. Remove impurities from our lives and transform us into your image so that the world may see that your presence is here on this earth. Help us reflect your glory and make us instruments of righteousness. Only you can do this transforming work in us. We are helpless without you.

Personal Notes and Prayers

Leviticus 23:3

שֵׁ֣שֶׁת יָמִים֮ תֵּעָשֶׂ֣ה מְלָאכָה֒ וּבַיּ֣וֹם הַשְּׁבִיעִ֗י שַׁבַּ֤ת שַׁבָּתוֹן֙ מִקְרָא־
קֹ֔דֶשׁ כָּל־מְלָאכָ֖ה לֹ֣א תַעֲשׂ֑וּ

שַׁבָּ֥ת הִוא֙ לַֽיהוָ֔ה בְּכֹ֖ל מוֹשְׁבֹתֵיכֶֽם׃

Six days is work done, and on the seventh day is a Sabbath of rest, a holy assembly; you shall do no work; it is a Sabbath to the LORD in all your dwellings.

Biblical Context

AFTER THE LAW IS given at Mount Sinai and the Tabernacle is built in the wilderness, God calls Moses and gives him instructions by which the Israelites were to live as priests among the nations. God mentions repeatedly that He longs for his people to be holy because He is holy. In this section of Leviticus, (chapters 17–27) the Israelites are given practical guidelines for holiness, including the customary celebration of the biblical feasts. The first festival that is identified is the Sabbath, a day of rest so significant that it is ordered as one of the Ten Commandments. In Exodus 20:8–11, we find the command to keep the Sabbath holy and to rest because God rested on the seventh day of creation. God knows that humans have a propensity to scurry about in their daily work and to pursue their own interests. The language of the commandment is clear "YOU SHALL DO NO WORK!" This is meant to be a strict prohibition against "our own work" on this special day, a day when God is honored and worshipped. However, the command does not preclude taking care of those who are in need, as confirmed by Jesus numerous times in the gospels (e.g., Mark 2:23–28; Luke 6:6–11). We are called to cease from "our own labor" but we are not called to stop from doing the LORD's work.

Life Application

You know your routine. Up at dawn, tend to yourself, tend to your nourishment, tend to your home life, tend to your vocation, tend to your ad-vocations, tend to your sleep and then do it all again the next day. One is more than likely to maintain this schedule each and every day of the week were it not for the strict prohibition to "DO NO WORK ON THE SABBATH." Our Father in heaven knows our weaknesses and the needs of our inmost being. He wants to refresh us and give rest to our soul, and for this reason, on the seventh day He says "STOP and rest!" Out of conviction, we want to obey, but we just need to do one more thing—fix this thing, clean this room or complete that task. Life's demands are great and will never cease to call us to action. We must make ourselves STOP from "our own labor" and take time to reflect on who God is, on what He has done, and on what He wishes to do in our lives. The command to STOP is not simply a legalistic decree. It is meant to be a time of rest, celebration, reflection and fellowship with our heavenly Father. Only there will we find the regenerating power to continue our work.

NT Scriptures

John 9:1–41; Hebrews 4:9–10

Prayer

O LORD, we thank you for calling us to rest. We desperately need to enter into your presence, to be close to you, to listen to your voice, and to fellowship with you. Help us be faithful to you in our work and in our rest. Refresh us as we come into your holy presence to gaze into your face. Transform us into your image from glory to glory. Holy are You, O LORD.

Personal Notes and Prayers

Numbers 6:24-26

יְבָרֶכְךָ יְהוָה וְיִשְׁמְרֶךָ: יָאֵר יְהוָה פָּנָיו אֵלֶיךָ וִיחֻנֶּךָּ: יִשָּׂא יְהוָה פָּנָיו
אֵלֶיךָ וְיָשֵׂם לְךָ שָׁלוֹם:

May the LORD bless you and keep you; may He make his face to shine upon you and be gracious to you; may the LORD lift up his countenance upon you and cause peace to settle upon you.

Biblical Context

IN 1979, ARCHAEOLOGISTS UNEARTHED a small silver amulet with the biblical Hebrew text of Numbers 6:24-26 (the Aaronic blessing) from a concealed burial chamber in Jerusalem, Israel. This artifact provides the earliest biblical text ever discovered. The amulet measures 1 x 1 ¾ inches. It was carefully rolled up, and was probably worn as a piece of jewelry around the neck, or possibly as a good luck charm belonging to a superstitious or religious individual. Since the message inscribed on the amulet is a divine blessing, it is possible that the piece of jewelry served to invite blessings on its owner and ward off any misfortune.

Life Application

Every word of this beautiful text is heavy with theological significance. The first verb, בָּרַךְ ("to bless"), echoes God's promise made to Abram when he was called out of Ur of the Chaldees. God promised that He would *bless* him and make him into a great nation. The second verb, שָׁמַר ("to keep"), reveals God's protection for his people. And in the light of Psalm 121:4, we are guaranteed that God keeps watch over his people twenty-four hours a day since He never slumbers nor sleeps. The third verb, אוֹר ("to shine"), reminds us of Moses's encounter with God on Mt. Sinai. So radiant was his face that he had to wear a veil over his head so as not to overwhelm the Israelites with the brightness of glory of the LORD. The end of the Aaronic blessing invites God to impart on his people peace, wholeness, healing, completeness, and quietness of heart, mind, and soul.

NT Scriptures

1 Corinthians 13:12; James 1:22–25

Prayer

Thank you LORD for your eagerness to bless us, to make your glory shine upon us, to grant us your perfect peace. In this uncertain world, you keep us safe and protect us. In this dark world, you are our light and our salvation. In this world of chaos, you are our peace that passes all understanding. Thank you O God our Father.

Personal Notes and Prayers

Numbers 11:12–13

הֶאָנֹכִ֣י הָרִ֗יתִי אֵ֚ת כָּל־הָעָ֣ם הַזֶּ֔ה אִם־אָנֹכִ֖י יְלִדְתִּ֑יהוּ כִּֽי־תֹאמַ֨ר אֵלַ֜י שָׂאֵ֣הוּ בְחֵיקֶ֗ךָ

כַּאֲשֶׁ֨ר יִשָּׂ֤א הָאֹמֵן֙ אֶת־הַיֹּנֵ֔ק עַ֚ל הָֽאֲדָמָ֔ה אֲשֶׁ֥ר נִשְׁבַּ֖עְתָּ לַאֲבֹתָֽיו׃

מֵאַ֤יִן לִי֙ בָּשָׂ֔ר לָתֵ֖ת לְכָל־הָעָ֣ם הַזֶּ֑ה כִּֽי־יִבְכּ֤וּ עָלַי֙ לֵאמֹ֔ר תְּנָה־לָּ֥נוּ בָשָׂ֖ר וְנֹאכֵֽלָה׃

[Moses speaking:] Did I myself conceive all these people? Or did I give them birth, that You would say to me, "Carry them in your bosom," just as a foster-father [carries] the suckling child upon the ground, which You swore to their fathers? Where will I get meat to give all these people? For they wail upon me, saying, "Oh please, give us meat that we may eat!"

Biblical Context

IN EXODUS 3–4, THE LORD promises Moses that He himself, with Moses as his instrument, would deliver the people out of Egypt and bring them into a land flowing with milk and honey. Moses is instructed to tell the people that it was God who promised to bring them out (Ex 3:17). The LORD tells Moses that He will be with him, that He will be the words in Moses's mouth and the power behind those words. Up to this point, He had been faithful to do all of this, but Moses and the people are dissatisfied. This situation is not what anyone wanted or expected. The people wanted freedom and abundance without delay and without any strings attached. Moses wanted to be left alone, or, barring that, to be permitted to lead in silence a people willing to be led. The people's expectations do not match their reality, and they expect someone else (Moses) to fix this. Moses's expectations do not match his reality, and he feels the unfairness of being expected to fix everything. So, the people wail. And Moses wails.

Life Application

Moses had a tendency to assume more responsibility than he could reasonably manage (see also Exod 2 and 18, and Num 20). The unfair expectation he felt to fix every situation was something he had taken upon himself. Moses himself later remembers that the LORD carried the people as a father carries his son (Deut 1:31). We can easily identify with Moses in his complaint. The people are clearly wrong. They have been given freedom from slavery, and they cry about meat and leeks. But Moses is also wrong. When we accept a call to serve God, do we recognize that it is God working in us through the agency of the Holy Spirit? Do we acknowledge our dependence on the Father who is carrying us as well as his people, his church, or do we attempt to control our environment, our ministry, and those under our care? Do we try to do everything ourselves, or do we accept help? (Part of God's response to Moses's weariness was to fill other leaders with His Spirit!) God invites us to work alongside Him in his own work, and in relying on his strength we find both power and freedom to fulfill our responsibilities.

NT Scriptures

Acts 6:1–4; Ephesians 2:10; Philippians 2:12–13

Personal prayer

Abba, we, like Moses, often fall into the trap of imagining that Your work depends on our strength. Forgive us for our self-importance. We cannot do everything. Help us to learn to lean on You. Thank You for Your kindness toward us, and for the help You provide through Your Spirit and through our fellow ministers. May You be glorified in our weakness.

Personal Notes and Prayers

Numbers 11:14

לֹא־אוּכַל אָנֹכִי לְבַדִּי לָשֵׂאת אֶת־כָּל־הָעָם הַזֶּה כִּי כָבֵד מִמֶּנִּי׃

*I alone am not able to carry all of these people,
for [this burden] is too heavy for me.*

Biblical Context

FOR A LITTLE OVER a year, the Israelites have been feeding daily on bread from heaven. By now, the people have grown sick of this miraculous manna so they come and complain to Moses about their craving for the food of Egypt—meat, cucumbers, melons, leeks, onions, garlic. This particular episode is especially troubling for Moses whose leadership skills have been tested time and time again by the Israelites (11:10). In many ways it looks as if Moses is at the brink of despair since he asks God repeatedly to kill him (11:15). Moses enters into a long discourse with YHWH and demands assistance in dealing with these troublesome people. God responds by appointing seventy leaders to come alongside Moses and walk with him in the anointing of the Spirit. These elders are not just figureheads but Spirit-endowed leaders who will bear the burden of the Israelites alongside Moses (11:16–17) and prophesy the word of the LORD to the Israelites (11:25–29). In addition to the new assisting leaders, God promises to provide meat for the people, "not for one day, or two days, or five days, or ten days, or twenty days, bur for an entire month" until it comes out of their nostrils and becomes loathsome to them (11:19–20). Moses's prayer is answered. He is not alone. The people will be satiated.

Life Application

Ministry is hard. Only a fool would think that ministry is a walk in the park. Numbers 11 reminds us that even the greatest and most humble leaders (Num 12:3) sometimes forget that "no man is an island." Paul had a thorn in his flesh to keep him humble (2 Cor. 12:7). It is also noteworthy that Paul never traveled alone. He was constantly in the company of friends who assisted him in ministry. Sometimes leaders need to pray to God for colleagues who will run alongside them in the race. This is true for pastors, missionaries, and people serving in the non-profit world. Life is long journey with many ups and downs, potholes, and heartaches. We have not been created to handle the burdens that come our way alone. In fact, the only way to fulfill the law of Christ is to bear one another's burdens (Gal 6:2) and to walk this journey together. We need one another. Let us never forget that in ourselves we are weak, but as we read in Psalm 133:1, "How beautiful it is when brothers and sisters in Christ dwell together in harmony."

NT Scriptures

2 Corinthians 12:7; Galatians 6:2; 1 Timothy 5:17–18; 2 Timothy 4:9–13

Prayer

O LORD, we thank you for calling us to serve you. We are weak in ourselves, but in You we find strength, wisdom and guidance. We thank you for the power of the Holy Spirit who indwells us. We surrender our gifts and callings to you and trust you to lead us until the end of the journey.

Personal Notes and Prayers

Numbers 12:7-8

לֹא־כֵן עַבְדִּי מֹשֶׁה בְּכָל־בֵּיתִי נֶאֱמָן הוּא׃

פֶּה אֶל־פֶּה אֲדַבֶּר־בּוֹ וּמַרְאֶה וְלֹא בְחִידֹת וּתְמֻנַת יְהוָה יַבִּיט וּמַדּוּעַ לֹא יְרֵאתֶם לְדַבֵּר בְּעַבְדִּי בְמֹשֶׁה׃

My servant Moses is not like this; he is trustworthy in all My house. Face to face and openly I speak to him and not in riddles while he sees the form of the LORD. Why were you not afraid to speak against My servant Moses?

Biblical Context

MIRIAM AND AARON WERE upset because Moses had married an Ethiopian woman. Instead of addressing openly their discontent with this family situation, they single-mindedly turned to their own personal status among the Israelites and spoke foolishly against Moses. They complained to an unknown audience that God had not only spoken through their brother Moses, but that God has spoken through them also. They were obviously jealous of their famous brother. Moses refrained from defending himself and remained silent before his accusers. However, we quickly find out that "the LORD heard it [the complaints]" (12:2). He was angered by Miriam and Aaron's statements against Moses and told the three siblings to meet Him outside the camp at the Tent of Meeting. The LORD came down in a pillar of cloud and defended Moses, stressing his faithfulness and his capacity to meet with God face-to-face until he could discern God's form. There is no response from Miriam and Aaron as they were probably ashamed at their earlier behavior. When the LORD departed the Tent of Meeting, Miriam became leprous. Aaron saw Miriam's infirmity, apologized to Moses and pleaded with him to intercede on her behalf. Moses did so and Miriam was eventually healed of her leprosy.

Life Application

When we try to defend ourselves against false accusations or rages of jealousy, our words can be ignored or come across as hostile words. Our natural tendency is often to retaliate, making the situation worse. But there is no need to defend ourselves against what we know is false. God hears and He is our defender. He knows the truth. We cannot control what others say to us or how they treat us, but we can control our reaction to them. Rather than getting defensive when falsely accused, we need to remain silent and let the LORD be our defender.

NT Scriptures

Luke 23:6–11; Acts 8:32 (cf. Isa 53:7)

Prayer

O LORD, you are our shield, our defender and our protector in times of trial and tribulation. We hide ourselves in you and find rest for our soul. Thank you for standing up for us, speaking for us and fighting for us. Give us wisdom to know when to speak and when to be silent. We trust in you alone.

Personal Notes and Prayers

Numbers 14:24

וְעַבְדִּי כָלֵב עֵקֶב הָיְתָה רוּחַ אַחֶרֶת עִמּוֹ וַיְמַלֵּא אַחֲרָי וַהֲבִיאֹתִיו
אֶל־הָאָרֶץ אֲשֶׁר־בָּא שָׁמָּה וְזַרְעוֹ יוֹרִשֶׁנָּה׃

*But my servant Caleb, because there was a different spirit
about him and he completely followed me, I will bring him
into the land where he went and his seed
will take possession of it.*

Biblical Context

THE LORD TOLD MOSES to send twelve men into the land of Canaan to explore. The men sent to scout out the land of Canaan returned and confirmed that it truly was a land flowing with milk and honey just as they had been told. Their report also included the notion that the land was filled with fortified cities full of powerful men. With this information these men had a choice; they could trust that God would remain true to his promise to give them the land, or they could shrink back in fear. Joshua and Caleb took the LORD at his word, and encouraged the people to go up and attack, and they were rewarded for their faith. The other ten men "spread a bad report among the Israelites," disregarding the promise of God and ultimately leading to the forfeit of his promise.

Life Application

The LORD rewards faith. This story highlights Caleb and Joshua's faith in the promise of God. The LORD had told the Israelites that He was giving them the land of Canaan, and for Joshua and Caleb it did not matter who was in the land, they believed that the LORD would be faithful to his promises. The story tells us that Caleb had "a different spirit about Him," and "he completely followed" the LORD. Caleb was not discouraged because the path looked difficult and he did not turn to his own human wisdom and understanding; he trusted God. Caleb is a shining example for Christians today. The LORD has left us plenty to do before

He returns and it would be easy to be overwhelmed and discouraged by the challenges and difficulties that we face as we seek to serve Him. But, like Caleb, a can-do attitude based on God's promises and whole-hearted devotion to God leads to eternal blessing, just as He has promised.

NT Scriptures

Matthew 6:33–34; Philippians 3:12–14; Hebrews 11:32—12:2

Prayer

O LORD, thank you for giving us eyes of faith and for showing us what you see. Forgive us for failing to trust you in all circumstances and for trying to find alternatives to your plan for our lives. Please show us the way into the promised land and grant us that we may remain on the right path, without turning to the left or to the right. We want to follow you all the way home.

Personal Notes and Prayers

Numbers 18:20

וַיֹּאמֶר יְהוָה אֶל־אַהֲרֹן בְּאַרְצָם לֹא תִנְחָל וְחֵלֶק לֹא־יִהְיֶה לְךָ
בְּתוֹכָם אֲנִי חֶלְקְךָ וְנַחֲלָתְךָ בְּתוֹךְ בְּנֵי יִשְׂרָאֵל:

The LORD said to Aaron: "You will have no inheritance in their land, nor will there be a portion for you among them, for I AM your portion and your inheritance among the sons of Israel."

Biblical Context

IN AN EARNEST CONVERSATION with the LORD, Aaron receives instructions about the awesome responsibility to serve as priest between a holy God and unholy Israel. Aaron is told that he and his sons will be in charge of offering sacrifices on behalf of Israel at the sanctuary. God then tells him that the Levites will serve under his care, responsible to assist with the work of the priests. In exchange for their service, the priests and Levites are to receive provisions for their sustenance in the form of tithes while the rest of the tribes will receive a land grant after they enter the promised land. This gift for the service of the priests and Levites was unique in that none of the other tribes would partake from the tithes taken from the sacrifices, but rather, land and property would be the inheritance of the rest of the tribes. Aaron is then told that their inheritance will be the greatest of gifts, it will be God himself.

Life Application

As partakers of the New Covenant, our inheritance is still the same: *the LORD is our inheritance.* He has made us into a holy priesthood to serve in his kingdom, so that we may declare his praises to the ends of the earth. When we are tempted to replace our comfort-driven material inheritance and indulge in our wealth, we must remember that Jesus, not things, is our true inheritance. There is no greater treasure on earth and in heaven than what we find in Jesus. He is our Provider, our Wisdom, our Guide, our Shield, our Refuge, our Strength, our Shepherd and our Salvation. He is our inheritance.

NT Scriptures

1 Timothy 6:17; 2 Peter 2:9–10; Revelation 21:1–8

Prayer

O LORD, preserve our hearts from the temptations of this world, from selfishness and from greed. Help us look to you and you alone for sustenance in spirit, soul and body. You yearn to reveal yourself to us in so many ways, every day of our lives. Shield us from the enticement to turn to the right and to the left, and find in us hearts that are completely surrendered to you.

Personal Notes and Prayers

Numbers 22:28

וַיִּפְתַּח יְהוָה אֶת־פִּי הָאָתוֹן וַתֹּאמֶר לְבִלְעָם מֶה־עָשִׂיתִי לְךָ כִּי הִכִּיתַנִי זֶה שָׁלֹשׁ רְגָלִים:

The LORD opened the mouth of the donkey. She said to Balaam, "What did I do that you have beaten me these three times?"

Biblical Context

BY THE TIME WE come to Numbers 22, the Israelites have been in the desert for four decades. God had just given them a major military victory over the Ammonites and they were now encamped near Moab. Needless to say, when Balak, the King of Moab, saw the size of their company and heard about the battle they had just won, he felt a bit threatened by their proximity. Balak sent some elders to Balaam (a prophet of God who lived by the Euphrates River) and offered to pay him if he would come and put a curse upon the Israelites. Balaam said he would need to pray about it, and he did. Balaam was not a stranger to God: he knew the voice of the LORD and spoke to him about the matter. God responded. At first, God said clearly, "No, do not go." But when Balak sent a larger group of princes who offered to pay an even steeper fee, Balaam beseeched the LORD again. This time, God said that under certain conditions He could go, but he must only do what the LORD would instruct him to do. This meant that he needed to pay close attention to when and what the LORD might say. Clearly he was not, for when the Angel of the LORD came and stood right in front of him, Balaam did not see. Perhaps he was preoccupied by the view, or was deep in thought about holy matters, or maybe he was thinking about what he would do with the huge divination fee he was about to receive from the king. For whatever reason, Balaam missed the message from God. When the donkey ran off the road, he assumed she was misbehaving and therefore, he beat her. God tried to reach Balaam twice more by standing right in his path. Twice more he missed it. Twice more his donkey tried to steer him off the road. And twice more he beat her for it. But when the LORD needed to get through to him, he found a way! "The LORD opened the mouth of the donkey..."

Life Application

I remember it was right around the time that the movie *Shrek* came out that I discovered this talking donkey in the Bible! At first I just considered this to be a fun and crazy story; but I think there is much more to it. We often expect God to speak to us in certain tried and true ways. Elijah expected God to speak through a mighty wind, an earthquake, or a burning bush. Instead, God's voice came as a whisper (1 Kgs 19:11–12). For Balaam, God got his attention through his talking donkey! It is easy for us to question our skills in discerning God's voice and worry about the divine messages we may be missing every day. However, while we may never hear the voice of Eddie Murphy emanate from a donkey, I think we can be certain that if God has something he wants to tell us, He'll get the message through to us loud and clear!

NT Scriptures

2 Peter 2:15

Prayer

O LORD, open our ears to the sound of your still small voice. Help us be sensitive to your call and respond in ways that are pleasing to you. Forgive us for being negligent in listening attentively to your instructions and messages of love.

Personal Notes and Prayers

Deuteronomy 4:7

כִּי מִי־גוֹי גָּדוֹל אֲשֶׁר־לוֹ אֱלֹהִים קְרֹבִים אֵלָיו כַּיהוָה אֱלֹהֵינוּ בְּכָל־קָרְאֵנוּ אֵלָיו:

For who is great nation for whom gods are near to it like the LORD our God, whenever we call out to him.

Biblical Context

THE PREAMBLE TO DEUTERONOMY reviews the recent history of Israel, setting the stage for the renewal of the covenant and the entry into the land of Canaan. Although Israel's forty years in the wilderness were both good and bad, the thing that was consistent was God's involvement with his people. God manifested himself by speaking, leading, fighting, delivering, comforting, providing, healing, rebuking, challenging, instructing and protecting. No other nation had a god like this who revealed himself in remarkable ways in the midst of the community. At that time, several features distinguished Israel from the great nations of the Ancient Near East. Israel did not have a mighty army. She did not have a human king, nor did she have a land to call her own. What she did have however was a great God who was always near and easily accessible. God was faithful to Israel in good times and in times of hardships. God could always be depended upon and trusted by his people.

Life Application

God has not changed; He is always near to his people (Ps 85:10; Jer 23:23). It is intrinsic to his very nature to be present at all times both with his Church as his Body and with individual believers. Despite Israel's faithlessness, God remained faithful and chose to dwell in the midst of his people. For the believer today, the same is true. God has chosen to dwell within those who have put their faith in Him, regardless of their past history. And as God engaged himself in the affairs of Israel, God is actively involved in our lives. He speaks to us, leads us, fights for us, delivers us, comforts us, provides for us, heals us, rebukes us, challenges us, instructs us and protects us. We can count on God in every situation of life.

NT Scriptures

John 14:4,7 Romans 10:12–13; Hebrews 10:19–23; James 4:8

Prayer

O LORD, where would we be without your presence. In this dark and lost world, you are our guide, our refuge, our light and our salvation. Help us be aware of your presence in this world. Open our eyes to see your glory and majesty. You call us to be faithful to you as you are to us. LORD, help.

Personal Notes and Prayers

Deuteronomy 4:37

וְתַחַת כִּי אָהַב אֶת־אֲבֹתֶיךָ וַיִּבְחַר בְּזַרְעוֹ אַחֲרָיו וַיּוֹצִאֲךָ בְּפָנָיו
בְּכֹחוֹ הַגָּדֹל מִמִּצְרָיִם:

*And underlying is that he loved your fathers and chose
their descendants after them, then brought you out of
Egypt with his own presence, in his great strength.*

Biblical Context

SHORTLY BEFORE THE ISRAELITES enter the Promised Land, Moses reminds them of the importance of keeping a healthy relationship with the God of their forefathers—Abraham, Isaac and Jacob. In his last farewell speech, Moses describes all that God had done for them and explains how they were to live sanctified lives in their new land. Moses recounts the incredible journey that led up to this point, a journey full of divine interventions. He reminds them that God alone made the heavens and the earth; therefore, He alone is to receive their complete devotion. No other god could ever do what their God had done; no other god deserved their attention. Moses warns the Israelites to avoid being corrupted by idolatry and to abstain from any temptation to worship other gods. However, even though the Israelites had experienced God's deliverance from Egypt and his guidance in the desert with clouds by day and with a pillar fire by night, they still struggled to trust God and to follow Him wholeheartedly.

Life Application

The entire prologue to Deuteronomy reveals that the God of Israel is unique, totally unlike other gods. He loves, cares, and pursues humans actively and unceasingly. No other god is like him; therefore, any form of idolatry is futile. When one gets caught up in idolatry, one is enslaved. The idols of today—self-image, success, comfort, money, education—demand relentless and fruitless efforts. As God' people, we are broken, underserving of his love, and unable to love Him as He deserves to be loved. But God knew this long before we existed, and He still chose to pursue us and to reveal his love for us. He knew of our rebellious nature, our problems with trusting him, our secrets lives, and our evil motives; nevertheless, He still loved us. He sent his Son to deliver us from slavery to sin. When we are crushed by the weight of one of our idols, we can simply turn to Him. We will quickly find out that He has kept his gaze on us far longer than we have had our backs turned against Him.

NT Scriptures

Ephesians 1:4-6; Romans 5:6-8

Prayer

O LORD, great is your faithfulness and your love for us. Forgive us for deviating from the path and turning to the right and to the left. We are weak, but you are strong. You carry us in your strong arms even when we fail to honor you. Have mercy on us and keep us in the shadow of your wings.

Personal Notes and Prayers

Deuteronomy 6:4–5

שְׁמַע יִשְׂרָאֵל יְהוָה אֱלֹהֵינוּ יְהוָה אֶחָד׃
וְאָהַבְתָּ אֵת יְהוָה אֱלֹהֶיךָ בְּכָל־לְבָבְךָ וּבְכָל־נַפְשְׁךָ וּבְכָל־מְאֹדֶךָ׃

Hear O Israel, YHWH our God YHWH is one.
Love YHWH your God with all your heart,
with all your soul and with all your strength.

Biblical Context

SHORTLY BEFORE HIS DEATH, Moses delivered his farewell address to the Israelites on the plains of Moab. The purpose of his speech was to prepare Israel for her new life in Canaan and to remind her of her covenantal responsibilities—to love YHWH and Him alone. Moses's command to listen carefully to God and to love him with every fiber of their being would be a lasting reminder of what God expected from them. The Israelites were to remember, as they entered a new and dangerously syncretistic land, that they should worship ONE God—YHWH—and him alone. This ONE God was to be loved and worshipped with all their heart, soul and strength. In the Ancient Near East, the heart and soul were considered one entity, so a wholistic idea such as the one uttered by Moses was easily grasped by the ancient Israelites.

Life Application

The *Shema* opens with the direct command to hear the instructions that follow. The Hebrew word for "hearing, listening" also carries the idea of "obeying." One may audibly *hear* or *listen to* instructions given by someone in authority—parent, superior, YHWH—and choose not to *obey*. This concept is especially apparent to those who have teenage children who are noteworthy for giving assent to directives, but quickly forget to follow through with action. In some ways, we are all challenged in this area. We hear God's instructions through his Word, but we quickly (and sometimes conveniently) forget. God calls each one of us to listen to him, to be attentive to his voice, to love him with our entire being, and to walk in his ways.

NT Scriptures

Matthew 22:34–38; John 14:23–24

Prayer

O LORD, how we have sinned against you and dismissed your instructions. Forgive us for our negligence and for arrogantly proceeding with our daily activities without paying attention to your Word. We thank you for calling us by name, for speaking to us individually, for calling us to walk in your paths, and for keeping us safe along the way.

Personal Notes and Prayers

Deuteronomy 6:13

אֶת־יְהוָה אֱלֹהֶיךָ תִּירָא וְאֹתוֹ תַעֲבֹד וּבִשְׁמוֹ תִּשָּׁבֵעַ׃

*Fear the LORD your God! Serve him
and swear by his name.*

Biblical Context

IN HIS LAST SERMON to the Israelites, Moses stresses the importance of keeping God's commands, decrees and laws. He highlights the need to teach these truths to the generations to come, so that they may enjoy life and increase greatly in the land God is giving them. In this text, the verbs "to fear" (יָרֵא), "to serve" (עָבַד) and "to swear" (שָׁבַע) are to be interpreted as imperatives, direct commands. These commands are not optional but prerequisites for long and fruitful lives. They come on the heels of the Shema where the Israelites are commanded to love the LORD their God with ALL their heart, mind and strength (6:5). This love is to be displayed in their daily walk and taught to the younger generation when they sit in their houses, when they walk by the way, when they lie down and when they rise up (6:7). The chapter ends with a clear explanation of why the Israelites were to "fear the LORD their God." Moses specifies that it is "for [their] good always, to keep [them] alive" (6:24).

Life Application

Today, it is uncommon for believers to discuss the meaning and implications of "fearing God." We are trained not "to fear" but to be self-reliant, and to depend on our own strengths and human abilities. We are taught that we are strong in Christ and need to fear nothing because "greater is He who is in us than He who is in the world" (1 John 4:4). However, the fear that is mentioned in Deuteronomy 6:13 is distinct from human fear. It implies honor, reverence, respect and devotion toward God. It speaks of humility, submission, dependence, obedience and trust—in other words, less of us and more of Him. God is our ultimate master, and we are called to submit to him before anyone else.

NT Scriptures

Hebrews 12:28–29; 1 Peter 2:17; Revelation 14:7

Prayer

"The fear of God is freedom, joy and peace, and makes all ills that vex us here to cease. Though the word "fear" some men may ill endure, 'tis such a fear as only makes secure . . . . Our hopes are all well-grounded on this fear. All our assurance rolls upon that sphere. This fear, that drives all other fears away, shall be my song, the morning of our day! Where that fear is, there's nothing to be feared; it brings from Heaven an angel for our guard. Tranquility and peace this fear does give" (*On the Fear of God* by Edmund Waller).

Personal Notes and Prayers

Deuteronomy 7:21

לֹא תַעֲרֹץ מִפְּנֵיהֶם כִּי־יְהוָה אֱלֹהֶיךָ בְּקִרְבֶּךָ אֵל גָּדוֹל וְנוֹרָא:

Do not be in dread before them, for the LORD your God is in your midst, a great God and one who is to be feared.

Biblical Context

IN DEUTERONOMY 7, MOSES is communicating God's statutes and instructions to Israel concerning her life in the land of Canaan. Her obedience to these ordinances will ensure that God's blessings are on the fruit of her womb, on the produce of her soil, on her grain, new wine, oil, herds and flocks. And eventually, Israel will be able to established herself in the land given to her by God and drive the Hittites, Girgashites, Amorites, Canaanites, Perizites, Hivites, Jebusites and their gods from her territorial inheritance. In Deuteronomy 7:17, Moses presents the following scenario: "Suppose you say in your heart: 'These nations are greater than I. How can I dispossess them?'" In verse 21, Moses reassures Israel that with the LORD God in her midst, she does not need to fear the inhabitants of Canaan. Her responsibility is to fear the LORD and not the people of the land. Throughout Deuteronomy 7, the LORD is portrayed as the mighty warrior who defeats the inhabitants of the land. While Israel is responsible to cooperate with the LORD's design to achieve victory, Israel is never portrayed as the source of victory. Instead, the source and cause of her victory is always the LORD. The LORD is the one who gives the inhabitants over to Israel (7:2, 16, 23, 24), the one who protects Israel (7:6, 10, 13, 16), and the one who confuses and ultimately destroys Israel's enemies (7:10, 15, 19, 22, 23).

Life Application

While the idea of the LORD being a mighty warrior may present a theological dilemma for Christians, in Deuteronomy 7, Moses reassures Israel that God is in control and fights on behalf of his people. Why should

Israel fear her adversaries if the true source of her victory—the LORD God—resides in her midst? For Christians who believe that the Spirit of the LORD indwells each believer, how could the fear of man ever be triumphant? Jesus said: "Do not let your heart be troubled. Trust in God; trust also in Me." The Spirit of the LORD—the God who is both great and to be feared—lives inside every Christian to teach, comfort, guide and bring triumph over God's enemies. As the apostle Paul wrote in Romans 8:31, "If God is for us, who can be against us?"

NT Scriptures

Matthew 10:28; Luke 12:4, 22–32; Romans 8:37–39

Prayer

O LORD, you are my light and my salvation—whom shall I fear? O LORD, you are the stronghold of my life—of whom shall I be afraid? (Ps 27:1) When I am afraid, I will trust in you (Ps 56:3). In God, whose word I praise, in you I trust; I will not be afraid. What can mortal man do to me? (Ps 56:4)

Personal Notes and Prayers

Deuteronomy 8:7

כִּי יְהוָה אֱלֹהֶיךָ מְבִיאֲךָ אֶל־אֶרֶץ טוֹבָה אֶרֶץ נַחֲלֵי מָיִם עֲיָנֹת
וּתְהֹמֹת יֹצְאִים בַּבִּקְעָה וּבָהָר:

*For the LORD your God is bringing you to a good land,
a land with streambeds (full of) water, springs and deep
rivers flowing out from the valleys and the hills.*

Biblical Context

THE BOOK OF DEUTERONOMY is a collection of farewell speeches uttered by Moses shortly before his death on Mt Nebo. God had miraculously rescued the Israelites from slavery in Egypt, sustained them through forty difficult years in the desert, and led them to the eastern border of the Promised Land. As Moses was facing the end of his life, the Israelites were preparing to receive their territorial inheritance and were ready to begin their new life in Canaan. In the book of Deuteronomy, Moses exhorts the Israelites to remain faithful to the covenant God established with them at Mt Sinai. He urges them to obey God without turning to the right or to the left. In Deuteronomy 8:7, Moses describes God's generous provision of water in terms of flowing springs and rivers, a plentiful supply to sustain them, their animals and their crops, while they live in the land. Water is a significant source of life. The land God prepared for them is described as a "good land." Why? Because it is filled with water for them, their animals and their crops. The abundance of water highlighted in this passage is an indication that the land was a place where they would flourish. An abundance of water is a source of hope for those who have only known the arid climate of the wilderness. This verse indicates that God's desire to bless and provide for his people flows as strong as the water promised to them in this new land.

Life Application

God's promise of water to the Israelites is important. God had sustained them through drought and slavery, simultaneously protecting and preparing them for abundant life in their new land. Just as flowing springs and deep rivers nourish land of milk and honey, so do God's blessings flow forth upon his people. Like the Israelites, believers can find comfort and hope in God's ongoing provision in their lives. God's design is good and his work is profitable for all. His continuous provision springs forth as a stream that will never dry up, flowing out of the deep well of God's own love for mankind.

NT Scriptures

Matthew 7:9–13; 1 Timothy 6:17

Prayer

O LORD, in times of drought, you bring refreshing. In times of sorrow, you bring comfort. In times of brokenness, you bring healing. You pour your love, mercy and grace upon us unceasingly. And you give us hope for the future. When the land is dry, you give us visions of living water. When the journey is treacherous and challenging, you show us the beauty of your creation. We thank you for showing us the way. Help us follow you with eyes wide open and ears that hear your calling. To you be the glory forever.

Personal Notes and Prayers

Deuteronomy 8:11

הִשָּׁ֣מֶר לְךָ֔ פֶּן־תִּשְׁכַּ֖ח אֶת־יְהוָ֣ה אֱלֹהֶ֑יךָ לְבִלְתִּ֨י שְׁמֹ֤ר מִצְוֺתָיו֙
וּמִשְׁפָּטָ֣יו וְחֻקֹּתָ֔יו אֲשֶׁ֛ר אָנֹכִ֥י מְצַוְּךָ֖ הַיּֽוֹם׃

Beware lest you forget the LORD your God, failing to keep his commands and his laws and his decrees, which I command you this day.

Biblical Context

THE ISRAELITES ARE FINALLY ready to enter into the Promised Land, after lingering in the desert for forty years. Moses gathers the people and reminds them of all that has happened since they left Egypt—the parting of the Sea of Reeds, the giving of the Law, the quail and manna for food, water from the rock, the serpent on the pole, and instructions on how to live their new land. In Deuteronomy 8, Moses reminds the people, as he has done many times before, that they must follow the commands of God. They must not forget that it was God who sustained them and provided for them during forty years in the wilderness. The Israelites must always remember that their survival did not depend on their own power or strength, but on God's alone.

Life Application

It is so easy, when things are going well, to forget the LORD. We forget to thank Him, to depend on Him, and to trust Him for the future. We forget that it is by his grace alone that we experience any good at all. As soon as we forget this truth, it becomes easier to fall into sins of pride, arrogance, self-reliance. Something in us begins to believe falsely that *we* did something to deserve the things we have. But, we couldn't be more wrong. As James said, "Every good and perfect gift is from above, coming down from the Father of the heavenly lights" (1:17). We are blessed because God blessed us. We are alive because God gives us breath. God commands us to remember and to make sure we never forget who He is and what He has done for us. His commands are for our own good—so that it will go well with us. When we remember what God has done for us in the past, we can continue to rely on Him for the future. He is the faithful God whose חֶסֶד ("mercy, grace, lovingkindness") endures forever. Remember. Do not forget.

NT Scriptures

Ephesians 2:11–14; Hebrews 3:7–19

Prayer

O LORD, forgive us for relying on our own strengths and for setting you aside as if you had not proven your faithfulness to us in the past. Forgive us for treating you as a side-lined spectator in the game of life. Forgive us for living with pride and arrogance, and for establishing our own rules for the game. Forgive us O LORD, and bring us back to you, the Author and the Finisher of our faith. We need you. We desperately need you.

Personal Notes and Prayers

Deuteronomy 9:5–6

לֹ֣א בְצִדְקָתְךָ֗ וּבְיֹ֙שֶׁר֙ לְבָ֣בְךָ֔ אַתָּ֥ה בָ֖א לָרֶ֣שֶׁת אֶת־אַרְצָ֑ם כִּ֞י בְּרִשְׁעַ֣ת הַגּוֹיִ֣ם הָאֵ֗לֶּה יְהוָ֤ה אֱלֹהֶ֙יךָ֙ מוֹרִישָׁ֣ם מִפָּנֶ֔יךָ וּלְמַ֜עַן הָקִ֣ים אֶת־הַדָּבָ֗ר אֲשֶׁ֨ר נִשְׁבַּ֤ע יְהוָה֙ לַאֲבֹתֶ֔יךָ לְאַבְרָהָ֥ם לְיִצְחָ֖ק וּֽלְיַעֲקֹֽב׃

וְיָדַעְתָּ֗ כִּ֠י לֹ֤א בְצִדְקָֽתְךָ֙ יְהוָ֣ה אֱלֹהֶ֔יךָ נֹתֵ֨ן לְךָ֜ אֶת־הָאָ֧רֶץ הַטּוֹבָ֛ה הַזֹּ֖את לְרִשְׁתָּ֑הּ כִּ֥י עַם־קְשֵׁה־עֹ֖רֶף אָֽתָּה׃

Not because of your righteousness or your uprightness of heart are you entering in order to possess their land, but because of the wickedness of these nations the LORD your God is causing you to possess them from before you, and in order to confirm the word that the LORD swore to your fathers, to Abraham, to Isaac, and to Jacob. Then you will know therefore, that not because of your righteousness is the LORD your God giving you this good land to possess, for you are a stubborn people.

Biblical Context

AFTER 40 YEARS OF wilderness wandering, Moses prepares the people to enter the Promised Land. He reminds them that they are God's chosen people, points them to the covenant at Horeb, and commands them to serve God *alone*. Before reminding the Israelites of their history, he tells them that they had done no special deed to deserve this territorial inheritance. God gave it to them as a gift, not because of their righteousness but because he had promised it to their forefathers centuries earlier. God knew the challenges his people would face in the land of Canaan and the risk they would face by living in the midst of idol worshippers. Nevertheless, he led them to the Promised Land and called them to be a blessing to all the nations of the world. What an amazing story, that such a broken and disobedient people witnessed the faithfulness and redemptive work of God.

Life Application

We are prone to believe that good things come to us because of our own righteousness. But in reality, we deserve none of the blessings we receive from God. We are simply the recipients his grace, goodness and faithfulness. Whether we obey or we disobey, God remains the same. He is true to his word and fulfills his promises. Let us therefore serve him with grateful and sincere hearts in response to his grace and faithfulness towards us.

NT Scriptures

Romans 1:17; 3:22; 2 Corinthians 5:21

Prayer

God, your promises are not quicksand or mirages. They are true and unchanging. You use them to carry out your will on this earth. Help us grasp hold of your plans and experience the joy of seeing your redemptive work on earth.

Personal Notes and Prayers

Deuteronomy 10:12–13

וְעַתָּה יִשְׂרָאֵל מָה יְהוָה אֱלֹהֶיךָ שֹׁאֵל מֵעִמָּךְ כִּי אִם־לְיִרְאָה אֶת־
יְהוָה אֱלֹהֶיךָ לָלֶכֶת בְּכָל־דְּרָכָיו וּלְאַהֲבָה אֹתוֹ וְלַעֲבֹד אֶת־יְהוָה
אֱלֹהֶיךָ בְּכָל־לְבָבְךָ וּבְכָל־נַפְשֶׁךָ׃

לִשְׁמֹר אֶת־מִצְוֺת יְהוָה וְאֶת־חֻקֹּתָיו אֲשֶׁר אָנֹכִי מְצַוְּךָ הַיּוֹם לְטוֹב
לָךְ׃

But now, Israel, what is the LORD your God asking from you but to fear the LORD your God, to walk in all his ways, and to love him and serve the LORD your God with all of your heart and with all of your being, to keep the commands of the LORD and his statutes, which I am commanding you today for your good?

Biblical Context

BEFORE THE NEW GENERATION of Israelites enters the land which God has promised them, Moses gives a series of speeches both to expound upon the Sinai covenant and to exhort this generation to keep the covenant and not repeat the failings of their ancestors. In chapter 9, Moses reminds the people that their own righteousness will not bring about their victory in the promised land; only due to the LORD's strength and faithfulness will Israel triumph. The Israelites must not allow themselves to fall prey to an egotistic self-righteousness which will lead them away from God. Moses illustrates this point—that the people have not earned their victories or standing with the LORD, but are wholly dependent on him—by recounting Israel's great sin with the golden calf and his intercession on their behalf. Verse 12 begins with a disjunctive *waw*, signaling a change in topic, or more precisely, the resumption of the topic Moses was discussing in chapter 6: loving the LORD their God, which is the heart of keeping the covenant. Verses 12–13 are punctuated by five verbs in the same infinitive construct form: fear, walk, love, serve, and keep. Love is the central verb and hearkens back to the *Shema* in 6:4–9. The entirety of the two verses are in the form of a rhetorical question, a device used for emphasis and to greater engage the listener.

Life Application

The five verbs of Deut. 10:12–13 are the focus of this passage. Fear and love are both attitudes (though not restrictively), while walk, serve, and keep are all actions. The pairing of fear and love is significant, for both are required in our approach to God. We fear God when we comprehend (as much as we are humanly capable) that he is the Creator, the only all-powerful God of the universe, and give him the homage and reverence due him. We love him both through our singular devotion to him and through our actions. Fearing and loving God will compel us to walk in his ways (his character and values are the model for ours), to serve him with everything we are and have, and to keep his commands (obedience). These attitudes are to result in these actions.

NT Scriptures

John 14:12–17

Prayer

LORD our God, may we always keep your faithfulness and love on our minds and in front of our eyes. May we continue to be grateful for who you are and all you have done for us, especially in sending your Son for us, so that we neither try to earn your favor, nor believe and act as though we deserve it. May our reverence, gratitude, and love for you spur us on to humble obedience and good works, through the power of your Holy Spirit, so that we may reflect your goodness to the lost and broken world around us.

Personal Notes and Prayers

Deuteronomy 15:15a

וְזָכַרְתָּ כִּי עֶבֶד הָיִיתָ בְּאֶרֶץ מִצְרַיִם
Remember that you were slaves in the land of Egypt.

Biblical Context

ONE OF THE MOST common themes of the Old Testament is that of "remembering." The Israelites were told time and time again "to remember" the mighty deeds of the LORD and to celebrate his greatness. The Israelites were instructed to observe the Sabbath (Exod 20:8), to remember God's mighty deliverance from Egypt (Deut 5:15; 15:15; 24:18), to honor God's leadership through the wilderness wanderings (Deut 8:2), to observe God's laws given to Moses on Mt Sinai (Deut 4:10), and to never forget the deeds they had seen God perform in their midst (Deut 4:9). Unfortunately, the Israelites were quick to forget. They subtly turned away from the path carved especially for them and chose to submit to the enticements that came their way. With their forgetfulness came their ignorance of the celebrations ordained by God, especially the Passover. Century after century, the prophets called them back "to remember" what God had done for them, and invited them to repent and turn from their wicked ways. They rejected the calls to repentance and the commands "to remember" the LORD their God, and consequently, they were called "stubborn" and "stiff-necked" (עַם־קְשֵׁה־עֹרֶף). They thought they were secure in the Temple, in the Priesthood, and in the Monarchy. How little they knew that all these would eventually be removed from their midst and that their security blanket would slip away from under their feet.

Life Application

Although as Christians we are not required to observe the Mosaic law nor to observe the feasts of the LORD, we are called "to remember" the mighty deeds of the LORD. How could we ever forget the price that Jesus paid on our behalf? How could we forget such great a salvation? Indeed, we are called to live in a state of continuous awareness that God's presence is with us and and that God expresses his love towards us continuously and in countless ways.

NT Scriptures

1 Corinthians 11:24–25; Ephesians 2:11–13

Prayer

O LORD, your eternal presence with us is overwhelming. We cannot comprehend it. You never leave us nor forsake us. You remember us according to your loving kind and not according to our sins and rebellion. We join with the psalmist and declare: "[We] will remember the deeds of the LORD; yes, [we] will remember your miracles of long ago" (Ps 77:11). Help us O LORD to you with our heart, with our mind, and with our deeds.

Personal Notes and Prayers

Deuteronomy 23:25–26

כִּי תָבֹא בְּכֶרֶם רֵעֶךָ וְאָכַלְתָּ עֲנָבִים כְּנַפְשְׁךָ שָׂבְעֶךָ וְאֶל־כֶּלְיְךָ לֹא תִתֵּן:

כִּי תָבֹא בְּקָמַת רֵעֶךָ וְקָטַפְתָּ מְלִילֹת בְּיָדֶךָ וְחֶרְמֵשׁ לֹא תָנִיף עַל קָמַת רֵעֶךָ:

If you go into your neighbor's vineyard, you may eat your fill of grapes, but you shall not put any in your bag. If you go into your neighbor's standing grain, you may pluck the ears with your hand, but you shall not put a sickle to your neighbor's standing.

Biblical Context

AFTER THE EXODUS FROM Egypt, God gave Moses laws that were intended to serve as standards of behavior for Israel. These standards were given to protect Israel and to provide boundaries within which she would find freedom to become all she was meant to be. In this passage, we read about a system of divine justice in which a neighbor was required to share his agricultural assets with a neighbor in need, however the one in need could not take advantage of his neighbor's generosity nor steal from his harvest. Israelites in need could enjoy as many grapes as they could eat from their neighbors's property but only within the boundaries of the vineyard. Such was also the case for eating a neighbor's grain. What could be consumed within the confines of the field could be devoured with great pleasure, but none of it could be carried beyond the borders of the property. Since God was the ultimate provider for Israel, God was entitled to establish the rules by which Israel was to live righteously. Her resources were to be shared justly so that all may be sustained with life. Should one take advantage of the divinely orchestrated system, God would ensure that the abuser received a just retribution.

Life Application

God provides much more than one could ever imagine or wish for. But with his provisions come boundaries that serve as limitations within which one may safely enjoy his blessings. Christian orthodoxy is generous; it allows for flexibility of interpretation, for the enjoyment of divine resources and for the sharing of God's blessings. As stated in Denver Seminary's vision, "charitable orthodoxy" even allows for disagreements in areas of theology and biblical interpretation. These are permitted as long as these are done with love and respect. Without a doubt, conflicts occurred in the neighbor's field when more than one Israelite entered into discussion about the ripeness of fruits, the quality of ears of grain, the process through which the produce was handled and the timing of the harvest. I can easily imagine the owner of the field mediating the occasional food fight on his property! May God help us navigate orthodoxy charitably and with respect!

NT Scriptures

Matthew 6:2–4; Luke 6:27–31; Acts 20:35; James 2:14–17

Prayer

O LORD, we thank you for giving to us exceedingly abundantly above all we can ask or think. You meet our needs from your abundance of blessings. Teach us to give generously as you have so generously given to us. Give us opportunities to give to those in need. Open our eyes so we may see the blessings you have bestowed upon us. Help us release them to others who have less than we have. To you be all the glory and honor.

Personal Notes and Prayers

Deuteronomy 32:10–11

יִמְצָאֵהוּ בְּאֶרֶץ מִדְבָּר וּבְתֹהוּ יְלֵל יְשִׁמֹן יְסֹבְבֶנְהוּ יְבוֹנְנֵהוּ יִצְּרֶנְהוּ
כְּאִישׁוֹן עֵינוֹ:
כְּנֶשֶׁר יָעִיר קִנּוֹ עַל־גּוֹזָלָיו יְרַחֵף יִפְרֹשׂ כְּנָפָיו יִקָּחֵהוּ יִשָּׂאֵהוּ
עַל־אֶבְרָתוֹ:

He found him in the wilderness and in a formless howling waste surrounded him. He cared for him, He watched over him like the pupil of his eye. Like an eagle rouses his nest of young, he hovered over it, he spread out his two wings, he took him, and bore him up with his wing-feathers.

Biblical Context

MOSES'S FINAL TESTIMONY TO Israel, a song composed before his death, paints a soaring word picture to describe how God cared for his people during their long forty years in the wilderness. Moses envisions a bird of prey stirring up its fledgling to take wing and then rescuing him when he fails to fly. This optimistic portrayal puts a hopeful face on some dark times: poisoned springs, a wasting disease from quail meat, an earthquake that swallowed up tents full of people, stinging desert vipers, hunger pangs and lack of water, pressure from an impatient and stiff-necked people. Moses remembers instead the dramatic supernatural help God provided: a cloud by day and a pillar of fire by night, a miraculous escape through the Red Sea from Pharaoh's army, bread from the skies in a barren land, water from a rock, tablets written by the finger of God, the tent of meeting, the ark of the covenant, military victories. Moses's focus was on God, on his providence, faithfulness and patience. The people however failed time and time again to remember that God was in complete control of their circumstances.

Life Application

How easy it is for us to concentrate on life's circumstances and become discouraged. All around us is sickness, violence, depression, poverty, injustice and death. We struggle to understand why so much depravity exists in the beautiful world God created for his children. Yet, God is very present. He manifests his goodness, his love and his faithfulness in multitudes of ways. He releases his angels to protects his own from the enemy. He encourages his children to spread their wings and fly. He provides, heals, strengthens, gives wisdom, and equips his children to care for his world. Yes, the enemy is at work and tries to steal, kill and destroy, but God is greater. And this must remain the focus of our lives on this earth.

NT Scriptures

John 10:10; 14:1, 6–7, 12–14

Prayer

O LORD, great is your faithfulness. You never leave us nor forsake us. You care for us in our times of need and reassure us of your constant presence in our midst. Help us trust you O LORD in every situation. We lift up our eyes to you from where our help comes. Deliver us from our own conceit and help us keep you at the center of our lives. To you and you only be all the glory for great things you have done.

Personal Notes and Prayers

Deuteronomy 32:11

כְּנֶ֙שֶׁר֙ יָעִ֣יר קִנּ֔וֹ עַל־גּוֹזָלָ֖יו יְרַחֵ֑ף יִפְרֹ֤שׂ כְּנָפָיו֙ יִקָּחֵ֔הוּ יִשָּׂאֵ֖הוּ עַל־אֶבְרָתֽוֹ׃

Just as an eagle stirs up his nest, and hovers over his young, He spreads out his wings, he takes hold of it. He raises it upon his wings.

Biblical Context

IN DEUTERONOMY, MOSES GIVES a farewell address to the Israelites before they cross into the Promised Land—the land of Canaan. Unfortunately, Moses does not make the trip with them. He climbs up Mount Nebo in the land of Moab, looks at the Promised Land across the Jordan and dies on the mountain. Before Moses ascends Mount Nebo, God instructs him to write a song and to teach it to the children of Israel (31:19). This song is meant to serve as a reminder to the Israelites that the God of Abraham, Isaac and Jacob who had delivered them from the bondage of Egypt and led them for forty years in the wilderness knew how weak and vulnerable they would one day become. God knew that his loving nurture and care for them would soon be forgotten (Deut 32:10–11). He knew that his efforts to bring them from infancy to maturity by stirring their nest and teaching them to soar on their own would eventually be fruitless. God knew that their love for Him would soon be replaced by love for foreign gods. With this song, Israel would one day recite and sing what had been spoken about them decades and centuries earlier.

Life Application

There is a time when a young eagle needs to learn to fly. Its mother stirs up the nest making it uncomfortable for the eaglet to remain in it. She withholds food from the eaglet, displaying the necessity for leaving the nest. The mother eagle eventually takes the eaglet onto her back, soars out into the open sky and then turns upside down, causing the eaglet to plummet downwards. She quickly catches the eaglet on her back, only to do it again and again, until the eaglet learns to fly. It is not surprising that God is described as a mother eagle. When we are adopted into God's family, we are immature in our faith and need spiritual nourishment to help us grow. There comes a time when we need to spread our own wings and share with others the wonderful truths of Scripture we learned in the nest. God, in his abounding love, takes us upon his wings and releases us into the world under his watchful eye. He neither leaves us nor forsakes us. He catches us when we fall and He teaches us to trust in Him as we grow to full maturity in Christ.

NT Scriptures

Matthew 25:14-30; Hebrews 5:11-14

Prayer

O LORD, thank you for faithfully watching over us as we grown in You, as we learn to spread our wings and as we bring the light of Christ into this dark world. Thank you for watching over us as we learn to serve you humbly and faithfully. What a privilege it is to know You!

Personal Notes and Prayers

Joshua 1:5

לֹא־יִתְיַצֵּב אִישׁ לְפָנֶיךָ כֹּל יְמֵי חַיֶּיךָ כַּאֲשֶׁר הָיִיתִי עִם־מֹשֶׁה אֶהְיֶה עִמָּךְ לֹא אַרְפְּךָ וְלֹא אֶעֶזְבֶךָּ׃

No man will stand against you all the days of your life. As I was with Moses I will be with you. I will not abandon you and I will not leave you.

Biblical Context

MOSES DIED SO GOD came to Joshua to tell him that the time had come for him to take the people into the Promised Land. Twice, before he died, Moses assured Joshua that God would not leave him or forsake him (Dt 31:6, 8). In Joshua 1:5, God himself is reiterating this promise to this new leader. Joshua could confidently go into the land of Canaan because no one would be able to stand against him, for God would be with him and would never abandon him. The two verbs used at the end of this verse could both be translated *abandon*. The first carries the idea of *to abandon, desert, leave in the lurch* (לֹא אַרְפְּךָ "I will not abandon you"). The second has the idea of *to leave, loose, forsake, abandon* (לֹא אֶעֶזְבֶךָּ "I will not leave you"). God is emphatically assuring Joshua that He can be trusted, that He can be depended upon.

Life Application

The writer of Hebrews quotes this promise, applying it to life in Christ (Heb 13:5). We invest our hearts in human relationships but then suffer the pain of betrayal and abandonment. Sometimes we are intentionally used and discarded, products of a disposable society. Sometimes we offer trust too quickly only to be abandoned when the wounds we carry are too much for the other to bear. Sometimes it is circumstances that lead to feeling abandoned like the small child whose mother is suddenly single due to death or divorce and must now go to work, leaving the child in the care of others. We learn not to trust for fear of being abandoned once more if we dare depend on another. But God knows all of our scars and insecurities, all of our fears and broken places and still, He promises that He will never leave us or abandon us. Resting in that promise, we can go forward with courage, loving others because we are loved; forgiving because we are forgiven; secure in the knowledge, that no matter how alone we may feel in the moment, we are not abandoned. God is with us. He promised.

NT Scriptures

Hebrews 13:5-6

Prayer

O LORD, our confidence comes from you. Our ability to pursue life with passion and purpose comes from you. You are with us. You never leave us nor forsake us. Even in moments when life is hard and challenges abound, you are there, leading us and guiding us. Who else would never leave us and forsake us but you O LORD. We bless you, honor you and proclaim your everlasting faithfulness to us.

Personal Notes and Prayers

Joshua 3:4

אַ֣ךְ ׀ רָח֣וֹק יִהְיֶ֗ה בֵּֽינֵיכֶם֙ וּבֵינָ֔יו כְּאַלְפַּ֥יִם אַמָּ֖ה בַּמִּדָּ֑ה אַֽל־תִּקְרְב֣וּ אֵלָ֗יו לְמַ֤עַן אֲשֶׁר־תֵּֽדְעוּ֙ אֶת־הַדֶּ֔רֶךְ אֲשֶׁ֣ר תֵּֽלְכוּ־בָ֔הּ כִּ֣י לֹ֧א עֲבַרְתֶּ֛ם בַּדֶּ֖רֶךְ מִתְּמ֥וֹל שִׁלְשֽׁוֹם׃

Surely there will be a distance between you and it [the Ark], a measurement of two thousand cubits. You will not approach to it, in order that you may know the way in which you will go. Because you have never crossed over on this road before.

Biblical Context

FORTY YEARS BEFORE THIS event, the sons of Israel had left Egypt and begun their long journey towards the Promised Land. After a difficult forty-year trek in the wilderness, the responsibility to acquire the land fell on the next generation, and on Joshua and Caleb. The LORD had chosen and anointed Joshua, prepared him to assume Moses's leadership, and instructed him to lead the Israelites into Canaan. In preparation for crossing the Jordan, Joshua gave the Israelites specific instructions for the journey from Shittim to the edge of the overflowing river. The Ark of the Covenant carried by the Levitical priests was to be the point of reference on which the Israelites would focus. "*Surely there will be a distance . . .*" As per Joshua's instructions, there was to be a distance of two thousand cubits (approx. ¾ of a mile) between the marching Israelites and the Ark. Not everyone could see the Ark however. The Israelites were to rely on those who were in front of them. They were to position themselves behind those who could see the Ark to ensure that they were advancing in the correct direction. Tribes followed tribes and individuals within the tribes followed other individuals within that tribe. This formation guaranteed that no one would go astray and miss the miracle of the crossing.

Life Application

Here, we find a good example of the way the Body of Messiah is to work together in unity. When God is on the move, we are to move with Him as one Body. At times, we see Him clearly and walk in step with him, while at other times, we fail to see Him and risk losing our way. As believers, we need one another to help ensure that we are proceeding in the right direction together. We cannot walk this journey alone lest we go astray. We must walk humbly with others and in unity with members of our faith family—brothers & sisters in the LORD, spiritual leaders—in order to ensure that we are following the path set before us by God. This way, we learn from one another ("Am I in the right position?"), care for one another ("Is my brother/sister in the right position?"), teach one another ("whispers to others 'You are too far in front!'"), and fellowship together ("Let us walk together.").

NT Scriptures

Acts 2:42; Ephesians 5:17-21; Hebrews 13:17

Prayer

O LORD, you called us to be one as you and the Father are one. Help us to let go of our arrogant individualism and teach us to walk together as one. Unite us with your word by the power of your Holy Spirit. Teach us to submit to and honor the leaders you have placed over us. Open our eyes so that we may see the path that you set before us. Open our ears so that we may hear your call and follow you voice. Thank you for remaining faithful to us even when we are unfaithful to you. Amen.

Personal Notes and Prayers

Joshua 5:9

וַיֹּאמֶר יְהוָה אֶל־יְהוֹשֻׁעַ הַיּוֹם גַּלּוֹתִי אֶת־חֶרְפַּת מִצְרַיִם מֵעֲלֵיכֶם
וַיִּקְרָא שֵׁם הַמָּקוֹם הַהוּא גִּלְגָּל עַד הַיּוֹם הַזֶּה׃

Then the LORD said to Joshua, "This day I rolled away the reproach of Egypt from upon you." So, the name of the place is called Gilgal to this day.

Biblical Context

SOON AFTER THE ISRAELITES crossed the Jordan into the land of Canaan, God told Joshua to circumcise all the men with new flint knives (5:2). Although the people who had come out of Egypt had been circumcised, this new generation had not (5:5–7). Circumcision was a physical mark on men who were in covenant relationship with the God of Abraham, Isaac and Jacob (see Lev 12:3)—Israelites and non-Israelites (e.g., Exod 12:48). In chapter 5, Joshua obeys the LORD's command and circumcises all the men at Giveʻat Haʻaralot (גִּבְעַת הָעֲרָלוֹת "the hill of foreskins"). The name of the site was then renamed Gilgal (גִּלְגָּל "rolling") where God "rolled off" the reproach of Egypt from the Israelites. It was a significant celebration of the renewing of Israel's covenant relationship with the LORD and a concrete separation from the past in Egypt. The Israelites were now in their God-given homeland, distant from Egyptian oppression. Egypt was behind them—rolled away, cut off, no longer relevant. They were about to take over their new land and live a new life, led by the LORD God himself. After the circumcision ceremony, the Israelites celebrated the Passover as instructed by God (Exod 13:1–10) and Moses (Deut 16:1). Before moving on, God reminded them that He had kept his promises to them in the past and He would definitely continue to do so in the future.

Life Application

When we become believers, God rolls away the reproach of our former rebellious life. Instead of bearing the marks of our former idols and sins, our hearts are circumcised with the mark of the everlasting covenant of the LORD. Although it can be a painful process to cut away the traces of our old lives, it is rewarding to be marked as a follower of the one true God. As the Holy Spirit painfully cuts away the reproach and stench of our old sins, God rolls away the lies we have believed and replaces them with his truth. God takes away our sin, invites us to be his own, and shows us how to live as people whose hearts are marked by the covenant with the everlasting God (Rom 2:28–29).

NT Scriptures

1 Corinthians 6:9–11; Colossians 2:9–14

Prayer

O LORD, how thankful we are that you put the sins of our past as far as the east is from the west. You freed us from bondage, delivered us from sin, healed us from shame and renewed our lives. You bound up our broken hearts, opened our prison doors, comforted us as we mourned and gave us beauty for ashes. You rolled away our reproach and set us on your path. THANK YOU.

Personal Notes and Prayers

Joshua 7:10–11a

וַיֹּאמֶר יְהוָה אֶל־יְהוֹשֻׁעַ קֻם לָךְ לָמָּה זֶּה אַתָּה נֹפֵל עַל־פָּנֶיךָ: חָטָא יִשְׂרָאֵל

Then the LORD said to Joshua, "Get up! Why are you falling on your face? Israel has sinned."

Biblical Context

JOSHUA WAS AT A loss to understand why the LORD would promise to go before Israel in battle yet let her suffer such a dramatic defeat at Ai. He cried out, questioning why God had brought her out of Egypt if it was only to let her be destroyed. But the problem was not with God nor with his faithfulness to his people. Unbeknownst to Joshua, one of his men—Achan—had violated the command of the LORD and taken forbidden plunder from Jericho. The LORD did exactly what He told Joshua He would do if anyone disobeyed. Joshua had misjudged God in this situation. He was not the one who had been unfaithful; it was Israel through Achan who had been unfaithful. It was not a time for mourning over the loss of men; it was time to get up and purge sin from the nation and uphold the end of the covenant God had established with them.

Life Application

When the LORD spoke to Joshua in this situation He wanted more than just a contrite heart. He wanted action. The LORD wanted Joshua to get up and get rid of the thing that was displeasing to Him. It sounds as if the LORD is almost chiding him for not knowing why they had suffered defeat. He had just told Joshua that destruction would come if they disobeyed Him (6:18). But Joshua was lamenting over the defeat instead of wisely solving the problem. It is easy to be consumed by the consequences of sinful actions and forget to actually deal with the problem that got us into the situation in the first place. God is ready to forgive and restore broken relationships but He also expects us to take action against our sin.

NT Scriptures

2 Timothy 2:13; Hebrews 12:1–2; 1 John 1:9

Prayer

O LORD, *"blessed is he whose transgressions are forgiven, whose sins are covered. Blessed is the man whose sin the LORD does not count against him and in whose spirit is no deceit. When I kept silent, my bones wasted away through my groaning all day long. For day and night your hand was heavy upon me; my strength was sapped as in the heat of summer. Selah. Then I acknowledged my sin to you and did not cover up my iniquity. I said, "I will confess my transgressions to the LORD"—and you forgave the guilt of my sin. Selah (Ps 32:1–5)*

Personal Notes and Prayers

Joshua 10:14

וְלֹא הָיָה כַּיּוֹם הַהוּא לְפָנָיו וְאַחֲרָיו לִשְׁמֹעַ יְהוָה בְּקוֹל אִישׁ כִּי יְהוָה נִלְחָם לְיִשְׂרָאֵל:

There has not been a day like it, either before or after, when the LORD obeyed to the voice of a man. Because the LORD fights for Israel.

Biblical Context

AFTER THE VICTORY AT Ai, Joshua was tricked by the Gibeonites who lied and convinced the leaders of Israel that they were from a distant land. Joshua agreed to allow them to live in peace in their inherited territory but quickly found out that they had deceived him with a fabricated story. When the king of Jerusalem heard that the Gibeonites had cut a covenant with the children of Israel, he feared greatly because Gibeon was a great city. He called on the Amorite kings of Hebron, Jarmuth, Lachish and Eglon to form a coalition and attack Gibeon. When the Gibeonites heard that the armies of the south were approaching their city, they called on Joshua who was in Gilgal and begged for his help. Joshua, eager to make up for his mistake rushed to battle on behalf of the Gibeonites. As he went, God promised him that He would fight for him and give him the victory. Having defeated the five Amorite kings in the Shephelah, Joshua commanded the sun and moon to stand still, and they did! As the text shows, God not only answered Joshua as we might expect, but he obeyed his words and made the sun to stand still until the battle was won.

Life Application

When did we last ask for something as large as the sun and moon standing still? Our tendency is to ask for small things, and even then, we often doubt that God will answer our prayers. Joshua did not fall into this trap. He believed he had a big God and he prayed accordingly. This story invites us to ask for the impossible and to trust that God will answer according to his will in ways that are far beyond what we can imagine. As Paul stated to the Ephesians: "Now to him who is able to do far more abundantly than all that we ask or think, according to the power at work within us, to him be glory in the church and in Christ Jesus throughout all generations, forever and ever. Amen" (Eph 3:20–21).

NT Scriptures

Matthew 8:23–27; 15:21–28; Ephesians 1:15–23

Prayer

O LORD our LORD, how majestic is your name above all the earth. In you we live and move and have our being (Acts 17:28). We are your ambassadors on earth, eager to establish your kingdom on earth as it is in heaven. You have granted us your authority, your power, your wisdom, your anointing so that we may do great and mighty things for you. Free us from our fears, our inhibitions and our unwillingness to do your will. Help us trust you fully for all you want to do through our lives. To you be the honor and glory forever. Amen.

Personal Notes and Prayers

Joshua 20:2–4

דַּבֵּר אֶל־בְּנֵי יִשְׂרָאֵל לֵאמֹר תְּנוּ לָכֶם אֶת־עָרֵי הַמִּקְלָט אֲשֶׁר־דִּבַּרְתִּי אֲלֵיכֶם בְּיַד־מֹשֶׁה:

לָנוּס שָׁמָּה רוֹצֵחַ מַכֵּה־נֶפֶשׁ בִּשְׁגָגָה בִּבְלִי־דָעַת וְהָיוּ לָכֶם לְמִקְלָט מִגֹּאֵל הַדָּם:

וְנָס אֶל־אַחַת מֵהֶעָרִים הָאֵלֶּה וְעָמַד פֶּתַח שַׁעַר הָעִיר וְדִבֶּר בְּאָזְנֵי זִקְנֵי הָעִיר־הַהִיא אֶת־דְּבָרָיו

וְאָסְפוּ אֹתוֹ הָעִירָה אֲלֵיהֶם וְנָתְנוּ־לוֹ מָקוֹם וְיָשַׁב עִמָּם:

Speak to the sons of Israel saying, "Appoint for yourselves cities of refuge, which I mentioned to you through Moses, that the one murdering a soul unintentionally and without knowledge may flee there. They will be for you a refuge from the avenger of blood. He will flee to one of these cities, he will stand at the entrance of the gate of the city, he will present his case in the hearing of the elders of that city and they will welcome him into the city to themselves. They will give him a place and he will dwell with them."

Biblical Context

THE ISRAELITES CONQUERED THE land of Canaan and began to take possession of it. As was commanded to Moses by God, six cities of refuge (עָרֵי הַמִּקְלָט) were set up throughout the land so that a refuge was always near for anyone who may need it. If someone killed another person accidentally (מַכֵּה־נֶפֶשׁ בִּשְׁגָגָה), without intending to do so (בִּבְלִי־דָעַת), he could flee to the gate of one of these cities of refuge to plead his case with the leaders. If he was believed, he was given admittance to the city, a place to live, a fair trial, and protection. Protection was necessary since someone from the family of the deceased would be pursuing the murderer to avenge the death of his family member (גֹּאֵל הַדָּם "avenger of blood"). Levitical priests were given these cities of refuge, along with many other cities, as their inheritance in the land.

Life Application

The modern-day city of refuge is the local church. God has purposely placed them throughout the land so that a refuge is always near for someone in need. Each of us will need a church at one point in our life, if we do not already have one. Our churches should be prominent and active in the community rather than remote or removed from the neighbors around it. Our churches should provide grace and protection for those who seek its shelter. Just as the cities of refuge were available for Jews, Gentiles, and the travelers among them, churches should be open and inviting to everyone regardless of race, gender, political affiliation, economic status, or life history.

NT Scriptures

Acts 15:4; Hebrews 13:2

Prayer

O LORD, with you there is no privileged race, gender, political affiliation, economic status or life history. We have all been created in your image, in your likeness, to represent you on the earth. Help us see beyond the color of people's skin, the riches they may or may not have, the background from which they come, the gifts they may or may not have. Teach us to see you in all human beings and to seek to enhance your presence in this world.

Personal Notes and Prayers

Joshua 23:14

וְהִנֵּה אָנֹכִי הוֹלֵךְ הַיּוֹם בְּדֶרֶךְ כָּל־הָאָרֶץ וִידַעְתֶּם בְּכָל־לְבַבְכֶם
וּבְכָל־נַפְשְׁכֶם כִּי לֹא־נָפַל דָּבָר אֶחָד מִכֹּל הַדְּבָרִים הַטּוֹבִים אֲשֶׁר
דִּבֶּר יְהוָה אֱלֹהֵיכֶם עֲלֵיכֶם הַכֹּל בָּאוּ לָכֶם לֹא־נָפַל מִמֶּנּוּ דָּבָר
אֶחָד:

I am about to go this day the way of all the earth. You know with all of your hearts and with all of you souls that not one word has failed from all the good words which the LORD your God spoke regarding all of you. They all came to pass for you, not one word has failed.

Biblical Context

JOSHUA LED THE HEBREW people into the promised land but he knew that it was not due to his own doing. He knew that without God's leading, power, anointing and support, the Israelites would never have made it into Canaan. They would no doubt have stayed in Egypt and perished there. Joshua 23 is Joshua's farewell address to all Israel through leaders, tribal chiefs, judges and officials. Acknowledging his old age and the imminence of his death, Joshua reminds the Israelites that God has been faithful to them without fault. He fought for them in battle, gave them victory over their enemies, performed wonders in their midst, led them into the promised land, and will continue to establish them in their homeland by driving out nations from before them. Everything the LORD promised them came to pass, and as they settle in the land, the LORD will continue to be with them. Though Joshua's body would soon fail and he would pass away—just as everything on earth does—Joshua reminds them that one thing is constant, the words and promises of the LORD are eternal. They stand forever.

Life Application

As seen throughout Scripture, when God makes promises, He fulfills them because He is faithful, truthful, and good. He promised to lead Israel into their homeland, and He did. He promised to sustain them with provision during the journey, and He did. He opened impossible doors (bodies of water) before them, and no one could shut them. We have much to learn from Joshua's farewell speech. First, as Joshua followed God until the day he died, we are called to do the same and to acknowledge his presence with us until death. We are responsible to seek him, love him and walk with him faithfully until our last breath. Then, we are commanded to teach the mighty deeds of the LORD to the next generation so that they may in turn follow the LORD with all their heart, mind and soul, and glorify him.

NT Scriptures

1 Peter 4:10; 3 John 3, 5

Prayer

O LORD, you have been faithful throughout all generations. You have never left your children to fend for themselves. You have always been there, ready to manifest yourself in the midst of your people. You never leave us nor forsake us. In our childhood, in our youth, in the prime of our lives, and in old age, you are always there. You will be there until our last breath, and then, you will welcome us into glory. What a day that will be!

Personal Notes and Prayers

Joshua 24:15

וְאִם רַע בְּעֵינֵיכֶם לַעֲבֹד אֶת־יְהוָה בַּחֲרוּ לָכֶם הַיּוֹם אֶת־מִי תַעֲבֹדוּן אִם אֶת־אֱלֹהִים אֲשֶׁר־עָבְדוּ אֲבוֹתֵיכֶם אֲשֶׁר בְּעֵבֶר הַנָּהָר וְאִם אֶת־אֱלֹהֵי הָאֱמֹרִי אֲשֶׁר אַתֶּם יֹשְׁבִים בְּאַרְצָם וְאָנֹכִי וּבֵיתִי נַעֲבֹד אֶת־יְהוָה׃

Now if it displeases you to serve the LORD, choose for you this day whom you will serve, whether the gods your fathers served that were across the river, or whether the gods of the Amorites when you were dwelling in their land. But as for me and my house, we will serve the LORD.

Biblical Context

AT THE END OF his life, Joshua reminds the children of Israel to continue to serve the LORD faithfully and to turn their backs on the temptation to participate in Canaanite cultic rituals. Joshua reminds them that God delivered them from the Pharaoh in Egypt, provided for them in the wilderness, led them to the promised land, granted them victory in battles, and delivered them from their foes. Yet the people of Israel still chose to dabble in syncretistic practices and turned away from the LORD. By this time, it is clear that the people had been worshipping foreign gods, and had not yielded themselves to the LORD. Joshua could not leave this earth without echoing the final message of Moses to the Israelites, "I have set before you life and death, blessing and curse. Therefore, choose life, that you and your offspring may live, loving the LORD your God, obeying his voice and holding fast to him, for he is your life and length of days, that you may dwell in the land that the LORD swore to your fathers, to Abraham, to Isaac, and to Jacob, to give them" (Deut 30:19–20). As for you and your families, serve the LORD!

Life Application

Joshua's firm stance in choosing to serve the LORD is inspiring. For Joshua, the prospect of standing in front of the assembly of Israel and declaring his choice may have been no big deal, but the thought of standing in front of my own family and making such a proclamation is sometimes frightening. I was not raised in a Christian home, and my being a Christian now has created a rift in my family, especially since my husband's family is Christian. Joshua's declaration has and continues to inspire me to make my own declaration. My husband and I have our own family now (just the two of us) and will grow that family in the future. We have our own choice to make and regardless of who we hurt or offend, there is only one choice that we can make: "we will serve the LORD."

NT Scriptures

Mark 12:28–31; John 12:26; Romans 1:16

Prayer

O LORD, you gave your own life so that we may receive abundant and eternal life. May we never forget your immense sacrifice for us. May we never find ourselves surrendering to evil. Help us be steadfast and immovable in our walk with you and take away our spirit of fear. Fill us with courage to do your will and to serve you all the days of our lives.

Personal Notes and Prayers

Judges 2:11

וַיַּעֲשׂוּ בְנֵי־יִשְׂרָאֵל אֶת־הָרַע בְּעֵינֵי יְהוָה וַיַּעַבְדוּ אֶת־הַבְּעָלִים׃

The sons of Israel did evil in the eyes of the LORD, and served the Baals.

Biblical Context

THE ISRAELITES WERE FINALLY in their homeland, living within their God given tribal allotments. They walked in the ways of the LORD during the days of Joshua and during the days of the elders who remained after Joshua (2:7). However, the next generation failed to remain faithful to the LORD and worshipped the gods of the nations around them. One wonders why this generation was so quick to deviate from the path—having forsaken Adonai and bowing down to the Baal and the Ashtaroth (2:12–13). Had the previous generation not taught their young the importance of worshipping *only* the God of Abraham, Isaac and Jacob? Had the previous generation failed to tell their children the stories of God's mighty deliverance from Egypt and miracles in the wilderness (2:10)? Seemingly unaware of the consequences of bowing down to other gods, this new generation of Israelites moved forward, breaking the covenant, engaging in syncretistic religious practices, and doing evil in the eyes of the LORD. Consequently, God gave them over into the hands of their enemies until they became severely distressed (2:14–15). This cycle—serving God then breaking covenant—was repeated numerous times during the period of the judges (3:7, 12; 4:1; 6:1; 10:6; 13:1). But God, in his wisdom and grace, raised up judge after judge to deliver the Israelites from the hands of their oppressors.

Life Application

While no one can guarantee that those who come after us will remain faithful to the LORD, we must remember to teach the next generation to follow God and his ways. In Deuteronomy 6:5 and 7, Moses commands the Israelites to love the LORD their God with all their heart, mind and strength. He instructs them to *"teach them [the Words of the LORD] diligently to your children, and talk of them when you sit in your house, and when you walk by the way, and when you lie down, and when you rise"* (Deut 6:7). In other words, the next generation should hear the Word of God continually and reflect on the mighty deeds God performed throughout history. Only then will God's children avoid doing evil in the eyes of the LORD.

NT Scriptures

1 Corinthians 10:12–13; 1 Timothy 4:12

Prayer

O LORD, how we thank you for revealing yourself to us and for teaching us what you have done and still do for those who are created in your own image. Help us be faithful to share your truth with younger generations and remind us to pray for them as they grow in wisdom and knowledge. Forgive us for selfishly keeping your gifts to ourselves and for failing to imitate your generosity. As others have shared the Good News with us, help us share the Good News with those who come after us. May the chain of your knowledge never be broken.

Personal Notes and Prayers

Judges 3:15a

וַיִּזְעֲקוּ בְנֵי־יִשְׂרָאֵל אֶל־יְהוָה וַיָּקֶם יְהוָה לָהֶם מוֹשִׁיעַ

The Israelites cried out to the LORD so the LORD raised up an anointed deliverer for them.

Biblical Context

WHEN IN A STATE of despair and chaos, the Israelites knew that turning to God carried important benefits. Time and time again, after the Israelites cried out to God, the LORD answered their cry. Throughout history, God raised up for them anointed leaders who would provide stability and security for the whole community. While in Egypt, God raised Moses to deliver his people out of bondage. During their wilderness wandering, God groomed Joshua to replace Moses. And after conquering Canaan, God provided judges to lead his people and to bring them to a place of safety and peace. Although God wanted to be their ultimate Leader, Judge, Provider, and their Everything, the Israelites thought they needed a visible and touchable figure who spoke their language and identified with their human struggles. Over and over again, God recognized their cries of desperation and provided leaders upon whom He placed his anointing and his seal of approval. Without the strength and inspiration of the Holy Spirit, these leaders could never have participated in delivering God's people, and led them into the plan God had for them.

Life Application

Throughout Scripture, God promises that He will never leave nor forsake his people. Regardless of circumstances, of location, of offenses committed, God's eyes are always on his people. His ears are always attentive to their cry. He is forever faithful to deliver, even when situations seem impossible to our human eyes. As the people of God, we are invited to turn to Him in times of trouble and to thank Him in times of peace. What a faithful Friend we have!

NT Scriptures

Acts 7:34–37; Revelation 7:17

Prayer

Thank you LORD for listening to our cries for help, to our calls for mercy and to our pleas for restoration. You are faithful to deliver us from our troubles—whether self-inflicted or inflicted by others. Help us keep our eyes on you in times of trouble for you are faithful to deliver.

Personal Notes and Prayers

Judges 7:7

וַיֹּ֨אמֶר יְהוָ֜ה אֶל־גִּדְע֗וֹן בִּשְׁלֹ֣שׁ מֵא֞וֹת הָאִ֣ישׁ הַֽמְלַקְקִים֮ אוֹשִׁ֣יעַ
אֶתְכֶם֒ וְנָתַתִּ֥י אֶת־מִדְיָ֖ן בְּיָדֶ֑ךָ
וְכָל־הָעָ֔ם יֵלְכ֖וּ אִ֥ישׁ לִמְקֹמֽוֹ׃

The LORD said to Gideon, "By means of the three hundred men who lap, I will save you. I will give the Midianites into your hand. However, all the (other) men will go, each man to his place."

Biblical Context

BY THIS TIME, THE land of the Israel had been ruined by the Midianites and the Israelites had lived under oppression for seven years. God was ready to give the land back to them, so he raised up Gideon to lead them. He may not have been the most likely character to be chosen for such a task since Gideon himself acknowledged that he came from the weakest clan of Manasseh and that he was the least of his father's household (Judg 6:15). But the fact that the LORD works in mysterious ways and through the lowliest among us would be illustrated dramatically through Gideon. When it came time for the Israelites to go up among the Midianites, God decided that the army was too large to perform the task. First, God instructed Gideon to send everyone who was afraid home. This cut his army of 32,000 down to 10,000 (7:3). Still the army was too big, so in a seemingly arbitrary way but under divine guidance, Gideon brought them to a pool of water and separated those who drank water by lapping it up like a dog from those who knelt down and used their hands to cup the water. Those who knelt down were sent home since they had shown that they were not sufficiently alert for battle with both knees on the ground and their faces in the water. Only three hundred men remained. The enemy forces, on the other hand, were as thick in abundance as a swarm of locusts and the amount of camels they had was compared to the amount of sand that is on the seashore (7:12). With an army of three hundred men who drink their water like dogs, led by the weakling of his clan, God saved Israel and drove their enemies from the Promised Land.

Life Application

The reason God sent so many men home is no mystery. God did not want to leave any room for them to boast in their own power to save themselves (7:2). It was God who fought their battles, God who brought them victory. The God who saved them saves us still. May we never forget the example of Gideon's army, and may we faithfully echo the words of the Apostle Paul, "I will not boast about myself, except about my weaknesses . . . For when I am weak, then I am strong."

NT Scriptures

2 Corinthians 12:1–10

Prayer

O LORD, forgive us for our arrogant boasting and proud utterances. In humility, we acknowledge that all gifts, abilities, skills and talents come from you, and without you, we are nothing. Every breath comes from you. Every day is a gift from you. Every relationship we hold dear comes from you. To you we owe everything. Today, our hearts are full of thanksgiving and praise for your love and goodness towards us. May we never forget and take for granted your wondrous gifts.

Personal Notes and Prayers

Judges 13:18

וַיֹּ֤אמֶר לוֹ֙ מַלְאַ֣ךְ יְהוָ֔ה לָ֥מָּה זֶּ֖ה תִּשְׁאַ֣ל לִשְׁמִ֑י וְהוּא־פֶֽלִאי׃

The angel of the LORD said to him [Manoah],
"Why is this that you ask for my name?
It is incomprehensible."

Biblical Context

MANOAH AND HIS WIFE were childless until a messenger of the LORD visited them and promised a son who would be set apart for God and begin Israel's deliverance from the Philistines. Manoah asked the messenger, "What is your name (who are you), so that we may honor you when your word comes true?" The messenger answered, "Why is *this* that you ask for my name?" In a similar story, Jacob also asks for the name of a messenger and receives the same response: "Why is *this* that you ask for my name?" (Gen 32:29). In both cases, the messenger of the LORD answers the question with a question, but only in the Manoah story is the name of the messenger revealed—it is פֶּלִאי which means "incomprehensible, wonderful, unusual, extraordinary." A word from the same Hebrew root appears in Isaiah 9:6 where God reveals himself as "Wonderful" (פֶּלֶא). Manoah's wife describes the angel of the LORD as awe-inspiring, and when Manoah offers a sacrifice to the LORD, the angel of the LORD does an extraordinary thing, ascending to heaven in the flame of the offering. Israel had lived under the oppression of the Philistines for forty years, yet Manoah and his wife believed in the LORD's promise of deliverance through their son. When their promised son arrived, they named him Samson (שִׁמְשׁוֹן "sun-like"). The LORD blessed him and raised him up to be a deliverer in Israel.

Life Application

It is comforting to know that God's name means "incomprehensible, wonderful, unusual, extraordinary," especially when life does not make sense and when circumstances seem to contradict God's character. Why do we seek to know his name, and are we ready to receive his special revelation? Even when we have to wait indefinitely in the midst of oppression and life's challenges, God is trustworthy and has a plan for deliverance. He will manifest himself in ways that are extraordinary and will bring deliverance through the most unexpected means.

NT Scriptures

Matthew 1:21–23; Revelation 19:11–13, 16

Prayer

O LORD, your name is above every name. In your name, we take refuge and find help. We call on your name and find safety and deliverance. Help us LORD live in a way that honors the beauty, majesty and power of your name. For we know that one day, every knee will bow and every tongue confess your name and acknowledge that you are the King of kings and LORD of LORDs.

Personal Notes and Prayers

1 Samuel 3:10

וַיָּבֹא יְהוָה וַיִּתְיַצַּב וַיִּקְרָא כְפַעַם־בְּפַעַם שְׁמוּאֵל שְׁמוּאֵל וַיֹּאמֶר שְׁמוּאֵל דַּבֵּר כִּי שֹׁמֵעַ עַבְדֶּךָ׃

The LORD came and standing at attention, He called again as he did before, "Samuel, Samuel". Then Samuel said, "Speak because your servant is listening."

Biblical Context

HANNAH WAS BARREN. SHE could not conceive with her husband Elkanah, whose second wife Peninnah was happily bearing children. Deeply distressed by her physical condition, Hannah poured her soul before the LORD, weeping bitterly. Praying in silence with only her lips moving, Eli noticed her and took her to be a drunken woman. After he learned of her unfortunate plight, he blessed her and prayed for God to grant her her petition. Miraculously, Hannah conceived and bore a son. She named him "Samuel" (שְׁמוּאֵל "God has heard") because he was the proof that God had heard and answered her prayer. Shortly thereafter, Hannah dedicated him to the LORD and took him to the prophet Eli for training in the service of the tabernacle. As a young man, Samuel had not yet come to know the LORD nor could he yet discern a divine call. When the LORD first called him, he mistook the voice for that of his guardian Eli. This happened twice before Eli realized that God was calling Samuel. It was only during the fourth appeal that Samuel responded to the call of God, as instructed by the prophet Eli. The LORD then opened Samuel's understanding and revealed to him what He was about to do in Israel.

Life Application

The first few chapters of the book of Samuel highlight the struggle human beings have in their ability to discern God's voice. In our passage, Eli, a prophet of God who should have known better, fails twice to recognize that God was calling the boy. Only the third time did Eli discern the voice of God. So, he instructed Samuel that, should the voice be heard again, he should answer: "Speak [LORD] because your servant is listening!" God had indeed been speaking all along but neither Eli nor Samuel had recognized the source of the call. God is still speaking today. He has never stopped speaking and revealing himself to his beloved. He yearns to speak to his children, to reveal his will and to make himself known. How else can we live successfully, productively and efficiently on this earth? Let us open our ears and heed his call.

NT Scriptures

Hebrews 1:1–2; 1 Corinthians 2:9–13

Prayer

O LORD, open our ears that we may hear your voice, for it is the voice of heaven, the voice that leads in the paths of righteousness. As the psalmist said, your voice is powerful and full of majesty; it shakes the wilderness and breaks the cedars of Lebanon. The prophet Isaiah heard the LORD saying: "Whom shall I send, and who will go for us?" Then he responded, "Here I am! Send me." May we be like Samuel and Isaiah who heard your voice and obeyed. May we follow you all the days of our lives.

Personal Notes and Prayers

1 Samuel 7:3

וַיֹּאמֶר שְׁמוּאֵל אֶל־כָּל־בֵּית יִשְׂרָאֵל לֵאמֹר אִם־בְּכָל־לְבַבְכֶם אַתֶּם
שָׁבִים אֶל־יְהוָה הָסִירוּ אֶת־אֱלֹהֵי הַנֵּכָר מִתּוֹכְכֶם וְהָעַשְׁתָּרוֹת
וְהָכִינוּ לְבַבְכֶם אֶל־יְהוָה וְעִבְדֻהוּ לְבַדּוֹ וְיַצֵּל אֶתְכֶם מִיַּד פְּלִשְׁתִּים:

Then Samuel said to the whole house of Israel, "If you return to the LORD with all your hearts, turn away from the foreign gods and the Ashtaroth that are among you, and fix your hearts on the LORD and serve him alone, then he will deliver you from the hand of the Philistines."

Biblical Context

THE ARK OF THE LORD had been captured by the Philistines and consequently, Dagon, the god of the Philistines, was destroyed, and the people of Gath and Ekron were afflicted with tumors (1 Sam 5:9, 12). Without the Ark in their midst, the Israelites lost battles, Eli died and the glory departed from Israel. Out of desperation, the Philistines sent the Ark back to Israel where it found a home, first in Beth Shemesh and then in Kiriath-Jearim, for a period of twenty years. It was at this time that Samuel addressed the people, pleading with them to turn back to God, remove from their midst "all foreign gods and Ashtaroth, and serve the LORD only." Only then would the LORD deliver them from the hand of the Philistines and give them victory over their enemies. This was not the first time the Israelites had sinned and allowed the gods of the nations to distract them from their devotion to the LORD. They were led astray and turned to foreign gods many times before. One more time, God gives them a chance to repent and forsake their evil ways.

Life Application

In life we are often distracted by the things of the world. We like the idea of living for God when it is easy and convenient, but at times, we prefer doing our own thing and follow our own desires rather than walking in the ways of the LORD. Departure from the center of God's will often starts with something seemingly insignificant and can turn into wrong habits that lead to slavery to sin. We are urged to turn away from these things, or to cause these things to depart from our life and serve the LORD, our God. We are commanded to love the LORD our God with all our heart, mind and strength. Only then can we be delivered from bondage to sin.

NT Scriptures

Matthew 18:7–9; Mark 12:30–31; Hebrews 12:1–2

Prayer

"Repentance is the abandoning of all false paths that have been trodden by men's feet, and men's thoughts and desires, and a return to the new path: Christ's path. But how can a sinful man repent unless he, in his heart, meets with the LORD and knows his own shame? Before little Zacchaeus saw the LORD with his eyes, he met Him in his heart and was ashamed of all his ways" (St. Nikolai Velimirovic, "The Thirty-Second Sunday After Pentecost: The Gospel on Repentant Zacchaeus, Luke 19:1–10," *Homilies Volume II: Sundays after Pentecost*).

Personal Notes and Prayers

1 Samuel 7:12

וַיִּקַּח שְׁמוּאֵל אֶבֶן אַחַת וַיָּשֶׂם בֵּין־הַמִּצְפָּה וּבֵין הַשֵּׁן וַיִּקְרָא אֶת־
שְׁמָהּ אֶבֶן הָעָזֶר

וַיֹּאמַר עַד־הֵנָּה עֲזָרָנוּ יְהוָה:

Then Samuel took a stone and he placed it between Mizpah and Shen. Then he called the place Eben-Ezer (the stone of help) and then he said: "Up till now the LORD has helped us."

Biblical Context

TWENTY YEARS EARLIER, THE Israelites had battled the Philistines at a place named Ebenezer. They had brought the Ark of the Covenant along, hoping that God would help them in the battle, but God did not help them because He was bringing judgment on the sinful house of Eli. Israel suffered defeat at the hands of the Philistines. The Ark was captured and taken to Dagon's temple in Ashdod. After being terrorized and afflicted by God at Ashdod, the Philistines returned the Ark to Israel, to Kiriath Jearim, where it remained for twenty years. After this time, the Israelites sought the LORD again. Samuel told the Israelites to put away their foreign gods and to serve the LORD. The Israelites listened to Samuel, put away their foreign gods and gathered at Mizpah to confess their sins and serve the LORD. While they were gathered there, the Philistines assembled to attack them, but this time the LORD intervened on behalf of his people and the Philistines were defeated. After this great victory Samuel set up a stone to commemorate the help they had received from the LORD; he called the place "the stone of help" or Ebenezer.

Life Application

Israel's fortunes changed completely after the LORD helped them. They had originally experienced defeat because of sin in the camp, but God had not abandoned them. When they turned to Him in repentance, He delivered them. This truth has echoed in the lives of many throughout history. A young man named Robert Robinson had experienced the defeat of a sinful life until he heard the gospel through the preaching of George Whitefield. He repented of his wicked lifestyle, turned to God and found salvation through Jesus Christ. In the hymn entitled "Come Thou Fount of Every Blessing" he penned the words "Here I raise my Ebenezer, here by Thy great help I've come." As he surveyed his life, he saw that the LORD had sought him out and rescued him from a sinful existence. Today, even though it is not easy to discern how the LORD works, those who put their trust in the LORD are able to testify to their Ebenezer, "Stone of help", where the LORD has helped, guided, protected and delivered.

NT Scriptures

Romans 8:28–29; Philippians 1:6; Hebrews 4:16

Prayer

O LORD, thank you for being there at our side ready to forgive us, cleanse us from sin and restore us to a place of victory. We recognized that you have been there as our "ebenezer" so many times along life's journey. We love your presence, your instructions, your deeds and your victories. We give you glory.

Personal Notes and Prayers

1 Samuel 12:10

וַיִּזְעֲקוּ אֶל־יְהוָה וַיֹּאמֶר חָטָאנוּ כִּי עָזַבְנוּ אֶת־יְהוָה וַנַּעֲבֹד אֶת־הַבְּעָלִים וְאֶת־הָעַשְׁתָּרוֹת

וְעַתָּה הַצִּילֵנוּ מִיַּד אֹיְבֵינוּ וְנַעַבְדֶךָ׃

Then they cried out to the LORD and said: We have sinned because we have abandoned the LORD and served Bealim and Ashtarot. So now, deliver us from the power of our enemies so that we may serve you.

Biblical Context

AFTER THE ISRAELITES HAD received the law at Mt Sinai, journeyed in the wilderness for almost 40 years, settled in the land of Canaan, and received their king from the LORD, they found themselves entangled in a web of confusion and oppression at the hand of their Philistine neighbors. Unable to bring about their own deliverance, they reacted as they had dome numerous times before—they cried out to the LORD, acknowledged their sins, and sought to be rescued by their Deliverer. The Israelites knew they had done evil in the eyes of the LORD. They had broken the first and most important of all the commandments—*You shall have no other gods before me*, Exod 20:3, Deut 5:7—and for this, they experienced the continued severe harassment of the Philistines. God had promised to Moses and Joshua that He would go before them and destroy their enemies. Had He forgotten to deal with the Philistines?

Life Application

God promises us peace, prosperity, joy, and health. Yet reality reminds us that we are still living in a fall world, where obstacles, inconsistencies, inconveniences, and conflicts plague our daily lives. God's promises are *yea and amen* to the glory of God, but some of these will be completely manifested only in the kingdom of heaven. Let us be steadfast, patient, wise, and determined to fulfill God's purpose for our lives, especially in the midst of difficulties.

NT Scriptures

2 Corinthians 1:8–11; James 1:2–7, 12

Prayer

O LORD, how many are the trials we face each day. Day after day, they afflict us and seek to draw us away from your presence. We thank you that in the midst of our troubles, you never leave us nor forsake us; you open you ear to our cry, and you protect us in times of trouble. May we remain faithful to you O LORD, especially when you seem so distant. You are more attentive to us than we will ever know. We thank you so much.

Personal Notes and Prayers

1 Samuel 12:24

אַ֣ךְ ׀ יְר֣אוּ אֶת־יְהוָ֗ה וַעֲבַדְתֶּ֤ם אֹתוֹ֙ בֶּאֱמֶ֔ת בְּכָל־לְבַבְכֶ֑ם כִּ֣י רְא֔וּ אֵ֥ת אֲשֶׁר־הִגְדִּ֖ל עִמָּכֶֽם׃

Only fear the LORD, and serve him in truth with all your heart, and consider the great things he has done for you.

Biblical Context

SAMUEL WITNESSED BOTH THE rise, the reign, and the fall of king Saul. The Israelites had requested a king like all the nations around them. In response to their cry, God chose Saul, of the tribe of Benjamin, to become king over them and to deliver them from the hand of the Philistines (1 Sam 9:16). Samuel anointed Saul as king, even though he knew that this was not what was best for the nation. God wanted to be Israel's king, but the people insisted that they should have a human king. Nevertheless, God anointed Saul with his Spirit, enabling him to prophesy with a band of prophets (1 Sam 10:10) and to declare the defeat of the Ammonites at Jabesh-Gilead. Some time later, Samuel delivers his farewell speech to the nation, reminding them to reflect on God's mighty deeds (e.g., God delivered them from their enemies on every side, 1 Sam 12:8–12). He urges them to fear the LORD, serve him, obey his voice, and observe his commandments (1 Sam 12:14). Samuel reminds them of the severe consequences of failing to do so (1 Sam 12:15). Samuel had served Israel faithfully since his youth and the people had great respect for him and for his message. However, before Samuel's death, the conditions in Israel decline and Samuel witnesses the change in Saul's reign, from his success to his downfall, when he failed to trust God at Gilgal. Rather than waiting for the appointed time to offer sacrifices with prophet Samuel, as per God's instructions, Saul reacted with fear and disobeyed God's command (1 Sam 13:13). His failure to trust God and exercise patience cost him the kingdom.

Life Application

We all go through periods of transition when we must exercise patience. Major events like births and deaths, school and job changes, and other events mark definite and permanent changes in our lives. Some of these events are what God has for us, and others are allowed by God for reasons we may not understand. No matter what happens during these periods of transition, we need to be patient, depend on God and consider all the things he has done for us. Remembering who he is helps us trust patiently, especially when periods of transition seem difficult. God is never late in revealing his plans for us. Let us wait for him.

NT Scriptures

Romans 8:22–25; James 5:7–11

Prayer

O LORD, you wait patiently for us when we are consumed with our human endeavors and fail to turn to you for guidance. You are long suffering and merciful, even when we fail to trust you. Help us walk in-step with you and wait for you to reveal your plan. Help us listen to your voice and allow you to lead the way. Forgive us for our impatience and for our failure to depend on you. We need you, every hour, we need you.

Personal Notes and Prayers

1 Samuel 14:6

וַיֹּאמֶר יְהוֹנָתָן אֶל־הַנַּעַר נֹשֵׂא כֵלָיו לְכָה וְנַעְבְּרָה אֶל־מַצַּב הָעֲרֵלִים הָאֵלֶּה

אוּלַי יַעֲשֶׂה יְהוָה לָנוּ כִּי אֵין לַיהוָה מַעְצוֹר לְהוֹשִׁיעַ בְּרַב אוֹ בִמְעָט:

Then Jonathan said to the young man carrying his armor, "Come, let us cross over to the garrison of these uncircumcised. Perhaps the LORD will act on our behalf, because nothing can hinder the LORD from bringing deliverance either by many or by few."

Biblical Context

IN 1 SAMUEL 14, Jonathan decides to challenge the Philistines garrisoned at Michmash (1 Sam 13:23). He resolves to break into their outpost by climbing up a treacherous pass in the craggy hills between Geba and Michmash. He explains to his young armor-bearer the best strategy to approach and defeat the Philistine soldiers. Jonathan tells his armor-bearer that an invitation from them to come up to their camp will serve as a sign that God has delivered the Philistines into their hand. However, none of this is certain. There is no evidence in the text that God had promised victory over the Philistines on that day. Jonathan says, "Perhaps the LORD will work on our behalf" (אוּלַי יַעֲשֶׂה יְהוָה לָנוּ). Even if Jonathan expresses uncertainty, his faith in God gives him the motivation to move forward with the plan. He recognizes these uncircumcised as the enemies of the LORD, and therefore, he formulates his plan of action with boldness and courage. Jonathan's faith is anchored in God's ability and determination to deliver his people from their enemies, as seen throughout Israel's history. Simply on the basis of God's might and willingness to work on the behalf of his own, Jonathan takes the leap.

Life Application

Sometimes we venture into uncertainty based on the hope that God will meet us. Like Jonathan we can take risks, which is not unreasonable in light of what we know of the LORD. He is a great and mighty God who works for us and not against us. There is nothing that he cannot do for us. The object of our faith is not always in the guaranteed promises of God, but in the person of God, in the power and willingness of God to give us success in undertakings that are in general alignment with his work on earth. Before we believe that God *will* act on our behalf, we must first believe that he is *able to* act. That is faith.

NT Scriptures

Matthew 9:27-29; Romans 4:16-21; Hebrews 11:1

Prayer

O LORD, we believe that you are willing, able and committed to establish your kingdom on earth. We are your children, your servants, your vessels, created to do your will. We seek to follow you wholeheartedly through the shadowy path of life. We walk by faith and not by sight. We trust you to lead us in your ways as we navigate life's dim journey. Help us remain faithful to you when the path is unclear and your voice is distant. We want to honor you with our lives and bring you glory with our words and deeds. We surrender ourselves to your will.

Personal Notes and Prayers

1 Samuel 17:33

וַיֹּ֨אמֶר שָׁא֤וּל אֶל־דָּוִד֙ לֹ֣א תוּכַ֗ל לָלֶ֛כֶת אֶל־הַפְּלִשְׁתִּ֥י הַזֶּ֖ה לְהִלָּחֵ֣ם עִמּ֑וֹ

כִּֽי־נַ֣עַר אַ֔תָּה וְה֛וּא אִ֥ישׁ מִלְחָמָ֖ה מִנְּעֻרָֽיו:

Then Saul said to David, "You are not able to go to this Philistine to fight with him. For you are a boy, but he has been a man of war since his youth."

Biblical Context

MOST PEOPLE HAVE HEARD the story of David and Goliath. The Philistines were encamped in the valley between Socoh and Azekah while Saul's men were based in the Elah Valley. David, the youngest of Jesse's sons, came to his brothers with a gift of grain, loaves and cheese, intending to return to his father with a report on the wellbeing of his brothers. However, when he entered the camp, the warriors were getting ready for battle against the Philistines. Conflict between the two camps was imminent, so both armies formed battle lines on the ridges of facing hills. Goliath, a huge Philistine military man, issued a challenge to Israel and offered to meet face-to-face with the best warrior Israel could offer. It is at this point that David's plans changed. He heard the challenge issued by Goliath and inquired into the Philistine's request. David's eldest brother rebuked him and tried to send him back home, but David would have none of it. He eventually approached Saul and revealing his credentials—he had killed a lion and a bear while protecting his flock—he offered to take up Goliath's challenge, for "who did this uncircumcised Philistine think he was!" With great confidence, David said, "The LORD who delivered me from the paw of the lion and from the paw of the bear will deliver me from the hand of this Philistine" (17:37). As is well known, David bravely went up against giant Goliath and killed him with a sling and a stone. He did so despite the fact that he was only a young shepherd boy. David's older brothers and Saul only saw David as a youth who knew nothing about fighting. But David trusted the living God and could not be stopped, even by a giant.

Life Application

Although everyone else saw David as an inexperienced child, David knew that God has equipped him for the task of defeating the giant. David's confidence in the LORD is an example Christians can take with them in their own tasks. When we feel God calling us to walk a difficult path, we can trust that God will equip us to accomplish the task he set before us. Even in the face of adversity, we can and must put our trust in the LORD and confidently go into the battle confidently and courageously.

NT Scriptures

2 Corinthians 1:8–10; 2 Timothy 4:16–18

Prayer

O LORD, out of the mouth of babes and infants, you have established strength because of your foes, to still the enemy and the avenger (Ps 8:2; Matt 21:16). The prophet Samuel walked with you from his youth (1 Sam 12:2). As a young man, King David defeated a giant. When Jeremiah said: "Ah, LORD God! Behold, I do not know how to speak, for I am only a youth" (Jer 1:6). You responded: "Do not say, 'I am only a youth'; for to all to whom I send you, you shall go, and whatever I command you, you shall speak. Do not be afraid of them, for I am with you to deliver you" (Jer 1:7–8). We thank you LORD for our youth.

Personal Notes and Prayers

1 Samuel 20:14–15

וְלֹא אִם־עוֹדֶנִּי חָי וְלֹא־תַעֲשֶׂה עִמָּדִי חֶסֶד יְהוָה וְלֹא אָמוּת׃
וְלֹא־תַכְרִת אֶת־חַסְדְּךָ מֵעִם בֵּיתִי עַד־עוֹלָם

If I am still alive, will you not show me the covenant love (chesed,חֶסֶד) of the LORD so I may not die, and do not cut off your covenant love (chesed,חֶסֶד) from my house forever.

Biblical Context

BY THIS TIME, DAVID had been anointed by prophet Samuel to be the next king of Israel. However, King Saul wished to stop this plan and plotted to kill David during a dinner at his palace. Aware of Saul's hatred towards him, David hid from Saul and met Jonathan in a field where they devised a plan to keep both of them safe from Saul's wrath. The two had previously established a covenant because they cared for each other with a deep love (18:3). In chapter 20, we are told that both of them relied on their covenantal love (חֶסֶד) for each other in order other to survive Saul's madness. This type of covenantal love (חֶסֶד) represents the highest kind of devotion and loyalty one could express towards another. David and Jonathan knew that this love (חֶסֶד) came from the LORD and did not come from them. It was supernatural, intense and genuine. This love was holy and unconditional, one that was established on a binding, steadfast and everlasting promise that could not be broken. It is the expression of this love between David and Jonathan that saved their lives from death at the hand of Saul.

Life Application

David and Jonathan sought *chesed* (חֶסֶד) from each other—a love that in actuality, no human could truly give. David and Jonathan depended on the LORD to be able to express this love towards each other. In our own flesh, we cannot love unfailingly, unfalteringly, unconditionally and faithfully at all times. We fail in loving those who are near and far. We need the LORD's empowering to love with *chesed* (חֶסֶד), as David and Jonathan demonstrated in this pericope. This *chesed* kind of love comes from God alone. *Chesed* (חֶסֶד) is the type of love with which God loves us—it is absolute, limitless and endless. It is a love that is all-forgiving, all-merciful and demands laying down one's life for another. Jesus expressed the fullness of *chesed* (חֶסֶד) towards us. He was all-forgiving, all-merciful and laid down his life for us. The LORD seeks out each one of us to receive *chesed* (חֶסֶד) from him. He alone gives us the ability to express *chesed* (חֶסֶד) towards others, to be all-forgiving, all-merciful and to lay down our lives for our brethren. Let us seek *chesed* (חֶסֶד) from Him. He will grant it to us freely.

NT Scriptures

1 John 4:9

Prayer

O LORD, teach us to have mercy and a covenantal love for one another. Teach us to be the kind of friends who love with chesed, for your word says, "A friend loves at all times" (Pro 17:17). "There is a friend who sticks closer than a brother" (Pro 18:24). "Greater love has no one than this, that he lay down his life for his friends" (John 15:13). Grant us the supernatural ability to love as you love us.

Personal Notes and Prayers

2 Samuel 6:20-21

וַיָּ֥שָׁב דָּוִ֖ד לְבָרֵ֣ךְ אֶת־בֵּית֑וֹ וַתֵּצֵ֞א מִיכַ֣ל בַּת־שָׁא֗וּל לִקְרַ֣את דָּוִ֔ד
וַתֹּ֗אמֶר מַה־נִּכְבַּ֨ד הַיּ֜וֹם מֶ֣לֶךְ יִשְׂרָאֵ֗ל אֲשֶׁ֨ר נִגְלָ֤ה הַיּוֹם֙ לְעֵינֵ֣י
אַמְה֣וֹת עֲבָדָ֔יו כְּהִגָּל֥וֹת נִגְל֖וֹת אַחַ֥ד הָרֵקִֽים: וַיֹּ֣אמֶר דָּוִד֮ אֶל־מִיכַל֒
לִפְנֵ֣י יְהוָ֡ה אֲשֶׁ֣ר

בָּֽחַר־בִּ֣י מֵאָבִ֗יךְ וּמִכָּל־בֵּיתוֹ֙ לְצַוֺּ֨ת אֹתִ֥י נָגִ֛יד עַל־עַ֥ם יְהוָ֖ה עַל־
יִשְׂרָאֵ֑ל וְשִׂחַקְתִּ֖י לִפְנֵ֥י יְהוָֽה׃

Then David returned to bless his house. Michal, Saul's daughter, went out to David saying, "How the king of Israel who uncovered himself today has dishonored himself before his female servants, uncovering himself like worthless fellows." David said to Michal, "Before the LORD who chose me instead of your father and all his household, to make me ruler over the people of the LORD, over Israel, so I will celebrate before the LORD."

Biblical Context

SHORTLY AFTER BEING ANOINTED king of Israel, David decided to bring the Ark of the LORD from Kiriath-Jearim to Jerusalem. To commemorate the occasion, David led a lively procession, singing, dancing and making music to the LORD. He expressed his delight publicly and joined the celebration from the house of Abinadab to the threshing floor of Nacon. At this location, Uzzah mistakenly placed his hand on the Ark and died, for no one was worthy to touch the Ark of the LORD. Disturbed by this seemingly unfair loss of life, David became angry and afraid, and decided to keep the Ark outside the City of David (Jerusalem). For three months, the Ark remained on the property of Obed-Edom whose house was richly blessed by the presence of the Ark. King David was told of this marvel and went to the house of Obed-Edom to retrieve the Ark and bring it to Jerusalem. When the procession reached the City of David, Michal witnessed David's public display of euphoric happiness. She became disgusted at the king's behavior and despised him in her heart. David dismissed Michal's criticism and continued to celebrate uninhibited before the LORD.

Life Application

We should learn from David and seek to be people who are willing to praise God with everything that is in us, regardless of what others think. There is no room for pride in worship and praise. What others think of open displays of praise should never deter us from expressing our affection for God. God is worthy of *all* praises. Scripture commands us to love the LORD with *all* our heart, *all* our mind and *all* our soul, and consequently, it is only natural for our *entire* body to want to express this love openly and without inhibition. Throughout Scripture, physical expressions of worship include clapping hands (Ps 47:1), dancing (2 Sam 6:14; Ps 149:3), playing musical instruments (Ps 150:3–5; 1 Chr 15:16), bowing down (Isa 45:14; Ps 95:6), singing (Judg 5:3; Ps 92:1), declaring the praises of God (Ps 51:15), bowing the head (1 Chr 29:20), and much more.

NT Scriptures

Luke 10:25–27; 1 Corinthians 4:10; Colossians 3:16

Prayer

O LORD, free us from our inhibitions and teach us how to praise you with every fiber of our being. We want to honor you and glorify you in word and deed. Use our hands, our mouth, our feet, our knees, our arms, our heart and our soul for your glory. Hinnenu! Here we are! Have your way in us and through us, from now and for the rest of our lives.

Personal Notes and Prayers

2 Samuel 9:13

וּמְפִיבֹשֶׁת יֹשֵׁב בִּירוּשָׁלַ͏ִם כִּי עַל־שֻׁלְחַן הַמֶּלֶךְ תָּמִיד הוּא אֹכֵל
וְהוּא פִּסֵּחַ שְׁתֵּי רַגְלָיו:

Now Mephibosheth dwelt in Jerusalem, for he ate at the table of the king continually; he was lame in both feet.

Biblical Context

DAVID WAS ANOINTED BY Samuel to be the next king of Israel. Saul was driven mad with jealousy against David, but amazingly Saul's son Jonathan responded very differently. He befriended David even though David was usurping his right to follow Saul on the throne. Jonathan was a mighty warrior and fit to be king, but he saw the hand of God upon David and loved him greatly. During a desperate time in David's life, while at Horesh in the Desert of Ziph, Jonathan finds David and encourages him (1 Sam 23:15-17). In what appears to be their last time together before Jonathan dies, they make a covenant (1 Sam 23:18). The text does not elaborate on the stipulations of the covenant, but when coupled with an earlier oath between Jonathan and David (see 1 Sam 20:42), it may have been a promise by David to care for Jonathan's descendants when David became king. This promise is later fulfilled in the story of Mephibosheth. We find only a brief introductory mention of Mephibosheth in 2 Sam 4:4. He was the son of Jonathan and had been injured in an accident at the age of five and was crippled in both feet. He comes back into the picture in 2 Samuel 9 when David, now the king, inquires whether there is anyone in Jonathan's family to whom he can show kindness for Jonathan's sake (and presumably to honor the oath he had made). Mephibosheth, now older, is brought before David and ends up being restored to his inheritance and invited with his family to eat at the king's table forevermore.

Life Application

David extended grace to Mephibosheth. Mephibosheth felt unworthy and his self-esteem was very low (*"What is your servant, that you should notice a dead dog like me?"* 2 Sam 9:8), but he was shown kindness on account of the relationship that David had with his father Jonathan. David treated him like a son and gave him access to an abundance of resources. Jesus Christ extends grace to us. We feel unworthy and our self-esteem is wanting, but we are shown kindness on account of the relationship of Jesus Christ to the Father, and because of his unsurpassable sacrifice for us. We are adopted as sons and daughters and given access to "the incomparable riches of his grace." We too are like one of the king's children!

NT Scriptures

Romans 8:32; Ephesians 1:5–6; 2:6–7

Prayer

O LORD, how great is your gift of grace to us. We are helpless without you. We need your grace and love to overcome our unworthiness. You provide for us in ways that far exceed anything David could have ever done for Mephiboshet. We rely on you for sustenance and life. Thank you LORD.

Personal Notes and Prayers

2 Samuel 12:23

וְעַתָּ֣ה ׀ מֵ֗ת לָ֤מָּה זֶּה֙ אֲנִ֣י צָ֔ם הַאוּכַ֥ל לַהֲשִׁיב֖וֹ ע֑וֹד אֲנִי֙ הֹלֵ֣ךְ אֵלָ֔יו
וְה֖וּא לֹֽא־יָשׁ֥וּב אֵלָֽי׃

*But now he is dead. Why should I fast for this? Am I able
to bring him back again? I will go to him,
but he will not return to me.*

Biblical Context

KING DAVID SHOCKED HIS inner circle. Seven days earlier, the child born to him from Bathsheba became very sick. So, David fasted and laid on the ground all day and all night, weeping and seeking God on behalf of the child. Not even his closest advisors could comfort him and make him eat his food. Seven days later, he learned from his servants that his child had just died. They expected David to do something terrible at the news of the child's death but David did not react as they expected. To everyone's surprise, he arose, bathed, anointed himself, changed his clothe, went to the Tabernacle to worship, and returned to the palace to eat a good meal. David's servants were dumbfounded by his strange behavior. They questioned him, unable to comprehend his nonchalance at the news of the child's tragic end.

Life Application

But now he is dead. There may be nothing more tragic than the death of your own child. The progression of burying one's parents and the potential to bury one's spouse are understandable in the natural order of things, but to bury one's child!! Something about that does not sit right with the human mind. It is a painful process for most people and the vacancy created by their child's death leaves a deep ache that lasts a lifetime. One year ago today, I learned the depth of David's faith in the LORD firsthand when my wife miscarried. David quickly turned into a role model for me. He took the appropriate actions, fasting, weeping, and laying on the ground, when there was still a chance that his child would survive. When his child died, David continued to take the appropriate actions. The situation was out of his hands, yet he did not blame the LORD. He did not lament day after day and month after month about "why did this happen to me?" He looked to the day he would see his child again. After our own tragedy, I got up on my feet as soon as I could, kept my family going, and got back to business as soon as possible, and did not lay blame. Today, our grief is still there, but there is solace in knowing that we will see our child again.

NT Scriptures

Philippians 4:4–7

Prayer

O LORD, we thank you for life on this earth and for life eternal in your presence. We thank you for keeping our deceased loved ones in perfect harmony with you in a kingdom that is not of this world. We look for the day when we will meet you face-to-face and reunite with those who have gone before us. In the meantime, grant us your peace.

Personal Notes and Prayers

2 Samuel 22:47

חַי־יְהוָה וּבָרוּךְ צוּרִי וְיָרֻם אֱלֹהֵי צוּר יִשְׁעִי׃

YHWH lives! Blessed be my Rock! Let God be exalted,
The Rock of my salvation!

Biblical Context

SECOND SAMUEL IS CENTERED around the reign of David and traces the significant events in his life as King. This includes his rise to the throne and his well-known failures of the rape of Bathsheba and the murder of Uriah. It also narrates the adverse effect these sins had on his family and the impact on the nation of Israel as a whole. At the end of his life, David composes a song after God rescued him from Saul and from the hand of his enemies. In this song, David praises YHWH for being his rock, fortress, deliverer, refuge, shield, horn of salvation, stronghold, and savior. David recounts the awesome deeds of YHWH and notes his own faithfulness to God. Verse 47 is a short extract from this "song of thanksgiving" and is typical of the tone of the larger song—an emotional recognition of the role God played in his life. The imagery found throughout this poem is very interesting. For example, David compares YHWH to a Rock to highlight God's steadfastness, strength, firmness, immutability, and dependability.

Life Application

There are many times in the life of a believer when what is most desired is an anchor—something to hold onto in a difficult situation. As believers, we need to live with the reality that a strong foundation supports us at all times, and that the solid and stable ground on which we stand is God himself. At the end of his life, David recognized God as his true foundation, as the Rock upon which he stood firm and secure. It serves us well to realize the same thing, many centuries after this song was first written, that God is our Rock and our firm Foundation.

NT Scriptures

Luke 6:47–48　1 Corinthians 10:1–4

Prayer

O LORD my God, "My hope is built on nothing less than Jesus's blood and righteousness; I dare not trust the sweetest frame, but wholly lean on Jesus's name. On Christ, the solid Rock, I stand; all other ground is sinking sand. All other ground is sinking sand." (Edward Mote, c. 1834)

Personal Notes and Prayers

2 Samuel 23:16

וַיִּבְקְעוּ שְׁלֹשֶׁת הַגִּבֹּרִים בְּמַחֲנֵה פְלִשְׁתִּים וַיִּשְׁאֲבוּ־מַיִם מִבֹּאר בֵּית־לֶחֶם אֲשֶׁר בַּשַּׁעַר

וַיִּשְׂאוּ וַיָּבִאוּ אֶל־דָּוִד וְלֹא אָבָה לִשְׁתּוֹתָם וַיַּסֵּךְ אֹתָם לַיהוָה:

Three of the warriors broke through in the camp of the Philistines and drew water from the cistern of Bethlehem, which was in the gate, and they brought it to David. But he was not willing to drink it. He poured it before the LORD.

Biblical Context

DAVID'S MIGHTY MEN WERE an elite group of warriors who were known for their ability to stand and fight when the rest of the Israelite army retreated. Three of these warriors, who could each single-handedly strike down a multitude of men in one encounter, were willing to risk their lives in order to serve David a drink of water. One day when David was stationed approximately twelve miles away from a Philistine outpost, he longed not only for water, but for the water from the well of his hometown, just inside the Bethlehem gate, which was where the Philistines were stationed. Knowing David's longing, these three warriors set out to fulfill it by going to Bethlehem, breaking through the Philistine camp, drawing water from the well inside the city, and carrying it back to David. However, even though they successfully brought the water back for David, he was not even willing to drink it. The very water he so badly craved was in his hands, but instead of drinking it, he poured it out before the LORD and said, "Far be it to me, O LORD, from drinking this! Is it not the blood of men who were going with their lives?"

Life Application

When David *poured* out the water, the root of the verb comes from *libation* or *drink offering*. A drink offering was a sacrifice poured out on the ground before a god as an expression of thanksgiving and dedication, usually consisting of wine and accompanying certain sacrifices and meal offerings. The water was too precious and valuable for David to drink; he considered it to be the blood of the three men and worthy only to be poured as a sacrifice before the LORD. What did the three warriors think when David poured out the water? Did they think it a waste after what they had just risked or were they touched that their lives meant that much to him? Sometimes the risks we take to touch the LORD's heart feel like a wasted bottle of costly wine poured all over the ground. However, I wonder now if some of our offerings are too precious and costly to consume. We should release as sacrifices to God everything that is precious and dear to us.

NT Scriptures

Philippians 2:17–18; 2 Timothy 4:6–7

Prayer

O LORD, our treasures come from you. We surrender them back to you. All that we are and all that we have come from you. We surrender ourselves and our possessions back to you. Please do with us and with our treasures what pleases you and glorifies your name. We pour ourselves out at your feet. Take us and make us who you want us to be, for your glory.

Personal Notes and Prayers

2 Samuel 24:10

וַיַּ֤ךְ לֵב־דָּוִד֙ אֹת֔וֹ אַחֲרֵי־כֵ֖ן סָפַ֣ר אֶת־הָעָ֑ם וַיֹּ֨אמֶר דָּוִ֜ד אֶל־יְהוָ֗ה חָטָ֤אתִי מְאֹד֙ אֲשֶׁ֣ר עָשִׂ֔יתִי

וְעַתָּ֣ה יְהוָ֗ה הַֽעֲבֶר־נָא֙ אֶת־עֲוֺ֣ן עַבְדְּךָ֔ כִּ֥י נִסְכַּ֖לְתִּי מְאֹֽד׃

David's heart troubled him after he counted the people, so David said to YHWH, "I have sinned greatly in what I have done. So now, YHWH, please remove the guilt of your servant, for I have acted very foolishly!"

Biblical Context

KNOWING FULL WELL THAT a census was unnecessary and contrary to God's will, David commanded his general Joab to go throughout the land from Dan to Beersheba and number the people. Joab cautioned him against this plan, but David refused to listen to his general's counsel and ordered the census taken nonetheless. The entire process took nine months and twenty days. After receiving the results—800,000 fighting men in Israel and 500,000 fighting men in Judah—David's heart was struck with guilt. David agonized and repented before God, acknowledging that he had not only sinned by ordering a census, but he had in fact "sinned greatly" and acted "very foolishly" (24:10). The next morning, the prophet Gad approached David with God's message and gave David a choice of penance: (1) three years of famine; (2) three months of warfare; or (3) three days of pestilence in the land. Distressed at the impending judgment, David surrendered to God and told the prophet, "Let us fall into the hand of the LORD, for his mercy is great; but let me knot fall into the hand of man" (24:14). In other words, David left the choice of penance to God since his own decisions were what brought trouble to Israel. God chose the three days of pestilence, and consequently, tens of thousands of David's men perished.

Life Application

When I think of doing something, or am in the process of doing something, and my heart senses trouble, I normally begin to experience anguish. If I continue to follow my own plans, guilt and sorrow increase. And unfortunately, this is precisely what I will sometimes do. It is strange to me why that would be the case. Clearly something within me knows the error of my ways, and yet something else pushes me forward with momentum. Perhaps this is what Paul refers to in Romans 7:15: "For what I am doing, I do not understand; for I am not practicing what I would like to do, but I am doing the very thing I hate." I do not believe that I will ever be completely free of this tendency in this earthly life, but like Paul, if I learn to recognize this inclination, perhaps repentance will come earlier and the consequences of my actions will be less painful.

NT Scriptures

Romans 7:15; 2 Corinthians 7:9–10; 2 Peter 3:9

Prayer

O LORD, I am weak and sinful. I thank you for convicting me of my sin and for letting me know that I have departed from your ways. I repent for failing to follow your instructions. I ask for mercy and for an increased awareness of your presence in my life. I ask for a clear mind and a sensitive heart to hear your voice and obey. Thank you for reordering my steps and leading me in the paths of righteousness.

Personal Notes and Prayers

1 Kings 15:4–5

כִּי לְמַעַן דָּוִד נָתַן יְהוָה אֱלֹהָיו לוֹ נִיר בִּירוּשָׁלָם לְהָקִים אֶת־בְּנוֹ אַחֲרָיו וּלְהַעֲמִיד אֶת־יְרוּשָׁלָם׃

אֲשֶׁר עָשָׂה דָוִד אֶת־הַיָּשָׁר בְּעֵינֵי יְהוָה וְלֹא־סָר מִכֹּל אֲשֶׁר־צִוָּהוּ כֹּל יְמֵי חַיָּיו רַק בִּדְבַר אוּרִיָּה הַחִתִּי׃

For the sake of David the LORD his God gave to him a lamp in Jerusalem, elevating his son after him and establishing Jerusalem. Because David did that which was right in the eyes of the LORD and did not turn from all that he had commanded all the days of his life except in the matter of Uriah the Hittite.

Biblical Context

DECADES AFTER DAVID'S REIGN, Abijam, his great-grandson, followed in the footsteps of his father Jeroboam and failed to follow the LORD. Yet, God preserved the house of David in Jerusalem *because David was faithful, except for the matter of Uriah*. Uriah had been one of David's mighty men, who devoted his life to support David and would willingly have died for him. But while Uriah was fighting with David's army away from Jerusalem, David committed adultery with Uriah's wife, called Uriah back from the field to get him drunk and have him believe that the child that had been conceived by David's tryst was Uriah's. When that did not work, he sent Uriah back to the battle, carrying his own death warrant.

Life Application

God knew all of David's weaknesses and strengths, successes and failures, when he created him in his mother's womb. God's plan for David, for Israel, for the world was created with intimate knowledge of the flaws that existed in his chosen vessels and he knew what would be required to help them fulfill his plans. I have heard Christians say, "Oh, God could not use me. You do not know my past." Some pastors have had spectacular public failures. Even after they have confessed and repented, we still hesitate to return them to leadership, as though there can be no restoration. Sins committed before salvation seem more forgivable than those after conversion. Consequently, the watching congregation members see their own sins as disqualifying them from service. But David, a man after God's own heart, who walk in the ways of the LORD all the days of his life, had his most spectacular failure after he had walked with God for many years. In that moment of basking in God's blessing, he committed adultery, deceived and betrayed a devoted friend, and had him murdered, using him as a messenger for his own demise, yet God blessed David. His gifts and calling are irrevocable and his grace is sufficient. God called you in full knowledge of your flaws and failures and he designed his plan with that in mind. Forgiven sins often lead to greater faith, like David, or Paul or Mary or Peter.

NT Scriptures

2 Corinthians 12:9; 1 John 1:5—2:2

Prayer

O LORD, how great are your mercies, your forgiveness and your healing power in our lives. Help us extend the same mercy, forgiveness and healing to all who transgress your laws. Help us see ourselves as you see us—as forgiven and loved with your everlasting love.

Personal Notes and Prayers

1 Kings 18:21

וַיִּגַּשׁ אֵלִיָּהוּ אֶל־כָּל־הָעָם וַיֹּאמֶר עַד־מָתַי אַתֶּם פֹּסְחִים עַל־שְׁתֵּי הַסְּעִפִּים אִם־יְהוָה הָאֱלֹהִים לְכוּ אַחֲרָיו וְאִם־הַבַּעַל לְכוּ אַחֲרָיו וְלֹא־עָנוּ הָעָם אֹתוֹ דָּבָר׃

Elijah approached all the people and said, "How long are you going to about limping between two opinions? If YHWH is God go after Him, but if Baal [is God] go after him," but the people did not answer him.

Biblical Context

LIKE OTHER KINGS OF Israel, Ahab the son of Omri turned away from the LORD and worshiped Baal. During a severe famine that was ravaging the land, God instructed Elijah to go to Ahab and tell him that he and his family were to blame for the punishing drought in Israel. When Ahab and Elijah met, Ahab called Elijah the "trouble maker of Israel" (עֹכֵר יִשְׂרָאֵל) and accused him of being the cause for the shortage of food. However, Elijah immediately pronounced a divinely inspired indictment on Ahab, and declared that he and his family were the real cause of the problem. Because they had abandoned the LORD's commands, followed the Baals, and led the inhabitants of Israel in idolatrous practices, God had sent a famine (18:18). Both the people and their animals suffered from a severe shortage of food and water. The inhabitants of the Northern Kingdom were in dire straights, and this was due to their abandonment of the God of Israel and their worship of foreign gods. The people were limping between YHWH and Baal, unable to decide who they would serve wholeheartedly. Elijah called the Israelites and the prophets of Baal to Mount Carmel to confront them with their sin and said, "How long will you waver/limp between two opinions" (18:21). Elijah gave them a choice: serve YHWH or serve Baal. "But the people did not answer him, not even a word" (18:21).

Life Application

When you find yourself in a quandary between two paths, it is quite normal to try and span the divide so as to allow time to decide which path might be the right choice. Maybe more information is needed or maybe the choices are not quite clear. Often there is a penalty for delaying or avoiding an important decision. One is in effect crippled and limping until the choice is made and acted upon. If the quandary is whether to serve God or earthly desires, the choice should be easy. "Serve God!" Jesus made it clear to his followers when he said, "No one can serve two masters, for either he will hate the one and love the other, or he will be devoted to the one and despise the other. You cannot serve God and money" (Matt 6:24; Luke 16:13). As Joshua told the Israelites during his farewell address, "Choose this day whom you will serve, whether the gods your fathers served in the region beyond the River, or the gods of the Amorites in whose land you dwell. But as for me and my house, we will serve the LORD" (Josh 24:15).

NT Scriptures

Matthew 4:10/Luke 4:8; Matthew 22:37; Ephesians 3:20–21

Prayer

O LORD, there is none like you. The gods of the earth are worthless. They are deaf, blind and mute. Forgive us O LORD for trusting in them. You the only living God, the Almighty God to whom all praise is due. You are trustworthy, faithful, loving, kind, merciful, compassionate and gracious. We put our trust in You alone.

Personal Notes and Prayers

1 Kings 18:21

וַיִּגַּשׁ אֵלִיָּהוּ אֶל־כָּל־הָעָם וַיֹּאמֶר עַד־מָתַי אַתֶּם פֹּסְחִים עַל־שְׁתֵּי הַסְּעִפִּים אִם־יְהוָה הָאֱלֹהִים לְכוּ אַחֲרָיו וְאִם־הַבַּעַל לְכוּ אַחֲרָיו וְלֹא־עָנוּ הָעָם אֹתוֹ דָּבָר׃

So Elijah drew near to all the people and said, "Up to now you have been limping on two opinions. If the LORD is God, walk after Him and if Baal is God, walk after him!" But the people did not answer him.

Biblical Context

BAAL WORSHIP HAD OVERRUN the land of Israel because of the wicked queen Jezebel and her patsy King Ahab. Ironically, the people looked to Baal for the rain so the LORD had caused a drought throughout the land, but now the stage was being set for the ultimate showdown between Baal and the LORD on mount Carmel. In one corner were four-hundred and fifty prophets of Baal and in the other corner was Elijah, the prophet of the LORD. As the people gathered to observe this contest Elijah called them out for trying to follow both the LORD and Baal. With a clever play on words he tells them two quit *limping* (פָּסַח) on two gods who do not mix together and *walk* (הָלַךְ) after the true God. As the story continues the prophets of Baal did everything they could to incite a response from Baal, they even *went limping* (פָּסַח) around the altar Elijah built but, to no avail because Baal was a fake. The LORD showed himself to be the true and living God that day.

Life Application

The Israelites were called to be separate from the nations that surrounded them and that included not bowing the knee to Baal. When they incorporated Baal into their monotheistic religious world it did not help them, instead, it hindered their relationship with the LORD God. It even provoked the LORD to send a drought on their land, the exact opposite of what they hoped Baal would do for them. The Israelites typify the Christians struggle to have "the best of both worlds." There are many things that the world embraces and follows after that are appealing to human nature but do not mix with faith in the One true God. When a believer has one foot in the world and one foot following God, the results are the same *limping around* that the Israelites experienced. To truly *walk* with the LORD means complete devotion to Him alone.

NT Scriptures

Matthew 6:33; Galatians 3:1–14; I Thessalonians 1:9b-10; I John 1:5–7

Prayer

O LORD, forgive us for worshipping worthless, useless and vain idols. How foolish we are to forsake you for what is dead and meaningless. "[We] are all senseless and foolish; [we] are taught by worthless wooden idols. Everyone is senseless and without knowledge; every goldsmith is shamed by his idols. His images are fraudulent; they have no breath in them (Jer 10:8, 10). All who make idols are nothing, and the things they treasure are worthless. Those who would speak up for them are blind; they are ignorant, to their own shame. (Isa 42:9) O LORD, forgive us and restore us to you.

Personal Notes and Prayers

1 Kings 18:27

וַיְהִי בַצָּהֳרַיִם וַיְהַתֵּל בָּהֶם אֵלִיָּהוּ וַיֹּאמֶר קִרְאוּ בְקוֹל־גָּדוֹל כִּי־אֱלֹהִים הוּא

כִּי שִׂיחַ וְכִי־שִׂיג לוֹ וְכִי־דֶרֶךְ לוֹ אוּלַי יָשֵׁן הוּא וְיִקָץ:

Around noon, Elijah mocked them saying, "Call out with a loud voice! For is he not a god? Maybe he is busy thinking or maybe he has gone away on a journey? Or maybe he is asleep and needs to be awakened?."

Biblical Context

THE 450 PROPHETS OF Baal and 400 prophets of Asherah are assembled to prove to the people that their gods are legitimate. Elijah challenges them to call down fire from heaven to consume their offering. As the day begins to wear on without results, Elijah taunts the false prophets and mocks their god! Elijah's address to the prophets of Ba'al is definitely not "polite."

Life Application

I remember discovering this Scripture on my way to a cross-country race in high school. The Living Bible embellishes the scene by adding, "or maybe he is sitting on the toilet?" which certainly grabbed my attention! I did not know a great deal about the Bible in those days, but to see such irreverence and attitude in this holy book certainly made an impression on me. The Bible does not sanitize stories. Unseemly events and attitudes are included in the narrative even when they do not reflect favorably upon God's people. One can sense the frustration in Elijah's tone as he sets about disproving the false prophets and their gods. Yet the people followed them and believed in them! It took a miraculous display of the true power and authority of God over nature before the false prophets were ridiculed and the worship of false gods was (temporarily) halted. It is comforting for me to hear Elijah's taunting. God's people can sometimes be incredibly annoying! As the account in 1 Kings 18 illustrates, this is nothing new. Since we serve the one true God, therefore we can have the confidence of Elijah, laughing in the face of false gods that advertise much but do not deliver. And because of this confidence, we owe it to one another to point out the false promises and counterfeits which we sometimes find ourselves adopting. Perhaps with as much wit as Elijah.

NT Scriptures

1 Corinthians 8:4; Acts 7:41–43

Prayer

O LORD, forgive us for the foolishness of following after gods who have mouths but cannot speak, who have ears but cannot hear, and who have eyes but cannot see. How foolish of us to replace you—the Living God—with dead idols. Revive us O God and turn us to you!

Personal Notes and Prayers

1 Kings 21:29

הֲרָאִ֗יתָ כִּֽי־נִכְנַ֣ע אַחְאָב֮ מִלְּפָנָי֒ יַ֜עַן כִּֽי־נִכְנַ֣ע מִפָּנַ֗י לֹֽא־אָבִ֤י הָֽרָעָה֙ בְּיָמָ֔יו בִּימֵ֣י בְנ֔וֹ אָבִ֥יא הָרָעָ֖ה עַל־בֵּיתֽוֹ:

Did you see that Ahab humbled himself before me? So because he humbled himself before me, I will not bring the calamity in his days. In the days of his son, I will bring the calamity on his house.

Biblical Context

OUR FIRST INTRODUCTION TO Ahab, king of Israel, reads thus: "And Ahab the son of Omri did evil in the sight of the LORD, more than all who were before him" (1 Kgs. 16:30). Ahab built a temple for Baal and Asherah, provoking the LORD to great anger. Even after Baal's defeat at Mt. Carmel, the LORD's sending rain on the land, and Ahab's God-given victory over Syria, he did not repent. Instead he complained to Jezebel, and acted more depraved as he took his neighbor's vineyard—that of Naboth the Jezreelite whose murder was crafted by Jezebel. Still, upon hearing Elijah's word that his house would be cut off, Ahab tore his clothes. It is is difficult to see that any repentance on Ahab's part could have been authentic. After his one act of humility, Ahab returned to his old ways, holding in contempt the one honest prophet of the LORD, Micaiah. Ahab was proof of the vast difference between one act of dejected humility and the kind of humility that comes from a submissive heart, such as that of Josiah. It seems somewhat confusing then, that the LORD would, for a time, relent of the disaster that he had promised. After all, Ahab had rejected the LORD's clear displays of power on his behalf. Yet, this God of seemingly endless chances keeps Ahab from the fruit of his actions, postponing the destruction of his house until the reign of his son.

Life Application

Christians seem to have a love/hate relationship with last minute conversions. Words like these often characterize our attitudes: "He lived his whole life in sin, now he is afraid to die and pretends to repent?" "She only acts like a believer when she is in a crisis." If left to us, the distribution of God's mercy would rely on life-long commitment or proof-positive repentance, not last-minute confession. Unfortunately, if we become stuck in this mindset, we will be less likely to cry out when we find ourselves in rebellion. Why should God listen to so disobedient a soul? The answer is clear—his mercy is disproportionate to our rebellion. It is according to his unfailing love (Ps 51:1). It is the character of the LORD to forego deserved destruction and grant undeserved mercy, and he will do it as he pleases (Exod 33:19). May the consciousness of our deserved punishment never stand between us and our request for compassion.

NT Scriptures

Luke 23:39–43; Romans 9:15–29

Prayer

O LORD, you forgive when we do not deserve it. You love us despite our sins. You are merciful beyond measure and faithful to all generations.

Personal Notes and Prayers

2 Kings 5:2b

וַיִּשְׁבּוּ מֵאֶרֶץ יִשְׂרָאֵל נַעֲרָה קְטַנָּה וַתְּהִי לִפְנֵי אֵשֶׁת נַעֲמָן:

They captured from the land of Israel a young woman who became servant for Naaman's wife.

Biblical Context

MOST BIBLICAL CHARACTERS WHO did great things for God are unnamed. Abraham, Isaac, Jacob, Moses, Joshua, Deborah, David, Solomon, Peter, Paul, Priscilla, Phoebe, and many more accomplished great things for God, but what about the messenger, the young man, the maidservant, the official, and the commander of the army? Where they not important also? In 2 Kings 5, we are told of *a young Israelite girl* (נַעֲרָה קְטַנָּה) who revealed to Naaman's wife that her husband could be healed of his leprosy through the prophet in Samaria. Intrigued by this prospect, Naaman visits the prophet, (reluctantly) obeys his instructions, receives healing and ultimately declares "I know there is no God in the whole world except in Israel" (2 Kgs 5:15). Who was this *young Israelite girl* (נַעֲרָה קְטַנָּה) whose simple message resulted in the conversion of a Syrian Gentile? In Esther 6, we learn that king Ahasuerus suffers from insomnia and orders that the book of the chronicles be read to him. In the chronicles, some of the king's attendants find and read the record of Mordecai's disclosure of the plot to assassinate the king. The king asks his personal attendant if Mordecai has been honored for this act of bravery. The attendant answers "nothing has been done" (Est 6:3). As a result, the course of events changes, Haman is hanged, Mordecai is promoted and the Jews of Persia are delivered from impending doom. Who were these men who read the chronicles and who was this personal attendant whose answer changed the course of history? We could add to this list the officials of Moses, able, God-fearing, trustworthy and bribe-hating men who provided counsel for the Israelites in the wilderness (Exod 18:17–26), the priests who could not continue to minister in Solomon's Temple because the glory of the LORD had filled the Temple (1 Kgs 8:10–11), and the choir members who sang glorious praises to God when the ark of the covenant was brought from the house of Obed-Edom to the City of David (1 Chr 15:22–28).

Life Application

Most of us feel like *unnamed minor characters* in the grand narrative of life. In reality, we are *that man* and *that woman* whose name is known only to God. What really matters in life is serving where we are planted, being faithful to God, loving those whom God brings into our lives and teaching the next generation to do the same. We never know how significant our small gestures are in the sight of God. What if our obedience in small things results in changing the course of history?

NT Scriptures

John 10:14, 27

Prayer

O LORD, you know our hearts, minds and our ways like no one else does, and still, you love us. You notice us when no one else does. You know our names and value us above all creation. Thank you. Thank you. Thank you.

Personal Notes and Prayers

2 Kings 5:11

וַיִּקְצֹף נַעֲמָן וַיֵּלַךְ וַיֹּאמֶר הִנֵּה אָמַרְתִּי אֵלַי יֵצֵא יָצוֹא וְעָמַד וְקָרָא
בְּשֵׁם־יְהוָה אֱלֹהָיו

וְהֵנִיף יָדוֹ אֶל־הַמָּקוֹם וְאָסַף הַמְּצֹרָע׃

Naaman went away angry and said, "Look, I said to myself that surely he would come out, stand and call on the name of YHWH his God, wave his hand over the area and remove the leprosy.

Biblical Context

NAAMAN WAS FURIOUS WHEN Elisha sent a messenger to him to tell him to dip seven times in the Jordan River in order to be healed of his leprosy. Naaman was the commander of the Syrian army (one of Israel's ongoing enemies throughout the 9th and 8th centuries B.C.) and was highly regarded by the Syrian king. He had traveled to Samaria in search of Elisha after learning about the prophet through a captive Israelite girl in his household. Having arrived in Samaria with an entourage and extravagant gifts in tow, the end of Naaman's journey entailed seven dips in the muddy Jordan river. Naaman vented, saying, "Could I not have been healed in the cleaner rivers back home in Syria?" Had he come this far only to jump in a dirty river? As Namaan turned to leave, his servants confronted him saying: "If the prophet had told you to do some great thing, would you not have done it? How much more then, should you dip and be healed?" Naaman had a role to play in his healing. He was to humble himself and simply obey the instructions of the man of God. Naaman's cleansing came from an unlikely source—a dirty river. As a result of his humble obedience, he received healing and confessed that the God of Israel was the one true God.

Life Application

Naaman was a powerful man who had traveled a long way to seek healing only to find that Elisha did not even come out to meet him, but gave him an unappealing command through a lowly messenger. Naaman had to take orders from someone below his rank. If Elisha had come out, waved his hand over him and called on the name of the LORD, would Naaman have worshiped Elisha instead of God? God was concerned with Namaan's spiritual health much more than with his physical condition. Naaman had to make a sacrifice that required humility and obedience. Stepping into a muddy river not once but seven times was a risk for such a prominent man. I can only imagine what he was thinking as he was getting in the fourth, fifth, sixth and seventh time. What is God wanting to do in you and what is he requiring of you? It may seem as ludicrous and as confusing as washing repeatedly in a dirty river until he accomplishes his deeper healing in your life. But God is faithful and will never asks us to obey his instructions without an eternal purpose. Let us obey, not reluctantly but fervently and enthusiastically.

NT Scriptures

Luke 4:27; 7:2–10; 17:11–19

Prayer

O LORD, we need your healing power in our lives. Teach us to humble ourselves and come to you with open hearts. Use the muddy rivers of life to heal us from our imperfections. Pour your living water on us to wash us from our sins. We thank you for healing us.

Personal Notes and Prayers

2 Kings 6:16–17

וַיֹּאמֶר אַל־תִּירָא כִּי רַבִּים אֲשֶׁר אִתָּנוּ מֵאֲשֶׁר אוֹתָם: וַיִּתְפַּלֵּל
אֱלִישָׁע וַיֹּאמַר יְהוָה פְּקַח־נָא אֶת־עֵינָיו
וְיִרְאֶה וַיִּפְקַח יְהוָה אֶת־עֵינֵי הַנַּעַר וַיַּרְא וְהִנֵּה הָהָר מָלֵא סוּסִים
וְרֶכֶב אֵשׁ סְבִיבֹת אֱלִישָׁע:

He (Elisha) said: "Do not be afraid because more are with us than are with them." Then Elisha prayed and said: "LORD, please open his eyes so that he may see." So the LORD opened the eyes of the boy and he saw! Unexpectedly, the mountain was filled with horses and chariots of fire all around Elisha.

Biblical Context

THERE IS DEEP DARKNESS on the face of the earth. Political, social and economic conditions around the world are unpromising. Conflicts abound, political tensions are rising in many countries, human rights are being violated, poverty is increasing, human suffering is intensifying and spiritual darkness is being felt deeply. Such is the picture the media is painting for its hearers and in many ways, such are the realities of our world. According to some, there seems to be very little hope for the future. "Where is God?" some ask. "Is He aware of our plight?" "Is He passively waiting for the destruction of mankind?" "Will He intervene in due time?" Over 2,500 years ago, a prophet named Elisha said to his servant: *"Do not fear, for those who are with us are more than those who are with them!"* (2 Kgs 6:16). But when the servant peeked out the window, all he saw was a large Syrian army with its multitude of horses and iron chariots. Turning to the prophet, he started counting: "One, two!" Peering a second time out the window, he thought to himself: "The pressure must be too great for my master. He is now unable to count!" Calmly, Elisha prayed: "LORD, open his eyes that he may see." Suddenly, the servant saw countless horses and chariots of fire appearing on the horizon and at that very moment, he knew that once he was blind and now he could see. God was there all along!

Biblical Context

If the story were to end there, it would be victorious but greater still are the events that follow! The prophet Elisha prays for God to bring blindness on his enemies. Now unable to proceed forward on their own, the Syrian military men who had originally intended to kill the prophet and his servant are led by Elisha to Samaria, to a place where the prophet orders: *"Set bread and water before them that they may eat and drink and go to their master." So he prepared for them a great feast; and when they had eaten and drunk, he sent them away, and they went to their master. And the Syrians came no more on raids into the land of Israel"* (6:22-23). What an amazing example of divine retribution! As Paul said to the believer in Rome, *"if your enemy is hungry, feed him; if he is thirsty, give him drink; for by so doing you will heap burning coals upon his head. Do not be overcome by evil, but overcome evil with good"* (12:20-21). Yes, the world is in chaos and the enemy seems more numerous than we are, but with the LORD's help, we can overcome evil with good one deed at a time, one day at a time for *"more are they that are with us than with them!"* Can you see God's army with its horses and chariots of fire? "LORD, open our eyes!"

NT Scriptures

Luke 10:19; 1 John 4:4; 5:1-5

Prayer

O LORD, with you there is no fear. Though the world rumbles and moans, we do not fear for you have said, "Peace I leave with you; my peace I give you. I do not give to you as the world gives. Do not let your hearts be troubled and do not be afraid."

Personal Notes and Prayers

2 Kings 6:17

וַיִּתְפַּלֵּל אֱלִישָׁע וַיֹּאמַר יְהוָה פְּקַח־נָא אֶת־עֵינָיו וְיִרְאֶה וַיִּפְקַח יְהוָה
אֶת־עֵינֵי הַנַּעַר וַיַּרְא
וְהִנֵּה הָהָר מָלֵא סוּסִים וְרֶכֶב אֵשׁ סְבִיבֹת אֱלִישָׁע:

Then Elisha prayed and said, "O LORD, please open his eyes so he can see." So the LORD opened the eyes of the young attendant, He looked and all of a sudden, the hill was full of horses and chariots of fire all around Elisha.

Biblical Context

ELISHA'S YOUNG ATTENDANT WAS afraid. Israel and Syria were at war, and the Syrian army had surrounded the city of Dothan in order to take Elisha captive for revealing to the King of Israel the Syrian military strategy. Elisha's attendant could see that the Syrian army surrounded them, but he could not see that his enemies were surrounded and outnumbered by a much greater army—the Army of the LORD. Elisha (אֱלִישָׁע "God is salvation") reassured his attendant saying, "Fear not, for those who are with us are more than those who are with them" (6:16). Then, Elisha asked the LORD to open his attendant's eyes. He used a verb that also appears in Genesis 3:5 when Adam's and Eve's eyes are opened to their nakedness, and Genesis 21:19 when God opens Hagar's eyes to a well of water in the middle of a desert. At first, Elisha's attendant could only see the Syrians's horses, chariots and army surrounding the city. He was unable to see what God was doing until God opened his eyes and showed him his own mighty army (6:17). What a relief it must have been for the prophet's attendant! In a reversal of events, God opened the eyes of the attendant and blinded the eyes of the Syrian military men. Elisha then led the blind Syrian warriors into the presence of the King of Israel who agreed to feed the them and granted them the freedom to return home. Through God's intervention, no one perished. Elisha and his attendant enjoyed God's protection and the Syrian army found freedom from sure defeat.

Life Application

How often we are defeated simply by what we see with our own eyes and by what we hear with our own ears. We fail to remember that God is greater than this natural realm and is always ready to work on our behalf. A seemingly hopeless situation is never the entire truth. God is at work. He yearns to show us his mighty deeds. Let us not forget to look up and seek God's perspective on every situation.

NT Scriptures

Luke 4:18–19; Acts 26:16–18; 1 John 4:4

Prayer

O LORD, some trust in chariots and some trust in horses, but we want to be like those who trust in the name of the LORD our God (Ps 22:7–8). Those who trust in earthly powers collapse and fall, but we want to rise up and stand strong in your power. We yearn to see the realities of your heavenly realm while we journey on this earth. Thank you for opening our eyes.

Personal Notes and Prayers

2 Kings 10:2–3

וְעַתָּ֗ה כְּבֹ֨א הַסֵּ֤פֶר הַזֶּה֙ אֲלֵיכֶ֔ם וְאִתְּכֶ֖ם בְּנֵ֣י אֲדֹנֵיכֶ֑ם וְאִתְּכֶם֙ הָרֶ֣כֶב
וְהַסּוּסִ֔ים וְעִ֥יר מִבְצָ֖ר וְהַנָּֽשֶׁק:

וּרְאִיתֶ֞ם הַטּ֤וֹב וְהַיָּשָׁר֙ מִבְּנֵ֣י אֲדֹנֵיכֶ֔ם וְשַׂמְתֶּ֖ם עַל־כִּסֵּ֣א אָבִ֑יו
וְהִלָּחֲמ֖וּ עַל־בֵּ֥ית אֲדֹנֵיכֶֽם:

Now, when this letter comes to you and the sons of your master are with you, along with chariots, horses, and a fortified city and weapons, seek the best and most upright from the sons of your master, place him upon the throne of his father, and fight for the house of your master.

Biblical Context

THIS TEXT IS PART of a message sent by Jehu to the elders of Samaria who were protecting the sons of king Ahab. Jehu found himself in the midst of a bloody civil war against the descendants of the infamous king Ahab. Jehu had been anointed to be king and commissioned by a young man sent by Elisha to destroy Ahab's descendants (2 Kgs 9:1–7). Even though Ahab was dead, the evil he had committed in Israel was being propagated by his sons and by those who remained loyal to his abominable ways. The LORD said through the young man sent by Elisha that Jehu was to "avenge the blood of my servants the prophets and all the servants of the LORD" (2 Kgs 9:7). This message provided a challenge for the elders who were forced to choose who they would serve. Would they follow the evil and idolatry of the house of Ahab and continue to worship Baal, or would they choose to obey the LORD and recognize that following other gods only leads to destruction and judgment?

Life Application

Once Jehu was called by the LORD and given a mission, he let nothing stand in his way. He was radically obedient to the LORD and called those around him to decide whose side they were on. If only my life was marked by such zeal to declare the love of God. Those who are not following God may not realize that they are in danger. Jehu sent a warning to the elders and gave them a chance to surrender. We cannot force people to choose Jesus, but we can tell them that if they choose another way, they are in eternal danger of damnation.

NT Scriptures

Matthew 10:32–39

Prayer

O LORD, you have given us the ability to choose you, to follow you, and to walk in your ways. Give us the wisdom to see clearly the difference between right and wrong, good and evil, and light and darkness. Draw us into your presence and give us the courage to let go of the things of this world. We want to glorify you in all we do and say. Help us LORD!

Personal Notes and Prayers

2 Kings 19:14

וַיִּקַּח חִזְקִיָּהוּ אֶת־הַסְּפָרִים מִיַּד הַמַּלְאָכִים וַיִּקְרָאֵם וַיַּעַל בֵּית יְהוָה
וַיִּפְרְשֵׂהוּ חִזְקִיָּהוּ לִפְנֵי יְהוָה:

Hezekiah took the scrolls from the hand of the messenger and he read them aloud. Then Hezekiah went up to the house of the LORD and spread it before the LORD.

Biblical Context

HEZEKIAH AND THE INHABITANTS of Judah were desperate. After making a brash decision to align themselves with Egypt against Assyria, the people faced certain death. Sennacherib, king of Assyria, had already looted the Temple in Jerusalem of all its silver and gold and was now threatening Hezekiah in a letter saying, "Do not let your God in whom you trust deceive you by promising that Jerusalem will not be given into the hand of the king of Assyria. Behold, you have heard what the kings of Assyria have done to all lands, devoting them to destruction. And shall you be delivered?" (2 Kgs 19:10–11). Hezekiah, and the whole kingdom of Judah knew that on their own, they could not survive the serious threat of the Assyrians. Hezekiah had already shown great faith in the LORD by tearing down all of the high places, smashing the standing stones and cutting down the Asherah poles (2 Kgs 18:4). However, everything was now on the line—Hezekiah's kingdom, his life, his people, and ultimately the reputation of his God. Hezekiah knew that coming before the LORD in worship and prayer for divine intervention was their only hope for survival. Before the LORD, he pleaded, "O LORD our God, save us, please, from his hand [Sennacherib's hand], that all the kingdoms of the earth may know that you, O LORD, are God alone" (2 Kgs 19:19). As later confirmed by the prophet Isaiah, God heard Hezekiah's petition and promised to deliver Judah from the hand of the Assyrians, and to punish the Assyrians for their treatment of his people.

Life Application

When things go wrong in my life, my first response is to strategize. I figure out where I am, what resources I have, and what my next steps should be. After all my planning, I ask God if I have made the right decisions and what He would want me to do. Hezekiah does not take this approach at all. He reads the threatening letter and goes straight to God. He never even thinks about what he could do on his own. He has already trained his heart and mind to rely on the LORD at all times. Even before he presents his petition before the LORD, he worships God and acknowledges that God is the only one in control of the heavens and the earth. May we always begin by seeking the LORD, at all times and in every situation, and acknowledge God's power and greatness over all.

NT Scriptures

Matthew 6:25-34; Romans 8:15; 2 Timothy 1:7

Prayer

O LORD, you instructed to "seek first the kingdom of God" and to leave the rest in your hands. Forgive us LORD for relying on our own resources first and for seeking you last, out of our own desperation. You have the wisdom, knowledge and power to take care of every detail of our lives. Help us O LORD to seek you first in every circumstance and to trust you with our lives.

Personal Notes and Prayers

2 Kings 19:19

וְעַתָּה יְהוָה אֱלֹהֵינוּ הוֹשִׁיעֵנוּ נָא מִיָּדוֹ וְיֵדְעוּ כָּל־מַמְלְכוֹת הָאָרֶץ כִּי
אַתָּה יְהוָה אֱלֹהִים לְבַדֶּךָ׃

*And now, O LORD our God, please save us from his hand,
so all the kingdoms of the earth may know that you,
and you alone, are the LORD God.*

Biblical Context

MANY KINGS OF ISRAEL and Judah had come and gone. Most of them were evil and had displeased the LORD by leading the people astray. Consequently, God gave Israel into the hands of the Assyrians (Is 8:7; Am 2:6–16). After the fall of the northern kingdom, Judah in the south was left in disarray and in fear of the oppressor, Assyria. Yet a ray of hope began to shine when Hezekiah came to the throne of Judah. Although he faced a full-on war with the Assyrians and the possible annihilation of his people, Hezekiah did what every leader of Israel should have done— he turned to God. After hearing the intimidating message of the Rab-Shakeh, the messenger of Sennacherib king of Assyria, Hezekiah tore his clothes, covered himself with sackcloth and went into the House of the LORD (2 Kgs 19:1). He asked the LORD to save Jerusalem for the sake of his own name. He pleaded with God and asked God to save Judah so that all the nations may know that the God of Israel is the Living God. The LORD heeded Hezekiah's prayer and saved Jerusalem because of Hezekiah's prayer. Sadly, after Hezekiah's death, Manasseh took over the throne and led the nation back into sin and idolatry. Eventually, Judah fell to the Babylonians who deported the Judeans to Babylon.

Life Application

The LORD listens to our prayers! How often we let the circumstances of life lead us into despair, discouragement and defeat. Hezekiah was not ignorant of the dangers facing him and his people. He knew what happened to the nations that stood against the Assyrians. It would have been easy for him to simply give in, curse the LORD and put his trust in Sennacherib, but instead, he turned to God. He pleaded with God. God listened to him. God answered his prayer and had mercy on Judah. God saved his people because of Hezekiah's prayer. There is much that can be learned from Hezekiah's actions. What would it look like to pray that God would act in our lives, not to make our lives better, but to make his name greater? While there were obvious motives of self-preservation involved in his prayer, Hezekiah was seeking the glory of the LORD. There are so many times that God can use our situations to reveal his Gospel if we will ask him to act in our lives. Though he may not always act how we think he should, the LORD always listens and responds to our prayers.

NT Scriptures

Matthew 7:7–11; Romans 8:31–39

Prayer

O LORD, thank you for hearing the prayers of faithful intercessors who turn to you and plead on behalf of others. We thank you for praying leaders who sacrifice themselves for the sake of the community. Teach us to pray sacrificially for those who need you in their lives. Teach us to pray as Moses, David, Hezekiah and Jesus prayed. Thank you for listening to our cries and for answering our petitions and for opening our eyes to your will for us.

Personal Notes and Prayers

Isaiah 2:5

בֵּית יַעֲקֹב לְכוּ וְנֵלְכָה בְּאוֹר יְהוָה:

*O house of Jacob, come, let us walk
in the light of the LORD.*

Biblical Context

THIS VERSE APPEARS AT the end of a beautiful passage about international peace, when all nations will flow from the north, south, east and west to Zion (Jerusalem), the mountain of Adonai and the place of the House of our God. Nations will gather in Jerusalem to seek the LORD, to learn his ways, and to follow his paths. The effects of this journey to Zion will be formidable and long lasting. Nations will acknowledge the LORD and submit to his commandments. Isaiah tells the people that peace will reign and no one will learn the art of war anymore. Nations will beat their swords into plowshares and their spears into pruning knives. Harmony and productivity will replace conflict and destruction. The prophet's eloquent appeal, placed at the end of this hopeful vision, exhorts God's people to walk in the light of the LORD so that all nations may witness the glory of God, forsake their evil ways and turn to God, the Judge of all the earth.

Life Application

As believers, we know that we are called to live in ways that testify to our faith in the LORD. However, we often set our responsibilities aside in favor of doing what is contrary to the call of God. The words of the prophet Isaiah challenge us to rise up and walk faithfully with our God. His words invite us to come into God's presence to be transformed by his Spirit, seek knowledge and wisdom, and become emissaries who are well equipped and efficient in the furthering of the Kingdom of God on earth. In practical ways, this may mean taking extra time to listen to a friend, sharing an encouraging word with someone who is distraught, buying a bag of groceries for someone who is struggling financially, going to places where the gospel is needed, assuming leadership in Christian matters, and proclaiming the gospel publicly in the religious and political spheres. Regardless of how we "walk in the light of the LORD," what we do is essential and matters, whether others recognize or do not recognize our work. We must live as examples to those around us at all times so that others may be drawn to the LORD, exalt him, walk in his ways and become witnesses to the gospel with us.

NT Scriptures

Matthew 4:12–17; 1 John 1:5–7

Prayer

O LORD, the world is getting darker and darker each day. What takes place around us is often disappointing, discouraging and contrary to your ways. Help us LORD remain faithful to you no matter what we face in this life. For we know that "neither death nor life, nor angels nor rulers, nor things present nor things to come, nor powers, nor height nor depth, nor anything else in all creation, will be able to separate us from the love of God in Christ Jesus our LORD." (Rom 8:38–39)

Personal Notes and Prayers

Isaiah 9:5

כִּי־יֶ֣לֶד יֻלַּד־לָ֗נוּ בֵּ֚ן נִתַּן־לָ֔נוּ וַתְּהִ֥י הַמִּשְׂרָ֖ה עַל־שִׁכְמ֑וֹ וַיִּקְרָ֨א שְׁמ֜וֹ
פֶּ֠לֶא יוֹעֵץ֙ אֵ֣ל גִּבּ֔וֹר אֲבִיעַ֖ד שַׂר־שָׁלֽוֹם׃

For a child is born to us; a Son has been given to us.
The ruling power is on his shoulder and his name
is called Wonderful Counselor, Mighty God,
Father of Eternity, Prince of Peace.

Biblical Context

THE MOST QUOTED AND beloved prophet of the Old Testament, Isaiah, has a stunning prophecy for Ahaz. Isaiah, a well-respected prophet, has accurately foretold world changing events during his own lifetime (eighth century BCE). In Isaiah 7:14, he mentions a sign to be given—a virgin will give birth and her son will be named Immanuel "God with us." Isaiah elaborates on this prophecy in chapter 9 where he states that "to us, a son is born and to us a son is given." The passive form of the verb "to give" (נתן) emphasizes that neither humans nor the child will have control over this event for it will be a gift to all from the Father. That gift will be so amazing that a wide range of descriptives apply to him—He will be "Wonderful Counselor, Mighty God, Father of Eternity, Prince of Peace." A Messiah would surely be most welcome during this troubled time in Israel, as dark days loom on the horizon. The typical Isaiah countrymen would be happy with a military-type savior, one who would thwart the threat of the Assyrians. Just as the gift of a son was out of their control, the type of Messiah to be given will far exceed their expectations as well.

Life Application

In our life time we may wish for a "messiah" to get us out of debt and to ensure a healthy existence for all of our families. More importantly, we wish for a "messiah" to provide certainty in the sea of doubts that swirls about us. The true Messiah does far beyond what we could ever imagine. Our

Messiah is a wonderful counselor, someone who is intuitively involved and knowledgeable of our plight. He is a Mighty God who has unlimited power to meet our needs. He is an Eternal Father who receives his troubled children with open arms. He is the Prince of Peace—the Prince of Shalom—who provides wholeness, security and tranquility. Not only do we now know that the Messiah has come for us, but he also knows that he arose from the dead assuring our salvation. In our darker days, we must not forget what Isaiah foretold and what we have been shown. Jesus our Messiah is the son of the virgin whose name is Emmanuel "God with us." Let us remembers his comforting words, "Do not let your heart be troubled. Believe in God; believe also in me" (John 14:1) and "Peace I leave with you; my peace I give you. I do not give to you as the world gives. Do not let your hearts be troubled and do not be afraid" (John 14:27).

NT Scriptures

Mathew 1:23

Prayer

O LORD, you are so far greater than what our minds can fathom. You are eternal and above all things. You know all things and see all things. You know every fiber of our beings. We are humbled that you would come to live among us and die for us. There are no words that can express our gratefulness for your gift of eternal life. We love you and trust you as we walk with you in humility. "Oh Love, that will not let me go, I rest my weary soul in Thee; I give Thee back the life I owe, that in thine ocean depths its flow, may richer, fuller be" (song by NYCYPCD).

Personal Notes and Prayers

Isaiah 28:9-10

אֶת־מִי יוֹרֶה דֵעָה וְאֶת־מִי יָבִין שְׁמוּעָה גְּמוּלֵי מֵחָלָב עַתִּיקֵי מִשָּׁדָיִם:

כִּי צַו לָצָו צַו לָצָו קַו לָקָו קַו לָקָו זְעֵיר שָׁם זְעֵיר שָׁם:

To whom will he teach knowledge? And to whom will he explain the message? Those just weaned from milk? Those just drawn from the breasts? For precept upon precept, precept upon precept, line upon line, line upon line, here a little, there a little.

Biblical Context

IN THIS CONTEXT, THE prophet Isaiah issues a rebuke to the leaders of Israel in the days of the divided kingdom. Isaiah criticizes especially the priests and prophets who should have been teaching God's Word to the people, but instead became proud and drunkards. The priests and prophets are accused of reeling from wine and staggering from strong drink. Their vision has become obscured by their unholy condition and they are unable to execute justice in the community. They have become useless, and consequently, the people are left in great ignorance and spiritual confusion. The rulers of Jerusalem are in no better condition. They have cut a covenant with death and made a pact with Sheol. They have made lies their refuge and hidden themselves under falsehoods. However, with God there is always a hope and a future. In spite of the failure of the leaders, there is still a reason to remain optimist. God promises to raise up a young and innocent generation. He will take those who are just weaned from the breastmilk and teach them his ways, line upon line and precept upon precept. Although they will not speak clearly at first, God will show them his ways until they are ready to replace the failed leaders of the land.

Life Application

Although this passage is a clear criticism of what was happening in Israel at the time, it also presents a positive side and a clear message. God does not expect his people, and particularly the leaders, to be ignorant and weak in their understanding of the things of God. Spiritual infancy is not acceptable, especially not for leaders. On the contrary, God expects spiritual maturity, ethical behavior, a sound mind, and a faithful walk with him. He requires that leaders continue to learn from God, in a systematic way, here a little and there a little, day after day, so that they may become proficient to teach others the ways of the LORD. The truths of Scripture are internalized a little at a time. One precept at a time. One insight upon another, built consistently over an extended period of time. Life with God is a journey that requires one step at a time, one decision at a time, a bite of learning here and a bite of learning there. Only then can one become the instrument God desires to use to further his Kingdom on earth.

NT Scriptures

Colossians 1:9–14; Hebrews 5:12–14; 1 Peter 2:1–3

Prayer

O LORD, we thirst for the living water you provide so abundantly. We hunger for the meat of the Word you gave so freely. Feed us O LORD and cause us to grow like cedars in Lebanon, planted in the house of Adonai. May we flourish in the courts of our God and still yield fruit in old age. May we be filled with the fresh sap that comes from your throne. And may our lives bring you glory as we seek you faithfully.

Personal Notes and Prayers

Isaiah 30:15

כִּי כֹה־אָמַר אֲדֹנָי יְהוִה קְדוֹשׁ יִשְׂרָאֵל בְּשׁוּבָה וָנַחַת תִּוָּשֵׁעוּן
בְּהַשְׁקֵט וּבְבִטְחָה תִּהְיֶה גְּבוּרַתְכֶם
וְלֹא אֲבִיתֶם:

For thus says the LORD God, Holy One of Israel, "In withdrawal and descent you will be saved. In quietness and in trusting, your strength will be." But you were not willing.

Biblical Context

ISAIAH SPOKE THE WORDS of the LORD to the people of Israel shortly before they fell to the Assyrians in 722 B.C. God used Isaiah to let the Israelites know that judgment would come upon them for their stubbornness and rebellion unless they repented and sought to live as He instructed. In this particular passage, what the LORD prescribes is withdrawing from the hustle and bustle, and slowing down the pace a bit. God asks that the Israelites just be still and trust that He has everything under control. This verse seems pretty straightforward. God is telling the Israelites exactly what they must do to be saved. He is telling them exactly where they can find enough strength for the battles they will face. However, the Israelites response is also explicit. In the next verse, Isaiah 30:16, we see that the Israelites insisted on their own fast horses to save them. Rather than placing their trust in the LORD, they thought they needed to be fast and efficient. Sound familiar?

Life Application

We often consider our fast-paced lifestyles to be a modern development in the history of the world—the human race keeps getting busier and busier. This may or may not be true, but this verse testifies that people's inability to slow down has been a problem to some extent for centuries. No matter how much we preach a gospel of grace, it seems we cannot escape the mentality that we have to do something to get something.

And so, even if we are able to avoid the worldly pursuit of money and power, we busy ourselves with "kingdom work." If anyone had a lot to accomplish on this earth, it was Jesus, and yet He knew very well his need for quality time with God. In the gospels we see that He made sure to withdraw from the crowds to "just be" with his Father. As the LORD instructed the Israelites, and as Christ demonstrated, let us seek solitude and silence in the midst of the hustle-and-bustle of life.

NT Scriptures

Matthew 14:13

Prayer

O LORD, forgive us for our addiction to busyness. Please forgive us for investing more time in the activities of the world than in seeking you. Help us set aside our own agendas and learn to sit at your feet to hear yours. Help us LORD set our priorities aright so that our lives may be productive for you and your kingdom.

Personal Notes and Prayers

Isaiah 40:11

כְּרֹעֶה עֶדְרוֹ יִרְעֶה בִּזְרֹעוֹ יְקַבֵּץ טְלָאִים וּבְחֵיקוֹ יִשָּׂא עָלוֹת יְנַהֵל׃

Like a shepherd he will tend his flock, by his arm he will gather the lambs together And he will carry them in his bosom; he will lead the nursing ewes (to a place of rest).

Biblical Context

ISAIAH 40 REPRESENTS A dramatic shift in the prophet's tone. After spending 39 chapters depicting the coming judgment of exile because of the sins of God's people, Isaiah now anticipates a time after the exile when God will restore his people and care for them as their shepherd. The verbs, which are in the imperfect form, act in the future continual aspect and, combined with God's sovereign and good character, reflect his sure promises and faithfulness to his people, even when they themselves have proven unfaithful. The LORD's arm, a metaphor that is so often used to demonstrate his transcendent power, now becomes the image of tender embrace and protection. In the ancient Near East, it was common to depict a ruler as a shepherd, for the metaphor emphasized the ruler's responsibility to gather, feed, lead, correct, and protect the people in their care. This image is applied to the LORD in a number of significant passages (see Ps 23; Ezek 34). Similar to Psalm 23, here God promises to bring the nursing ewes to a safe place where they and their vulnerable newborn can rest without fear of encountering danger. In the previous 39 chapters, Isaiah emphasized God's holiness, transcendence, sovereignty, might, and ability to enact judgment on those who break his covenant; now, Isaiah reveals God's compassion, mercy, nearness, faithfulness, salvation, and redemption for the very ones who broke the covenant. Both images of God are necessary and complementary, for there is no justice without condemnation of sin. Yet this depiction of God provides unique hope in the form of grace to those who deserve none. As their shepherd, God actively welcomes his people back into the fold by gathering them together. Ultimately, God will take an even greater step into solidarity with his people by becoming not only a lamb like them, but also the sacrificial "lamb of God who takes away the sin of the world!" (John 1:29).

Life Application

The image of God as shepherd reflects both his incredible power to protect his people and his tender care of them. With God as shepherd, we see both God's omnipotence and goodness acting in harmony: we can trust God to protect us precisely because he is capable and willing to do so. This does not guarantee that nothing bad will happen to us; after all, this promise comes immediately after one of the longest compilation of judgment oracles in the Old Testament. Yet we learn here that God does not abandon his people even in the midst of such judgment. Rather, he acts faithfully on our behalf, administering grace and redemption so that we might be returned to the fold. When we scatter, he gathers us back and when we are vulnerable, he protects us and brings us to a place of rest. Truly God is our good shepherd.

NT Scriptures

John 1:29; 10:1–18; Revelation 5:1–4; 14:4

Prayer

Good shepherd, we praise you for your faithfulness to us. We ask forgiveness for the ways in which we have strayed from your good care. Bring us back into the fold so that we might experience your tenderness once again. Gather us into your arms so that we might receive your mercies anew. Teach us to follow you wherever you might lead, for the glory of your name.

Personal Notes and Prayers

Isaiah 40:15-17

הֵ֤ן גּוֹיִם֙ כְּמַ֣ר מִדְּלִ֔י וּכְשַׁ֥חַק מֹאזְנַ֖יִם נֶחְשָׁ֑בוּ הֵ֥ן אִיִּ֖ים כַּדַּ֥ק יִטּֽוֹל׃

וּלְבָנ֕וֹן אֵ֥ין דֵּ֖י בָּעֵ֑ר וְחַיָּת֕וֹ אֵ֥ין דֵּ֥י עוֹלָֽה׃ כָּל־הַגּוֹיִ֖ם כְּאַ֣יִן נֶגְדּ֑וֹ מֵאֶ֥פֶס וָתֹ֖הוּ נֶחְשְׁבוּ־לֽוֹ׃

Surely the nations are like a drop in a bucket and are considered like dust on scales. Surely he weighs the islands as fine dust. Lebanon is insufficient for burning; its animals are insufficient for burnt offerings. All the nations are as nothing before him; they are regarded by him as nonexistent and worthless.

Biblical Context

AFTER THIRTY-NINE CHAPTERS OF pronouncing judgment on both Israel, Judah and the nations, Isaiah finally introduces a positive message: "Comfort, comfort my people" (40:1 נַחֲמ֥וּ נַחֲמ֖וּ עַמִּ֑י). Yet, this message of "comfort" is by no means intended to create complacency in Israel. Rather, it is meant to teach the people that God is bigger than all circumstances of life and far greater than all nations. They are "like a drop in a bucket" (15). God is not like them. He holds all the waters of the earth in the palm of his hand, weighs the mountains in scales, understands all things and exercises justice perfectly (12–14). He sits above the earth and spreads out the skies like a curtain (22). He controls the elements (24), never grows tired or weary, and renews the strength of those who wait for him (28–31). There is none equal to him (25). In these truths, Israel can find "comfort." God will never leave his people. He will lead, guide, give counsel, meet needs, give strength and might, and cause those who follow him to soar on wings like eagles. Israel need not fear her enemies for God is with her. Israel must be faithful to God in order to find this gift of "comfort."

Life Application

Whether many of us in the American Church would admit it or not, the United States is one of the nations which God regards "as nothing before him" (כְּאַיִן נֶגְדּוֹ). Though we can count ourselves blessed to live in a country that respects religious freedoms, we would be foolish to place our ultimate hope in a nation whose leaders are just as susceptible to corruption as the leaders of ancient Israel, and whose masses are just as easily led astray as the Israelites of old. Whatever evils our government may practice or legalize for the general population, it is up to the Body of Christ to be faithful to God's commands and serve as a witness to Him in a world full of evil, lest we fall under the same judgment that awaits the nations.

NT Scriptures

Romans 12:1–2; 1 Peter 2:11–12; 4:12–19

Prayer

O LORD, open our eyes to our sins and bring us back to you. Forgive us for our failure to place our trust in you. Forgive us for being unfaithful to you and for engaging in the sins of the world. You know how weak we are and how prone we are to deviate from your paths. Today we ask you to redirect our attention towards you. Show us your ways and keep us from falling. We need you LORD. Be our eternal Guide.

Personal Notes and Prayers

Isaiah 41:10

אַל־תִּירָא כִּי עִמְּךָ־אָנִי אַל־תִּשְׁתָּע כִּי־אֲנִי אֱלֹהֶיךָ אִמַּצְתִּיךָ אַף־
עֲזַרְתִּיךָ אַף־תְּמַכְתִּיךָ בִּימִין צִדְקִי׃

Do not fear for I am with you. Do not be dismayed for I am your God. Indeed, I will strengthen you; indeed, I will help you. I will support you with my righteous right hand.

Biblical Context

AFTER MANY YEARS OF living in the land, the Judahites knew that God could discipline his children with exile. They had seen it happen to their brothers to the north and had witnessed the complete destruction of their territory by the Assyrians. The thought of being taken away from their homeland by foreigners to an unknown and distant nation created terror in the hearts of the people. Fear was an accurate response to the military might and brutal relocation program of the Assyrians. Over seven hundred years later, the same plot of land would feel the wrath of the Romans who instilled fear in their subjects. Numerous times, God reassured his people with these words: "Do not fear!" Beginning with the announcement of Jesus's birth to the shepherds, the messenger declared "Do not fear!" (Luke 2:10). In a boat on the Sea of Galilee, Jesus commanded his disciples "Do not fear!" (John 6:20). In the garden, Jesus said to them "Do not fear!" (Matt 10:26–28). And to the church in Smyrna, Jesus commanded "Do not fear!" (Rev 2:10).

Life Application

Humans often become fearful when the future—immediate or distant—is unknown. Although fear is a common human response to the unknown, it is unhealthy and can lead to wrong decisions. What happens when we give that fear to Jesus our Savior? Indeed, He strengthens us! Indeed, He helps us. He supports us with his righteous right hand! God calls us to lay our fears at his feet and to embrace his plan for our lives with confidence that he will take care of us.

NT Scriptures

Matthew 8:26; Mark 14:48; Luke 2:9; Revelation 2:10

Prayer

LORD, fear often causes us to lose sight of you instead of making us run to you. When we do not know the future, we fear your creation rather than you. When we are in dire circumstances, we fear our situations rather than you. Help us! Strengthen us, O LORD, to embrace your righteous right hand and save us in times of distress. Help us rely on you rather than on ourselves. We know you hold our future and we rest in your victorious right hand.

Personal Notes and Prayers

Isaiah 42:8

אֲנִ֥י יְהוָ֖ה ה֣וּא שְׁמִ֑י וּכְבוֹדִי֙ לְאַחֵ֣ר לֹֽא־אֶתֵּ֔ן וּתְהִלָּתִ֖י לַפְּסִילִֽים׃

I am the LORD, that is my name! My glory I will not give to another nor my praise to a graven image.

Biblical Context

ISAIAH IS A COMPLEX book, and its authorship and origin have been vigorously debated. Regardless of whether one believes that a single author or multiple authors wrote Isaiah, one can find unity of purpose and consistent themes throughout the book. One of the overarching themes is the belief in a sovereign God, the LORD, the God of Israel. He is "high and exalted" (6:1 רָ֥ם וְנִשָּׂ֖א), "the Rock eternal" (26:4 צ֥וּר עוֹלָמִֽים), "the everlasting God, the creator of the ends of the earth" (40:28, אֱלֹהֵ֤י עוֹלָם֙ בּוֹרֵא֙ קְצ֣וֹת הָאָ֔רֶץ), and Israel's "Holy One ... Creator ... King" (43:15 קְדוֹשְׁכֶ֔ם בּוֹרֵ֥א יִשְׂרָאֵ֖ל מַלְכְּכֶֽם). Another theme in Isaiah is that of judgment and salvation, and the first thirty nine chapters of the book cycle this theme repeatedly. For its sins, Israel finds herself in exile. But Israel is not the only recipient of judgment. The prophet also speaks of other nations such as Egypt, Assyria and Babylon. Ultimately though, the focus is not on Israel or the nations, but rather on the God who sovereignly governs all. The remaining chapters (40–66) emphasize the hope of Israel. This hope takes numerous forms including restoration to their land, the re-establishment of Jerusalem, a return to the covenant relationship with God, and ultimately a Messiah. But again, the focus is rightly place on the LORD who is over all. Here, in the midst of declarations of hope for the nation, God redirects Israel's focus on himself, the living God.

Life Application

When I think of the book of Isaiah I think of God, and I believe that this is what the author intended. In my opinion, this particular verse (42:8) is an abstract of that intent. In it, the LORD once again identifies himself and reveals his expectations to the people in simple terms: "I am the LORD, that is my name! My glory I will not give to another nor my praise to a graven image." He is the LORD, and he alone deserves glory and honor and praise; he and no other. Personally, the challenge in this passage is to not only accept this truth intellectually but to live it out day by day. It is relatively easy to say that he is LORD of my life, but quite a bit more difficult to submit to that Lordship. It is relatively easy to say that I have no other idols in my life, but then I look around and have to acknowledge that there are numerous things in my life that claim my worship. Giving all of our praise to God should be easy, but it is not, especially when we are called to let go of our idols. Thankfully, we serve a God who is gracious and compassionate, and though he demands perfection, he accepts and loves imperfect people.

NT Scriptures

John 8:58, 1 Timothy 1:17; Revelation 4:11; 5:13

Prayer

O LORD, there is none like you. None is just, compassionate, loving, patient, understanding, and generous like you. You see our sins and you call us back to you. You see our failures and you encourage us. You see our weaknesses and you strengthen us. Teach us to be faithful to you as you are faithful to us. Yes, the glory belongs to you.

Personal Notes and Prayers

Isaiah 43:19

הִנְנִי עֹשֶׂה חֲדָשָׁה עַתָּה תִצְמָח הֲלוֹא תֵדָעוּהָ אַף אָשִׂים בַּמִּדְבָּר
דֶּרֶךְ בִּישִׁמוֹן נְהָרוֹת:

*"See! I am about to do a new thing now, it will spring up.
Do you not know it? I will even establish a way in the
wilderness, a stream in the desert."*

Biblical Context

MOST SCHOLARS AGREE THAT this chapter in Isaiah was written after the fall of Assyria to the Babylonian Empire, but before the destruction of Jerusalem in 586 BCE. Following the warnings of the impending judgment described in Isaiah 1–39, the second book of Isaiah brings a glimpse of hope to Israel. Although the nation is doomed to destruction at the hands of the Babylonians, God calls out a remnant who will remain faithful to Him. In chapter 42, Isaiah announces the coming of a Savior who will bring justice to the nations, open the eyes of the blind, and cause the deaf to hear. In chapter 43, the Savior announces protection, guidance, and salvation for his people. And just as the LORD made a way in the desert for his people after they came out of Egypt, He promises to do it again for the faithful remnant. He will "pour water on the thirsty land, and streams on the dry grounds. He will pour his Spirit on the offspring [of Israel] and his blessings on their descendants" (44:3). So, while judgment is unavoidable for Israel, the grace of God will prevail in the end, and the Savior will come and bring redemption to his people.

Life Application

What a wonderful promise. The LORD speaks clearly and shows his people that He is going to do something new, something amazing and life changing. In Isaiah, God's message of judgment is followed by a message of hope—a declaration that a Savior is coming. The promise has been fulfilled and the Savior has now come. Jesus is this Savior. He is God incarnate. He is the "new thing" promised by Isaiah. He is the way in the wilderness and the stream in the desert. He opens our blind eyes and our deaf ears. And He promises to bring us home where we belong.

NT Scriptures

Matthew 11:4–5; Mark 7:37; 10:46–52; Luke 2:11

Prayer

O LORD, we were blind and you gave us sight. We were deaf and you opened our ears. You promised to come for us and you did so, giving your life for us. We thank you for redeeming us from the powers of darkness and for bringing us into the light. We can now see you and hear you. Lead us in your ways and show us the path on which you want us to journey. Help us be faithful to you as you are faithful to us.

Personal Notes and Prayers

Isaiah 49:6

וּנְתַתִּיךָ לְאוֹר גּוֹיִם לִהְיוֹת יְשׁוּעָתִי עַד־קְצֵה הָאָרֶץ׃

I will make you a light to the nations to be my salvation unto the end of the earth.

Biblical Context

PIECE BY PIECE THE prophet Isaiah fills in the picture of this puzzling figure, "the Servant" (עֶבֶד יְהוָה). In the second "Servant Song," Isaiah's audience learns that the Servant was called for a special purpose before He was born, He was sent to do a work that would seem to have been done in vain but ultimately approved by the God himself. Finally, the work would serve a dual purpose; first, to bring a remnant of Israel back to God, and second, to be the LORD's salvation to the end of the earth. This gives a clear picture of the mission of the Servant, but at the same time, it raises the question "How will the Servant become salvation?" The answer to this comes in chapter 53 when the Servant takes upon himself the "iniquity of us all" when He is stricken, smitten, pierced, crushed, punished, and wounded on our behalf. Some have correctly translated the Servant's mission in Isaiah 49:6 as "that you may bring my salvation to the ends of the earth." The Servant does bring salvation, but more than that, He *is* salvation. It is through Him and in Him only that God saves.

Life Application

The supreme epitome of the Servant is Jesus. Many New Testament Scriptures go out of the way to connect Jesus with the Servant of Isaiah, leaving little doubt that He is the Servant par excellence. He is the ideal Servant, but He is not the only servant. The nation of Israel was supposed to be God's servant, but they disobeyed. For believers today, Jesus is the model Servant after whom we are supposed to fashion our lives and be servants. Even his teaching includes phrases that echo the Servant in Isaiah 49; "you are the light of the world" (Matt 5:14). We are called to be witnesses of Jesus—our salvation—to the ends of the earth (Matt 28:19–20; Acts 1:8). The words of Isaiah 49:6 inspire us to worship the One who is salvation. These words compel us to serve Him as He has served us and take the gospel to the ends of the earth.

NT Scriptures

Matthew 1:21; John 1:9, 29; Ephesians 1:3–14

Prayer

O LORD, you are our salvation. You came to seek and save us as we wallowed in our sin. Thank you for your great salvation and for sending us to share this good news to all the nations of the earth. How we want everyone to know that you are indeed the salvation they seek. Help us share the message of salvation to all those you place on our paths. Make us aware of your presence at all times. Remind us of the price you paid for our salvation. We are blessed beyond measure by your salvific work in our lives. To you be the glory!

Personal Notes and Prayers

Isaiah 53:3

נִבְזֶה וַחֲדַל אִישִׁים אִישׁ מַכְאֹבוֹת וִידוּעַ חֹלִי וּכְמַסְתֵּר פָּנִים מִמֶּנּוּ
נִבְזֶה וְלֹא חֲשַׁבְנֻהוּ׃

*He was despised and rejected by men, a man of sorrows
and acquainted with disease, and like one from whom
men hide their faces. He was despised
and we did not value him.*

Biblical Context

IN THIS PASSAGE, THE suffering Servant is ostracized, banished, and relegated to living on the margins of society. His suffering appears to start early in life. Isaiah tells us that he is unremarkable and unattractive as a young shoot out of dry ground. We normally do not think of the Messiah living this way. We prefer imagining a Messiah who is powerful, winsome and who walks head and shoulders above the crowd, not one who suffers like us. This Messiah in Isaiah 53 is somewhat obscure, almost alienated from the community, even before he experiences suffering at its worst. Applying this to Jesus, we can recognize not just the disfigurement of the cross, but the earlier pain of living his life as one who was rejected and persecuted. Not only did he suffered *for* us, but he also suffered *like* us. He was openly despised, rejected, isolated, and debased. No one who understood him for who he was. People turned away from him and hid their faces at his cruel suffering. This makes suffering the perfect disguise.

Life Application

Today, we still prefer to look the other way. We find it difficult to stare at the ugly, the crippled, or the disfigured. This is natural. Created in God's image, we are predisposed to prefer beauty. However, our culture goes a step farther. It reveres glamour and the pretty people, and punishes the unremarkable. As believers we too can find it hard to be patient with even the mild suffering of others, much less accept the ugliness of the cross of

Christ. There is a limit to how much despair and anguish we can witness in others. We do not want to accept the possibility that we might suffer as well, so we deny it or ignore it in others. We are sometimes drawn into the conspiracy of pretense that we can control life and always delete the parts we do not like. Yet Jesus found a way to gaze long at the leprous, demon-possessed, diseased and unappealing, to see the individual beneath the surface. Being acquainted with disease, he was willing to linger in the presence of the sick. Being acquainted with suffering, he was willing to linger in the presence of those who suffered. This is good news for those of us who are sick and sorrowful. We can do what the Messiah did; we can learn to linger with those who mourn and those who are sick, and become a source of eternal blessings for them.

NT Scriptures

Matthew 10:8; Luke 13:10–13; 14:12–14

Prayer

O LORD, open our eyes to see those who suffer around us as you see them. Give us hearts of compassion to help those who have been marginalized and ostracized because of their infirmities. Use us to reach them with your love, compassion and mercy. Make us instruments of redemption for the sake of your Kingdom.

Personal Notes and Prayers

Isaiah 55:1

הוֹי כָּל־צָמֵא לְכוּ לַמַּיִם וַאֲשֶׁר אֵין־לוֹ כָּסֶף לְכוּ שִׁבְרוּ וֶאֱכֹלוּ
וּלְכוּ שִׁבְרוּ בְּלוֹא־כֶסֶף וּבְלוֹא מְחִיר יַיִן וְחָלָב:

Ah! All who are thirsty, come to the waters; and you who have no money, come, buy and eat. Come, buy wine and milk without money and without price.

Biblical Context

THESE WORDS, SPOKEN BY the prophet Isaiah to the exiles returning from captivity, had broader significance than a promise of physical provision. Throughout the Hebrew Bible, the imagery of drinking, tasting, and feasting are used to illustrate *spiritual* and *emotional* nourishment. The biblical Feasts are living metaphors for the celebration of the LORD's salvation of his people. And in fact, the recipients of Isaiah's message can be Jews or Gentiles, as *all* are invited to be in relationship with the LORD. The images of thirst and hunger are powerful; they represent core needs that must be met. This three-fold invitation begins with a request to "Come" (לְכוּ), and implies stepping toward the LORD, acknowledging an inability to save or sanctify oneself. Then, in a state of pennilessness to obtain fulfillment in our own strength or pursuits ("that which does not satisfy," v. 2), there is a recognition that spiritual longings can only be met through a relationship with a living God. Yet, "without money," why is there still a directive to "buy" (שִׁבְרוּ), the "richest of fare" (v. 2)? Here "buying" is turned on its head, as there is a next step of purposely *entering into* the "everlasting covenant" relationship with Him (v. 3). And then to partake (אֱכֹלוּ), to eat of the free gift of life and blessing, to "taste and see that the LORD is good" (Ps 34:8), and experience a "filling up" of deep contentment that only his Holy Spirit can provide.

Life Application

What are ways we can come, buy, and eat? Within the new covenant, we *recognize* Jesus Christ as our Messiah and then *receive* his sacrifice as the payment already made on our behalf, allowing for a relationship with Him. We feed on Scripture with its transforming power spiritually, just as food grows us up physically. And we converse with our LORD in prayer, and live with his presence in us and with us, knowing He alone is the "living water" (John 4:10) and the "bread of life" (John 6:48) that quenches and feeds our soul and spirit.

NT Scriptures

John 6:35; 7:37; Revelation 22:17

Prayer

O LORD, how I hunger and thirst for you. "The communion bread is laid on my tongue so gently. But I am ravenous; I want to gnaw the whole loaf. We know already we are his body, but taking in this crumb of the earth's generous flesh, this sip of its given blood, presses Incarnation into our flesh. By way of imagination we take in the symbol and the substance to become more vividly vessels filled with Christ, so that even as we step away from the altar and out the church door we keep living the liturgy and the urge to Eat and Drink. The wine burns still in my throat. I have a shred of bread stuck in my teeth. O, how to feed the hunger and thirst of the world?" ("Crunching Jesus" in *Thumbprint in the Clay: Divine Marks of Beauty, Order and Grace* by Luci Shaw, 68–69).

Personal Notes and Prayers

Isaiah 61:3

לָשׂוּם לַאֲבֵלֵי צִיּוֹן לָתֵת לָהֶם פְּאֵר תַּחַת אֵפֶר שֶׁמֶן שָׂשׂוֹן תַּחַת אֵבֶל

מַעֲטֵה תְהִלָּה תַּחַת רוּחַ כֵּהָה וְקֹרָא לָהֶם אֵילֵי הַצֶּדֶק מַטַּע יְהוָה לְהִתְפָּאֵר:

In order to establish those mourning in Zion, to give to them a crown of joy instead of ashes, oil of gladness instead of mourning, a garment of praise instead of a faint spirit. One will call them oaks of righteousness, a plantation of the LORD, in order show his glory.

Biblical Context

THIS VERSE POINTS TO the coming of a Messiah who will be anointed by the Spirit of the LORD to proclaim good news to the poor, to heal the broken-hearted, to bring freedom to the captives, to deliver those who are imprisoned, to comfort those who mourn, and to declare the year of the LORD's favor. The anointed One—the Messiah—will enact a complete reversal of their wretched condition. The Messiah will change their mourning into gladness and their faint spirit into a life of praise. As a result, those who are touched by the Messiah will be known among all the peoples of the earth as those whose mourning has ended and whose sorrow has turned to joy. They will be recognized as the ones who produce the fruit of righteousness and as those whom God has blessed.

Life Application

The Messiah's role was to be one of caring for the people of God, one of turning adversity into freedom and mourning into fullness of joy. Two thousand years ago, at the beginning of his earthly ministry, Jesus revealed his identity as the long awaited Messiah whose deep concern was for the outcast, the sick, the oppressed, and the brokenhearted. After he read Isaiah 61:1–3 in the synagogue in Nazareth (Luke 4:16–19), he proclaimed, "Today, this Scripture has been fulfilled in your hearing" (Luke 4: 21). To this day, God has not abandoned his people. He is still freeing and delivering from bondage of sin, sickness and oppression those who call on his name. In the eschaton, mourning, poverty, brokenness, captivity, imprisonment, and sorrow will vanish away. When Christ returns to earth to receive his bride, the full extent of the prophecy in Isaiah will be realized. Those who mourn in this life will one day be clothed splendidly and will be full of joy. They will be like strong trees that cannot be shaken by the storm.

NT Scriptures

Acts 2:17–18; 2 Timothy 1:7

Prayer

O LORD, how thankful we are that you never leave us nor forsake us; that you turn our mourning into joy, deliver us from bondage and oppression, and heal us from our diseases. You will forever be faithful to your promises. We come before you and lay our struggles, weaknesses and brokenness at your feet. We trust you with our lives and we know that the "sufferings of the present time are not worth comparing with the glory that will be revealed to us" as we walk with you forever.

Personal Notes and Prayers

Jeremiah 1:7–8

וַיֹּאמֶר יְהוָה אֵלַי אַל־תֹּאמַר נַעַר אָנֹכִי כִּי עַל־כָּל־אֲשֶׁר אֶשְׁלָחֲךָ
תֵּלֵךְ וְאֵת כָּל־אֲשֶׁר אֲצַוְּךָ תְּדַבֵּר׃

אַל־תִּירָא מִפְּנֵיהֶם כִּי־אִתְּךָ אֲנִי לְהַצִּלֶךָ נְאֻם־יְהוָה׃

Then the LORD said to me, "Do not say, 'I am a child.' For to all whom I will send you to, you will go, and all that I command you, you will speak. Do not be afraid before them, for I am with you to rescue you,' declares the LORD."

Biblical Context

THE CALL OF EVERY prophet was different and required complete submission to the will of God. However, Moses argued that he could not be God's instrument because he was "not a man of words" and had "a slow mouth and a heavy tongue" (Exod 4:10). Isaiah exclaimed that he was a man of unclean lips, unworthy to speak the word of God (Is 6:5). Jonah ran away from the call of God because he despised the Assyrians who would eventually receive his message. Jeremiah was scared because he felt he was only a child. He was afraid of what the people he spoke to would do to him. Jeremiah must have felt like he was in shoes that were much too big for him. Who would listen to him, especially because he was called to speak words of judgment and warning to the people of Israel? But God offered reassuring words saying, "Today, I have set you up as a fortified city, an iron pillar and bronze walls against the whole land, against the kings of Judah, its princes, against its priests, and against the people of the land. Though they will fight against you, they will not win, for I am with you to deliver you" (Jer 1:18–19).

Life Application

As Christians, we have been called to a similar task. We have been commissioned to go out and proclaim before the people the good news of Jesus Christ. We are to bring the message of salvation to a people of unclean lips and rebellious spirit. For many, including myself, this is a daunting task. We are consumed with thoughts of insecurity and ask ourselves, "What will people think of me? I am young and have no great life experience or store of wisdom. I am not a great speaker and I may be rejected by my audience. I do not feel . . . and I do not know . . . ." But God does not send us out into the world without first equipping us and without providing a divine helper. The Holy Spirit goes with us and empowers us for the task. It is He who speaks through us, and it is He who does the convicting. We do not need to depend on our persuasive arguments or outstanding list of facts. It is God upon whom we must rely, even when our fears and doubts try to tell us otherwise.

NT Scriptures

Matthew 10:26–33; Hebrews 13:6

Prayer

O LORD, you are our fortress and our deliverer. You are the rock in whom we take refuge. You are our shield, and the horn of our salvation, our stronghold and our strength. We trust you to lead us to those who need to know you and to embolden us to declare your word in the face of adversity. Help us surrender our will, our mind and our emotions to you. Make us your instruments so that the world may know that you are the living God.

Personal Notes and Prayers

Jeremiah 9:23–24

כֹּה אָמַר יְהוָה אַל־יִתְהַלֵּל חָכָם בְּחָכְמָתוֹ וְאַל־יִתְהַלֵּל הַגִּבּוֹר בִּגְבוּרָתוֹ אַל־יִתְהַלֵּל עָשִׁיר בְּעָשְׁרוֹ:
כִּי אִם־בְּזֹאת יִתְהַלֵּל הַמִּתְהַלֵּל הַשְׂכֵּל וְיָדֹעַ אוֹתִי כִּי אֲנִי יְהוָה עֹשֶׂה חֶסֶד מִשְׁפָּט וּצְדָקָה בָּאָרֶץ כִּי־בְאֵלֶּה חָפַצְתִּי נְאֻם־יְהוָה:

Thus says the LORD, "Let not the wise boast in his wisdom, and let not the mighty boast in his might; let not the rich boast in his riches. For in this, let him who boasts boast that he is prudent and knows me, that I am the LORD who does loving kindness, justice and righteousness on earth, for in these I delight," declares the LORD.

Biblical Context

THE BOOK OF JEREMIAH reveals the struggles of the prophet to call Judah back from the brink of judgment. In the early chapters, Jeremiah pronounces impending judgment and in chapter 7, he calls Judah to reform her ways. He exhorts the Judahites to deal with one another justly, to stop oppressing the aliens, orphans and widows, and to follow YHWH only (vv. 3–6). In 9:11–26, we find a graphic depiction of God's judgment on the people for their failure to reform their ways. In the midst of this disquieting text, the LORD provides a glimpse of what it means to truly know Him. In the verses translated above, Jeremiah relegates wisdom, strength and riches to a low level of importance when compared with the knowledge of the LORD. Further, he describes what truly delights the LORD—loving kindness, justice, and righteousness. These are defining traits of their God, and to truly know their Him, the Judahites should have been emulating these traits. Unfortunately they were not, and as a result they were sent into exile.

Life Application

There is a precarious balance between knowing about God and knowing God. We may read the Bible and know *about* God's concern for the marginalized in society—the orphan, the widow, the alien, the sick, the lost, etc.—but unless we commit to ministering to these, we do not really know Him. To truly know God, we must delight in those things that delight Him, namely loving kindness, justice and righteousness.

NT Scriptures

Luke 19:10; James 1:27; 2:1–8

Prayer

O LORD, forgive us for loving wisdom, might and riches more than those who need you. Help us love you and your people more than the gifts you give us. Help us live with kindness towards those who are hurting, with justice towards the oppressed and with righteousness before you. We want to boast in You, and in You alone.

Personal Notes and Prayers

Jeremiah 20:8–9

כִּי־מִדֵּי אֲדַבֵּר אֶזְעָק חָמָס וָשֹׁד אֶקְרָא כִּי־הָיָה דְבַר־יְהוָה לִי
לְחֶרְפָּה וּלְקֶלֶס כָּל־הַיּוֹם: וְאָמַרְתִּי
לֹא־אֶזְכְּרֶנּוּ וְלֹא־אֲדַבֵּר עוֹד בִּשְׁמוֹ וְהָיָה בְלִבִּי כְּאֵשׁ בֹּעֶרֶת עָצֻר
בְּעַצְמֹתָי וְנִלְאֵיתִי כַּלְכֵל וְלֹא אוּכָל:

For whenever I speak, I cry out and proclaim violence and ruin. For the word of the LORD has become to me reproach and derision all the days. But if I say, "I will not remember him and will not speak anymore in his name," it is in my heart like a burning fire shut up in my bones, I am weary to hold it in; indeed I do not have the power.

Biblical Context

THE PROPHET JEREMIAH WAS the quintessential prophet of "doom" as he proclaimed God's word of judgment to Judah prior to the Babylonian invasion and subsequent destruction of the Temple and city of Jerusalem. His personal struggles and ministry are vividly recounted in Scripture, more so than any other prophet. Despite the fact that he was ridiculed and derided for his prophetic words, he was unable to hold back the word of the LORD because it was like a *fire* in his bones. There is no human way to contain the power and propulsion of God's Word. No less than thirteen verbs in these two short verses attest to this intense pressure to speak the truth.

Life Application

Because human nature never changes, what took place in Judah centuries before Jesus came is often a reality in our churches today. Many reject the Word of God—as they did in Jeremiah's day—and refuse to heed its message. Anointed by the Spirit, Jeremiah could not contain God's truth, even though he attempted to do so. He was a true and faithful mouthpiece for the LORD. Christian leaders today hold the same responsibility in our churches. The natural consequence of their study of God's word should be to speak forth truth with courage, boldness and conviction. Where spiritual fire burns in the bones of leaders, the church is awakened and revived by the flames that pour forth from the preaching of God's Word.

NT Scriptures

Titus 1:7—2:1

Prayer

O LORD, set us on fire with your Word and Spirit. Do not let us rest until we burn with zeal, with love, and with passion for the lost. Awaken in the depth of our hearts the desire to preach, teach, share, lead, minister and proclaim your message to the world. Make us like Jeremiah, unafraid, unintimidated, unmoved and unshaken. Strengthen us for the task and establish us in strategic places where we can deliver your message and bring people to you. Enable us to complete the work of your Kingdom on earth. Do not let us sleep and slumber. Set us on fire, O God!

Personal Notes and Prayers

Ezekiel 18:31–32

הַשְׁלִיכוּ מֵעֲלֵיכֶם אֶת־כָּל־פִּשְׁעֵיכֶם אֲשֶׁר פְּשַׁעְתֶּם בָּם וַעֲשׂוּ לָכֶם
לֵב חָדָשׁ וְרוּחַ חֲדָשָׁה

וְלָמָּה תָמֻתוּ בֵּית יִשְׂרָאֵל: כִּי לֹא אֶחְפֹּץ בְּמוֹת הַמֵּת נְאֻם אֲדֹנָי
יְהוִה וְהָשִׁיבוּ וִחְיוּ:

Cast off from upon you all of the transgressions that you have committed then make yourselves a new heart and a new spirit. For why should you die, O house of Israel? "For I have no pleasure in anyone's death!" says the LORD the LORD. "Now repent so that you may live!"

Biblical Context

THE LORD CALLED EZEKIEL to serve as prophet over the house of Israel *after* he was carried off into exile. Much of Ezekiel's ministry included warning God's people of their sin and proclaiming the LORD's judgment on Jerusalem. Ezekiel tells them that each individual would be judged for their own sin and declared that, (1) the righteous shall live and the sinner shall die (vv. 5–20), (2) the sinner who repents shall live and the righteous who repents (from righteousness) shall die (vv. 21–29). Having been found guilty of sin, Israel is commanded to (1) cast off (הַשְׁלִיכוּ) ALL of their transgressions; (2) make (וַעֲשׂוּ) for themselves a new heart and spirit; and (3) repent/turn (וְהָשִׁיבוּ) so that they may live (וִחְיוּ). The first two imperatives show the meaning of the third: repentance requires casting off sin AND making oneself right towards God. The fourth imperative shows the result of such actions: those who obey shall live and not die. These commands are interrupted by the LORD's comments, *"Why should you die, O house of Israel?"* and *"I have no pleasure in anyone's death."* Both statements emphasize the LORD's desire for his people: LIFE. Though Israel was guilty of sin and beginning to experience their deserved death, the LORD shows mercy and compassion by telling them what to do to obtain life.

Life Application

Many people struggle with a loving God who judges sin. After all, the penalty of sin is death (Rom. 6:23). God does and will judge all people according to their way of life, but He takes *no pleasure in the death of anyone*. Just as the LORD desired for and commanded Israel to repent so they would live, He desires and commands all people everywhere to do the same today (Acts 17:30). The LORD wants *you* to live and not die. And you can live. *Repent so that you may live*. Repentance requires casting off *all* of our sins and making a new heart and spirit for ourselves, living in right relationship with God. The good news is that by repenting and believing in the LORD Jesus, we receive the Holy Spirit who enables us to live with that new heart and spirit. Though God does judge sin, He desires for us to repent so that we may live and not die. Please! Do not ignore the LORD's command to repent, *for why should YOU die, O beloved of the LORD? Repent so that you may live!*

NT Scriptures

Mark 1:14-15; Luke 5:32; 24:47; 2 Peter 3:9

Prayer

Heavenly Father, thank you that you do not desire anyone's death, including mine. Though I do not deserve to live, for I have transgressed against You and others, I praise You for the life You desire me to have. I cast off ALL of the transgressions I have committed, I shall make for myself a new heart and new spirit which delights in You by the power of the Holy Spirit whom You have given me. I repent from all my sins and I praise You for I know that I shall live! I pray these things in the name of Jesus Christ my LORD, Amen!

Personal Notes and Prayers

Ezekiel 34:2b

כֹּה אָמַר אֲדֹנָי יְהוִה הוֹי רֹעֵי־יִשְׂרָאֵל אֲשֶׁר הָיוּ רֹעִים אוֹתָם הֲלוֹא הַצֹּאן יִרְעוּ הָרֹעִים:

Thus the LORD God said, "Woe shepherds of Israel who have been feeding themselves. Should not those shepherding be shepherding the flock?"

Biblical Context

THE PROPHECIES OF EZEKIEL occur entirely within the context of exile in Babylon. In captivity, God gives Ezekiel a prophetic voice and he becomes a human messenger to the exiles, speaking both condemnation and hope. The words of God that come through Ezekiel in the beginning of chapter 34 echo and expand upon the words of Jeremiah 23:1–6. The "shepherds of Israel" (i.e., the kings) are condemned for their failure to care for the sheep (i.e., the people of Israel). In Jeremiah 23, the shepherds are accused of destroying and scattering the sheep. In Ezekiel 34, they are accused of caring only for themselves, neglecting the weak and sick, and ruling harshly. As a result, the sheep have become "food for the wild animals" (Ezek 34:5). In each book though, the prophetic condemnation is followed by a messianic hope. Through Jeremiah God promises that a new king will come who will do what is just and right in the land (23:5). Through Ezekiel, God not only promises that He will place over the people a new shepherd to tend them but that He himself will look after them—two complementary promises pointing to a messianic hope (34:11, 23).

Life Application

While the words of the prophet Ezekiel point to the hope of a Messiah, it is important to be aware of some of the issues that led Israel to despair in exile. They were a chosen people, called out to God for holiness and to be blessing to the nations. While Israel had issues throughout her history, some of her biggest problems arose during the time of the monarchy. As monarchic rule evolved in Israel, the chosen people became more and more like the nations around them, which, ironically, is exactly what they asked for in 1 Samuel 8:19-20. This was largely a result of the character, or lack thereof, of the kings that successively ruled over the nation. God desires that his people be holy and that they delight in the things He delights in—loving-kindness, justice and righteousness (see Jer. 9:22-23). We see here in Ezekiel 34:2 however that the nation was struggling because the shepherds of the nation thought more highly about themselves than they were about their responsibility to lead the people. People will only be as good as the leaders that lead them. Thus, we as spiritual leaders of God's people today must lead selflessly, lest we scatter our people to become "food for the wild animals."

NT Scriptures

Matthew 23:11-12; Romans 12:3; Philippians 2:3-8

Prayer

O LORD, what responsibility you have given us—to lead, shepherd and protect your people from being vulnerable and at the mercy of the enemy. Grant us that we may lead wisely, model the Good Shepherd and protect your people from the evil one.

Personal Notes and Prayers

Hosea 2:16 [14]

לָכֵ֗ן הִנֵּ֤ה אָֽנֹכִי֙ מְפַתֶּ֔יהָ וְהֹֽלַכְתִּ֖יהָ הַמִּדְבָּ֑ר וְדִבַּרְתִּ֖י עַל־לִבָּֽהּ׃

Therefore, I will gradually entice her and lead her into the wilderness, and then I will speak to her heart.

Biblical Context

THE PROPHET HOSEA SPEAKS to Israel during a time when Israel lived in great prosperity. Though blessed with material possessions, the Israelites were not following the LORD. As they had done many times before, they had turned to the Baals and worshipped them in word and deed. Consequently, divine judgment was looming. Once again, God raises up a prophet to preach a message of doom, to announce the imminent fall of Israel and the exiling of its inhabitants. In the first chapters of the book of Hosea, the relationship between God and Israel is depicted in marital covenant language. Hosea is called to marry a woman (i.e., Israel) who would ultimately be unfaithful to him. This unfaithfulness severs the marital relationship and brings pain and hardship on the union. The wife is rebuked and instructed to remove the unfaithfulness from between her breasts (2:2). Her refusal to do so will cause her to become like a desert, a parched land slain with thirst (2:3). Her children will be unloved and she will become naked, without wool and linen to cover her body (2:9). Her feastings will cease and wild animals will devour her (2:12). A terrible outcome for unfaithfulness to the one who loved and cared for her. However, in love she is wooed into the wilderness and treated tenderly with affection, intending to repair the broken relationship. Promises of blessings and restoration are uttered, and the one who was once called "not my beloved" will receive love from her beloved.

Life Application

We are often like Israel. God has extended his grace to us through his Son Jesus Christ, but we have neglected to live as he commanded. We lust after sin, just as Hosea's wife lusted after other men. We are the unfaithful wife in our relationship with God. But our God lovingly lures and entices us away from our sinful behavior, capturing our attention with his intense pursuit of us. Our God reminds us that with his outstretched hand, he delivered us out of slavery. Our God constantly seeks to remind us of the great love he has for us. In thankfulness for this grace, we must strive by the power of the Holy Spirit to acknowledge his love toward us and to lead godly lives for his glory.

NT Scriptures

Romans 5:5; Ephesians 2:1–7; Revelation 21:1–5

Prayer

O LORD, I have been unfaithful to you. I have turned away to follow my own desires. I repent of my inclination to follow ways that are not from you. Forgive me and restore me to yourself. I seek your mercy and grace. Draw me to your bosom and surround me with your loving arms. I love you LORD.

Personal Notes and Prayers

Joel 2:16

אִסְפוּ־עָם קַדְּשׁוּ קָהָל קִבְצוּ זְקֵנִים אִסְפוּ עוֹלָלִים וְיֹנְקֵי שָׁדָיִם יֵצֵא
חָתָן מֵחֶדְרוֹ וְכַלָּה מֵחֻפָּתָהּ׃

Gather the people, sanctify the assembly and assemble the elders. Gather the children and the ones nursing at the breast. Let the bridegroom come out from his room and the bride from her chamber.

Biblical Context

THE FIRST TRUMPET BLOWN in Zion proclaimed the coming of the day of the LORD (2:1). It would be a day of darkness and anguish (2:2, 6), when the earth would shake as the LORD went out before his army (2:10–11). Generally speaking, the prophet does not mention the specific reason why judgment was being proclaimed over Judah. Whatever its sin, Joel is quick to communicate that God being gracious, merciful, slow to anger, and abounding in love is reason enough to blow another trumpet, the trumpet of repentance. "Who knows whether he will not turn . . . and leave a blessing behind him?" (2:14). Just as the coming of the the LORD would affect the entire community of Judah, so repentance involves the entire nation. Not only the regular assembly and elders (see 1:14), but newlyweds who might otherwise be exempt from cultic observances, and young children . . . even those too young to fully comprehend what was happening. Even as all people, young and old are here involved in repentance, so the LORD will pour his Spirit upon all flesh. Sons and daughters will dream, young and old will prophesy (2:28), and the fortunes will be restored to Judah and Jerusalem (3:1).

Life Application

In our culture, worship often becomes such a private affair that we tend to individualize even the most communal actions in Scripture. A person might skip out on community to have "church alone." Truth is left unspoken because of the fear of imposing one's own beliefs on someone else. Both damaging behavior and darkest depression will go unnoticed for long periods of time. Eventually, nothing is any longer anyone's business. Yet, when God became jealous (2:18), he became jealous for a people. When he saved, he saved a nation. The individual appropriation of God's saving act was never at odds with the community of worshippers, from youngest to oldest. Neither should we think that our worship (even our repentance) will ever bear fruit if it all takes place in a closet, or in the wilderness. May we always know the richness and reward that comes from joining with others in the worship of our Creator.

NT Scriptures

1 Corinthians 12:12–26; Hebrews 10:24–25

Prayer

O LORD, we often live in secret, failing to share our hearts, minds, struggles, and victories with the members of your Body. We rob ourselves of your blessings. Teach us to be transparent with one another and to live in harmony with those who are around us. Teach us to be honest with those who love us and teach us to love them with your unconditional love. Help us work together for the sake of your Kingdom and for your glory.

Personal Notes and Prayers

Amos 4:12

לָכֵן כֹּה אֶעֱשֶׂה־לְּךָ יִשְׂרָאֵל עֵקֶב כִּי־זֹאת אֶעֱשֶׂה־לָּךְ הִכּוֹן לִקְרַאת־
אֱלֹהֶיךָ יִשְׂרָאֵל:

Therefore, thus will I do to you, O Israel. Because I will do this to you, prepare to meet your God, O Israel!

Biblical Context

MANY TODAY, EVEN WELL-INTENTIONED Christians, find the God of the Old Testament to be cruel and overly bent on exacting judgment—an outmoded model, they would say, supplanted in the New Testament by the indiscriminating love and compassion of Jesus. No doubt, they would find the same kind of vindictive God in Amos 4. Yet, however alarming this oracle actually is, what is often overlooked is the manifold mercy of the LORD, especially in light of the relentless impenitence of Israel. These were the very people loved and chosen by YHWH himself, delivered from Egyptian bondage, given direction in the Law and Prophets, and led victoriously into the Promised Land (Amos 2:4, 9–11; 3:1–2). Yet time and time again, in their injustice, idolatry and ritualism, they were sufficiently warned (see Amos 3:7). Time and time again, they refused to repent and were judged as a result (4:6–11), and time and time again, they failed to get the recuperative gist of it all. Despite famine, drought, mildew, plague, sword and decay (i.e., judgments that should have convinced Israel to repent), we find the oft-repeated refrain, "Yet you have not returned to me" (Amos 4:6, 8, 9, 10, 11 וְלֹא־שַׁבְתֶּם עָדַי). As a result, Israel is now commanded to prepare to meet her God in even greater judgment—in military devastation and exile from the land (Amos 3:9–15; 4:2–3; 5:1–3, 27). Yet even in the midst of this gloom and doom, the LORD's mercy, in light of 9:11–15, sheds a glimmer of hope. Indeed, YHWH proves himself merciful and abounding in steadfast love and faithfulness (Exod 34:6).

Life Application

Lest we become like the Israelites (see Rom. 15:4; 1 Cor. 10:6–12), Christians today would do well to grow in gratitude for what our heavenly Father has done for us, is doing for us, and will do for us, especially in Christ and through his Spirit—better yet, to grow in gratitude for the Triune God himself! Undoubtedly, this will require an appreciation for whole-Bible reading and reflection, private and communal prayer and thanksgiving, and perhaps even journaling and listing. Alternatively, we should periodically remind ourselves that the LORD sometimes uses the hardships of our lives to discipline or reprove us for our sin. Such a reality requires that we examine our hearts regularly and confess our sins to God and to one another. As leaders in the church, we would also do well to implement times of silence and solitude in our corporate worship gatherings for such introspection and confession.

NT Scriptures

Matthew 11:20–24; Acts 5:1–11; Romans 15:4; 1 Corinthians 10:6–12; 1 John 1:8–10

Prayer

O LORD, how great is your love, that you would call us to repent, that you would extend grace and mercy, and that you would forgive us our sins. You are willing to place our sins as far as the east is from the west. You are willing to erase them from our lives and replace them by your amazing love. How blessed we are to serve you, O Living and Eternal God.

Personal Notes and Prayers

Jonah 1:16

וַיִּירְאוּ הָאֲנָשִׁים יִרְאָה גְדוֹלָה אֶת־יְהוָה וַיִּזְבְּחוּ־זֶבַח לַיהוָה וַיִּדְּרוּ נְדָרִים׃

The men feared the LORD greatly, so they sacrificed to the LORD and made vows.

Biblical Context

GOD TOLD JONAH TO arise and go to Nineveh. Jonah, unwilling to deal with the Assyrians, made his way to the coast and boarded a ship headed in the other direction, towards Tarshish. While they were sailing on the sea, God sent a terrible storm that threatened to tear the ship apart. While Jonah was sleeping below deck, the sailors became very afraid and cried out to their gods, but nothing happened. The waters became increasingly turbulent. The captain found Jonah sleeping on the lower deck and urged him to cry out to his god. When it was finally made clear that Jonah was the cause of the storm, the men asked Jonah what they should do. Jonah told them to throw him into the sea but the men first refused and tried unsuccessfully to row to shore, while crying out to God for their lives. They were afraid that if they killed Jonah this great and terrible storm-god would destroy them as well. But when they finally threw Jonah into the sea, suddenly, the calm seas returned. In verse sixteen, we find out that the sailors "feared the LORD." Three significant verbs appear in verse sixteen: "to fear," "to sacrifice," and "to vow." Each is repeated in idiomatic phrasings that intensify the meanings of the statements: They "feared *a great fear*" (וַיִּירְאוּ יִרְאָה גְדוֹלָה), they "sacrificed *a sacrifice*" (וַיִּזְבְּחוּ־זֶבַח), and they "vowed *vows*" (וַיִּדְּרוּ נְדָרִים). Repetition is often used in Hebrew to highlight a concept, to emphasize an event and to draw attention to certain actions. These men were in complete awe of this great, awesome and fearsome God. Jonah had not borne witness of his God but the sailors recognized Him nonetheless.

Life Application

When the storm came up, the sailors were afraid of dying because they knew that in storms, sailors sometimes perish. On hearing that Jonah had angered his God, they were very afraid. He had told them that he was running from God, but they had not expected God to pursue him. However, it is not until the storm abated that they cried out to Jonah's God. This God controlled the sea and storm, and had proven himself powerful. This part of the story reminds me of the reaction of the disciples when Jesus calmed the storm on the Sea of Galilee. The disciples had been afraid of drowning. After Jesus rebuked the wind and the waves and calmed the storm, they were afraid and marveled at the One who could command the wind and the sea. We should stand in awe of the power and majesty of the God we serve. The God who commands the storms, holds us in his hands, pursues us when we flee, and loves us undeservedly.

NT Scriptures

Luke 8:22–25; John 16:33

Prayer

O LORD, how great is your mercy towards us sinners. You love us when we fail to love you. You are faithful to us when we fail to be faithful to you. We do not deserve your grace yet you extend it freely and free us from our sins. How thankful we are today that you pursue us relentlessly every day.

Personal Notes and Prayers

Jonah 2:9 [8]

מְשַׁמְּרִים הַבְלֵי־שָׁוְא חַסְדָּם יַעֲזֹבוּ׃

*Those holding on to the emptiness
of vanity forsake their loyalty.*

Biblical Context

UP TO THIS POINT Jonah has done just about everything wrong. He heard the word of the LORD and then did just the opposite. He was supposed to go in one direction and instead, he boarded a ship going almost exactly in the opposite direction. God sent a storm while Jonah hid in the bowels of the vessel. Everyone else on the ship took vows, prayed and did their best to find the cause of their guilt. Jonah knew that he was the reason that the sailors were in danger but he did nothing. Only as a last resort did the sailors reluctantly throw him overboard. Now in the belly of a great fish, Jonah laments his fate and eventually comes to his senses. Sloshed around by the waves and billows, with weeds wrapped around his head, Jonah talks about redemption and the hope of looking once again to God's holy Temple. He knows that despite his own unfaithfulness, God will remain faithful to him. Up until this point, Jonah could easily have been one of the people described by this verse—one who holds on to the emptiness of vanity and forsakes his loyalty. But he knew better. He remembered the Lord, prayed and promised to pay his vows to God with a voice of thanksgiving. He threw himself on the mercy of God, knowing that "salvation belongs to the LORD" (v.9). God rescued him and put him back on the right path.

Life Application

The "emptiness of vanity" is a very strong phrase. The Hebrew word הֶבֶל ("emptiness") points to something that is vaporous, evanescent, transitory, unsubstantial and insignificant. The Hebrew word שָׁוְא ("vanity") implies nothingness, irrelevance and worthlessness. It is hard to imagine anything of less value than the "emptiness of vanity," or the "insubstantiality of nothingness," or the "insignificance of worthlessness." Why anyone would foolishly hold on to such things is puzzling, however, it is unfortunately a reality in the lives of many of God's people. Holding onto empty things is just what causes us to forsake our loyalty to God. However, as Jonah's story reminds us, God's faithfulness to us is based on his never ending love for us and his constant pursuit of us. God never leaves us nor forsakes us, even when we try to run away from him or hold on to vanity. What a great God we serve.

NT Scriptures

2 Corinthians 4:18; 2 Timothy 2:11–13; Hebrews 13:5

Prayer

O LORD, we are feeble and easily distracted. We are attracted to the things of the world, to things that are meaningless in the light of eternity. Teach us what is important to you. Open our eyes to what you value in this world. Help us let go of our worthless idols and concentrate on you and your Kingdom. We need you LORD.

Personal Notes and Prayers

Jonah 4:10–11

וַיֹּ֣אמֶר יְהוָ֗ה אַתָּ֤ה חַ֙סְתָּ֙ עַל־הַקִּ֣יקָי֔וֹן אֲשֶׁ֛ר לֹא־עָמַ֥לְתָּ בּ֖וֹ וְלֹ֣א גִדַּלְתּ֑וֹ שֶׁבִּן־לַ֥יְלָה הָיָ֖ה וּבִן־לַ֥יְלָה אָבָֽד׃

וַֽאֲנִי֙ לֹ֣א אָח֔וּס עַל־נִֽינְוֵ֖ה הָעִ֣יר הַגְּדוֹלָ֑ה אֲשֶׁ֣ר יֶשׁ־בָּ֡הּ הַרְבֵּה֩ מִֽשְׁתֵּים־עֶשְׂרֵ֨ה רִבּ֜וֹ אָדָ֗ם אֲשֶׁ֤ר לֹֽא־יָדַע֙ בֵּין־יְמִינ֣וֹ לִשְׂמֹאל֔וֹ וּבְהֵמָ֖ה רַבָּֽה׃

But the LORD said, "You take pity on the plant for which you did not labor and did not grow. It grew in one night and died in one night. Should I not take pity upon Nineveh the great city in which there are one hundred and twenty thousand people who do not know between their right and left, and has many beasts?"

Biblical Context

GOD CALLS RELUCTANT JONAH to go to Nineveh to proclaim repentance, lest judgment come upon the city. After hearing the call, Jonah flees from God and heads in the opposite direction. God dramatically stops him in his tracks and redirects him towards Nineveh. Although Jonah is physically in the city, his heart has not changed—he is still heading for Tarshish. He reluctantly and halfheartedly preaches to his foes. Though Jonah preaches God's message, he is disgusted when the people of Nineveh repent. He is offended when God relents from bringing destruction upon them. While waiting and hoping for the destruction of Nineveh, Jonah finds shelter under a plant that is eventually destroyed by a divine messenger—a worm. Alone and deceived, Jonah falls into despair.

Life Application

How often our hearts are misguided by prejudice. As Christians, we say we want what God wants, but in our hearts, we are deceived and withhold the truth from our foes. Though Jonah was a prophet of God who had heard God's call, his prejudice against the Ninevites made him unwilling to have compassion on them. We are often like Jonah, withholding unconditional love from those who have offended us. We, like Jonah, give mental ascent to God's will but we are reluctant to give our all to reach the lost. According to the words of Moses, what God desires of us is that we love and serve him with all our heart, mind and strength (Deut 6:5). God calls us to join our passions to his and to share the Good News without prejudice with all who are lost—friends and foes.

NT Scriptures

Matthew 5:43–48; Luke 10:25–37; 1 John 4:20–21

Prayer

O LORD, forgive us for withholding the truth from those who so desperately need it. We confess that we often pursue our own interests rather than following your call on our lives. Heal our hearts and pour your compassion in us so that we may love all those you place on our paths.

Personal Notes and Prayers

Micah 6:8

הִגִּיד לְךָ אָדָם מַה־טּוֹב וּמָה־יְהוָה דּוֹרֵשׁ מִמְּךָ כִּי אִם־עֲשׂוֹת מִשְׁפָּט
וְאַהֲבַת חֶסֶד וְהַצְנֵעַ לֶכֶת עִם־אֱלֹהֶיךָ:

He has made known to you, man, what is good. And what does the LORD seek from you? Nothing but to do justice and to love mercy and walk humbly with your God.

Biblical Context

THE PROPHET MICAH IS speaking to the nation of Judah in hopes of transforming its people from their unjust behavior to avoid God's destructive wrath. Having been set apart as the LORD's people, Judah is guilty of unjust behavior among their own people as well as spiritual blindness in their worship of the LORD. In order to restore their relation to God, Judah is commanded by Micah to do three things in v. 8: to do justice, to love mercy, and to walk humbly with God. These three things are in line with the will of God, and his good and perfect will has been made known to his people long before Micah's time. But because of Judah's consistent sin God spells it out once more. First, the people of Judah are "to do justice" (עֲשׂוֹת מִשְׁפָּט) by aligning every aspect of one's life in accordance to the LORD's will. In loving mercy (חֶסֶד), Judah is also to live lives in solidarity with God as well as each other, despite gender or social and economic status. The verb "to love" (אָהֵב), is used when speaking of חֶסֶד. It is the deepest love of which a wife has for her husband or a child for his/her parents. Third, God requires his people "to walk humbly" (הַצְנֵעַ לֶכֶת) with Him. They are to be in constant communication with Him while acknowledging their desperate need for Him. Their desires are to come from Him, their lives are to be constantly inspired by his will. Though the people of Judah may think they are living lives worthy of God's affirmation, they are lacking in reverence and obedience to the One they are ever dependent on.

Life Application

As Christians we must understand the implications of Micah 6:8 for our lives. As seen above, God is concerned about the inner spirituality of his people rather than religious displays of piety (vv. 6–7). God requires good of his people in acting with justice, maintaining a covenant loyalty with Him and others, and daily walking in dependence in Him. As Christians we are called to bring about the just and good will of our Creator while living in a constant relationship with Him. How else can we know how to fulfill his will? And just as our initial existence is dependent on Him, we must continue relying on God in every aspect of our life.

NT Scriptures

Matthew 5:1–11, 6:25–34; Romans 12:1–2, 9–21; Ephesians 4:1–6, 5:1–2; James 2:14–26

Prayer

O God, our almighty Creator and Sustainer, thank you for your perfect will and your unending love for all of creation! May your will be accomplished through your people and may we remain faithful to you always. May we seek your justice in this world. And may we remain in unity as we daily seek your wisdom and trust in you in all things. Amen.

Personal Notes and Prayers

Nahum 1:3

יְהוָֹה אֶרֶךְ אַפַּיִם וּגְדוֹל־כֹּחַ וְנַקֵּה לֹא יְנַקֶּה יְהוָה בְּסוּפָה וּבִשְׂעָרָה
דַּרְכּוֹ וְעָנָן אֲבַק רַגְלָיו׃

The LORD is slow to anger and great in power. (However)
He certainly does not acquit the guilty. His way is
in the storm and in the whirlwind,
and a cloud is the dust of his feet.

Biblical Context

ONE HUNDRED AND FIFTY years before Nahum, Jonah cried out to Nineveh with a message of repentance. God forgave the inhabitants of the city because they heeded Jonah's message and chose to repent from their evil ways. However, during the time of Nahum, evil had returned to Nineveh. God could no longer stand the cruelty and wickedness of the great city, and abhorred the way Assyria had treated Israel. By this time, the city of Nineveh was once again full of lies, full of violent inhabitants, committing promiscuity. It had become a stench to the nations. Consequently, God determined to destroy her and to send his prophet Nahum to declare its pending destruction. The message was harsh and to the point: God would pursue the Ninevites (his enemies) and would consume them like dry stubble. He would destroy their leaders and plunder their riches. God would bring ruin and desolation to the inhabitants of Nineveh, burn their chariots and put to the sword their armies. Hope was gone. It was time for God's wrath to be poured out on those who abused his people.

Life Application

The New King James version of this verse reads: "The LORD has his way in the whirlwind and the storm, and the clouds are the dust of his feet." When I was a child, growing up in tornado country, I was overjoyed to find this in my *Precious Moments Bible*. When a thunderstorm approached our area, the threat of tornados sent me trembling to the basement. This verse however told me that God was in control, even over winds that could suck people right out of their beds at night and destroy their homes. What a comfort this was to me. God could be relied upon during major storms, and I did not need to fear because God was in control. But for the sinners and the wicked (e.g., Nineveh), the whirlwind and the storm can be extremely threatening because God often uses natural elements to display terrifying power against the unjust. God is patient, kind, good and slow to anger but He is holy and will not disregard evil forever.

NT Scriptures

Romans 1:18–23; 9:22–24

Prayer

O LORD, you are our hiding place. You protect us from those who plot evil against us and from those who would seek to destroy our lives. You know those who devise wicked schemes and seek to harm the innocent. Build a hedge of protection around your people and deliver us from evil. For yours in the Kingdom, and the glory and the power forever and ever. Amen.

Personal Notes and Prayers

Nahum 1:7

טוֹב יְהוָה לְמָעוֹז בְּיוֹם צָרָה וְיֹדֵעַ חֹסֵי בוֹ׃

YHWH is good, a stronghold in the day of trouble.
He knows those who trust in Him.

Biblical Context

NAHUM (נַחוּם) MEANS "COMFORT" or "consolation." The name is a short form of Nehemiah (נְחֶמְיָה) which means "comfort of YHWH." As a prophet, Nahum the "comforter" is assigned the difficult task of pronouncing judgment upon Nineveh, the city that had repented after hearing the words of Jonah. Sadly, the next generation of Ninevites failed to remain faithful to the God of Israel and followed the evil schemes of the counselor of Belial, an enemy of YHWH (1:11). The Ninevites reinstated the worship of the Assyrian gods and returned to the practices of fornication, divination and sorcery (3:4). God took notice of their unfaithfulness, arrogance and pride, and pronounced upon them the same fate they had inflicted upon his people in Judah and Samaria a century earlier—destruction of vineyards, demolition of ramparts, deportation of people into exile, death of city dwellers. At the hand of the Babylonians, judgment eventually came upon Nineveh until Nahum's prophecy was fulfilled—the city was completely destroyed and masses of corpses filled the Assyrian capital (3:3). The God who was once their stronghold in the day of trouble had executed his judgment and removed his protection from them.

Life Application

Interspersed within the painful prophecy of Nahum are revelations of the character of the God of Israel. First, Nahum tells us that "God is good." One of the first things we learn as children is that God is good and that his goodness is available to all who turn to Him. What would life be if this truth were not the case? Could we love and respond to an all powerful Creator if we did not have the assurance that He is completely good? Second, we read that God is "a stronghold in the day of trouble." No human is immune to "days of trouble" and based on the words of Nahum, God is a fortress to all those who seek his protection during the difficult times of life. God does not promise a trouble-free existence but he does promise to provide protection and refuge. Third, God knows our thoughts and the intent of our hearts. Nothing is hidden from him. He "knows those who trust in him" and rewards them with his unfailing presence. As the name of Nahum reveals, we can find comfort in the certainty that these three divine attributes are absolutes.

NT Scriptures

2 Timothy 2:19

Prayer

O LORD, be our refuge and fortress in time of trouble. Deliver us from the schemes of the enemy. Hide us in the shadow of your wings and protect us from danger. Help us trust you with every fiber of our being and teach us how to live each day with the awareness that you are near. We love you LORD.

Personal Notes and Prayers

Nahum 1:7

טוֹב יְהוָֹה לְמָעוֹז בְּיוֹם צָרָה וְיֹדֵעַ חֹסֵי בוֹ:

The LORD is good, a stronghold in the day of need.
He knows those who take refuge in him.

Biblical Context

LIKE MOST OF THE prophets, Nahum was not one to sugar-coat his words. Prior to his brief message concerning the LORD's goodness (1:7), Nahum poses two questions, "Who can stand before his indignation? Who can rise up in the heat of his anger?" (1:6). The reader has no reply, no less the people of Nineveh. As powerful as the Ninevites may have once been, Nahum declares that their city will now be ravaged (3:7), her children will be killed (3:10), her leaders will be bound with chains (3:10), and her inhabitants will be helplessly scattered (3:18). Upon her exile, Nineveh will be found in her own desperate time of need. On that day, Nineveh will seek refuge from her enemies (3:11), but her former victims will be more ready to rejoice over her demise than to offer a helping hand (3:19). Though the Ninevites may have once sought refuge in the LORD and experienced his great compassion and mercy (see Jonah 3), it is clear that by Nahum's time this was no longer the case. The people had abandoned the LORD and returned to their wicked ways.

Life Application

What is clear in Nahum is that God's goodness and compassion are not at odds with his justice. God "knows those who take refuge in him" (1:7) and promises to be their stronghold and refuge. And even though "he is slow to anger," he will also "by no means acquit the guilty" (1:3). Those who have once known him and turn away from him open themselves up to divine retribution. Turning one's back on the LORD is synonymous with seeking refuge elsewhere—in other gods, in earthly things, in self. God will protect those who love him, but those who forsake him also forsake his goodness and protection. May our prayers concerning this ever be, "God, you are both good and just. Be our stronghold forever. May other forms of comfort be found lacking so that we might put our hope in you, and you alone."

NT Scriptures

2 Peter 3:9–10; 2 Timothy 2:19

Prayer

O LORD, why would we ever want to turn away from you? You are our refuge, our stronghold, our protector, our provider, our redeemer, and the lover of our soul. Help us remain faithful to you and give us the wisdom to forsake all other gods. There is none like you O LORD. In you alone we trust.

Personal Notes and Prayers

Habakkuk 1:2-4

עַד־אָ֤נָה יְהוָה֙ שִׁוַּ֣עְתִּי וְלֹ֣א תִשְׁמָ֔ע אֶזְעַ֥ק אֵלֶ֛יךָ חָמָ֖ס וְלֹ֥א תוֹשִֽׁיעַ:
לָ֣מָּה תַרְאֵ֤נִי אָ֙וֶן֙ וְעָמָ֣ל תַּבִּ֔יט וְשֹׁ֥ד וְחָמָ֖ס לְנֶגְדִּ֑י וַיְהִ֧י רִ֦יב וּמָד֖וֹן יִשָּֽׂא:
עַל־כֵּן֙ תָּפ֣וּג תּוֹרָ֔ה וְלֹא־יֵצֵ֥א לָנֶ֖צַח מִשְׁפָּ֑ט כִּ֤י רָשָׁע֙ מַכְתִּ֣יר אֶת־הַצַּדִּ֔יק עַל־כֵּ֛ן יֵצֵ֥א מִשְׁפָּ֖ט מְעֻקָּֽל:

How long, the LORD, do I cry out for help but you will not hear? I cry out to you "Violence!" but you do not deliver. Why do you cause me to see wickedness and cause me to look at trouble? Violence and devastation are before me. There is strife, and contention abounds. Therefore, the law grows ineffective and justice never goes forth,
 for the wicked surround the just.
 Therefore, crooked justice goes forth.

Biblical Context

THE OPENING VERSES OF Habakkuk are written in the form of a lament. The prophet is crying out to God about social injustice in the land. Scholars have proposed two interpretations for this passage. Some have suggested that the occurrences of רָשָׁע ("wicked") in verses 4 and 13 both refer to the Babylonians while others attribute the designation of "wicked" to the Judahites in verse 4 and to the Babylonians in verse 13. I agree with the latter, that it is more likely that in verse 4, Habakkuk is lamenting the glaring injustices perpetrated by the "wicked" Judahites rather than by the "wicked" Babylonians. It is ironic that the same adjective—"wicked"—is used to describe both the Israelites and the Babylonians. Habakkuk is deeply distressed by what he sees in Judah. So he asks why God has not delivered the innocent from their (Israelite) oppressors, and why He is allowing the righteous to suffer at their hand. Though Habakkuk has been praying for some time, God has not yet answered his prayers.

Life Application

This passage reveals two important truths. First, it is not wrong to pray and lament as Habakkuk did. When God responded to Habakkuk, He did not condemn him for his outcry. God himself lamented over Israel's rebellion in the wilderness (Exod 16:26; Num 14:11). When those who are violent behave unjustly and oppress the weak, it is acceptable for God's children to cry to Him for help. It is acceptable for Christians to lament before God. Second, we learn from Habakkuk that even when our deliverance seems delayed, we must continue to trust in God, even if we do not understand the reason for our suffering. God is faithful. He will deliver.

NT Scriptures

Luke 13:34–35; James 5:10–11

Prayer

Dear LORD, we pray that you would continue to deliver our nation from the injustice and wickedness that is oppressing it and the people within it. Help us not grow weary while waiting for Your deliverance. Forgive us for the times we have become impatient, and help us to continue to trust in you when we suffer, especially when we do not understand why.

Personal Notes and Prayers

Habakkuk 1:11

אָז חָלַף רוּחַ וַיַּעֲבֹר וְאָשֵׁם זוּ כֹחוֹ לֵאלֹהוֹ׃

Then as wind passes through and goes on, so the guilty one, whose strength is his god.

Biblical Context

HABAKKUK IS LAMENTING THAT evil surrounds him in Judah and asks how long he will have to tolerate it. God answers him saying that the violence and injustice in Judah will be met with even more violence. God is raising up the Babylonians to be his instrument of judgment upon the house of Judah. The verse above describes the Babylonians as unstoppable and guilty. The guilty (Babylonians) would bring the judgment of God upon the guilty (Israelites). Such were the consequences of disobedience and rebellion against God. God had no choice but to enact the judgment described in the covenant stipulations (see Deut. 28:15, 25). God was bound by his own covenant. As Israel—the Northern Kingdom—was punished for committing glaring sins and refusing to repent, so would Judah—the Southern Kingdom—experience the wrath of God. As with Israel, the people of Judah committed violence, injustice, evil, selfish acts, rebellion, religious syncretism, and responded with arrogance. God's call to repentance was ignored time and time again, therefore, God had no choice but to execute judgment upon Judah. The judgment on Judah was motivated by nothing but God's love and mercy for his chosen people.

Life Application

The Babylonians made strength their god. They did not ascribe power to the LORD, the Creator of the heavens and the earth, but to their own military might. Ultimately God would judge them for their guilt, but not yet. When we rely on our own power, ability and strength to move through life, we too become guilty. Relying on ourselves rather than relying on God may work for a while, but soon we discover that we have to repent from our pride and overconfidence, and turn back to the One who is all powerful and almighty, that is, if we want to survive. And when we experience misfortunes and calamities because of other people, we should remember that God is fully in control and knows how to deal with every situation. Therefore, let us not ask "Why me?" but rather let us acknowledge that God is greater than all things, and let us draw back to Him in repentance and praise.

NT Scriptures

Romans 9:33 (/Romans 10:11/1 Peter 2:6); 2 Corinthians 12:7–10

Prayer

O LORD, you judge sin, rebuke us for turning away from you, and punish us for our arrogance and pride. Forgive us LORD for our stubbornness. Have mercy on us for we are very weak. Teach us to live humbly before you and to follow you with abandon.

Personal Notes and Prayers

Habakkuk 2:4

הִנֵּה עֻפְּלָה לֹא־יָשְׁרָה נַפְשׁוֹ בּוֹ וְצַדִּיק בֶּאֱמוּנָתוֹ יִחְיֶה:

Notice the proud/the one puffed up, his soul is not upright within him. But the just shall live by his faith.

Biblical Context

THE PROPHET HABAKKUK QUESTIONS God saying, "How long shall I cry out to you and you refuse to hear and answer?" (1:2) "How long will you force me to look at iniquity, destruction and violence and do nothing?" (1:3) Habakkuk is desperate for an answer from God but when God finally speaks, the answer is not what the prophet wants to hear. God says, "I am raising the Chaldeans/Babylonians to commit violence against you and take you captive" (1:6–9). "What??" says the prophet. "You who are from everlasting, holy, a rock, and pure. How can you allow this to happen to your people?" (1:12–17 paraphrased). God instructs Habakkuk to write a plain message on tablets so that the people may read it and act upon it. The message is as follows: "Some are puffed up and dishonest but whoever puts their uncompromising faith and trust in me, and lives by faith and not by sight during these impending difficult times, will live and not die" (2:4 paraphrased). The concept of the just (צַדִּיק "righteous") living by faith (אֱמוּנָה "faithfulness, fidelity, trust, steadiness") is a fundamental one in Scripture. God delights in the those who live by faith in him (Pro 12:22) wholeheartedly (2 Chr 19:9). God showers blessings on such people (Pro 28:20). God's message to Israel was plain and simple. Faithfulness and trust in me will save your lives during these ferocious times. Look to me and nowhere else for there is only hope in me. Habakkuk understood the message and though he was aware of the challenging times that lay ahead, he concluded, "Though the fig tree does not blossom, nor fruit is on the vines, the produce of the olive fails and the fields yield no food, the flock is cut off from the fold and there is no herd in the stalls, yet I will rejoice in the LORD; I will take joy in the God of my salvation. God, the LORD, is my strength; he makes my feet like the deer's; he makes me tread on my high places" (3:17–19).

Life Application

Although it seems simple enough, living by faith through righteousness is difficult. A common interpretation to living a righteous life is to perform good works. Some believe that the foundation for a healthy relationship with God is based on the accumulation of good works. From God's point of view however, nothing could be further from the truth. The idea of building a relationship with God through holy or good works is dangerous. Faithfulness to God must come from the heart and by faith, and eventually be displayed through doing God's work. Good works should come as a result of faithfulness to God, not to gain favor with God. The prophet Isaiah made it clear that "all our righteous acts [צְדָקָה] are like filthy rags" (Is 64:6). We do not gain acceptance with God based on our righteous acts, rather, we live in the presence of God by faith and with a steadfast trust in Him. Sadly, much of the "joy of the LORD" is lost unnecessarily when pursuing salvation and righteousness through works.

NT Scriptures

Romans 1:16–17; Ephesians 2:8–9; Hebrews 10:37–38

Prayer

O LORD, our deeds are as filthy rags in your sight. Help us live in awe of YOUR deeds and help us look for them every day of our lives. For your deeds are praiseworthy, majestic, and awesome. Give us eyes to see who you are and what you do for us.

Personal Notes and Prayers

Habakkuk 2:14

כִּי תִּמָּלֵא הָאָרֶץ לָדַעַת אֶת־כְּבוֹד יְהוָה כַּמַּיִם יְכַסּוּ עַל־יָם׃

For the earth is filled with the knowledge of the glory of the LORD as the waters cover the sea.

Biblical Context

THE PROPHET HABAKKUK IS believed to be a contemporary of the prophets Zephaniah and Jeremiah (end of seventh century BCE). He prophesied to the people of Judah about the pending judgment of God at the hand of the Babylonians. Habakkuk's contemporaries and prophets before them had called the people to turn back to God, but to no avail. The Judahites were set in their evil ways and refused to repent. Habakkuk cried out to God in distress, but his pleas seemingly fell on deaf ears (1:2). God remained silent. Habakkuk complained about the chaotic life he witnessed in Judah and sought divine intervention, but it did not happen. God could not force his people to serve Him. God had done his part. He had provided instructions for righteous living, established a covenant with his people, gave them a homeland, blessed them with a Temple, raised prophets to call them back to God, gave them victory over enemies, and waited patiently for their repentance, but the people ignored the prophets and even killed some of them. Although the situation in Judah was chaotic and grim, Habakkuk knew that the knowledge of the LORD was available on earth as the waters cover the sea. Unfortunately, knowledge was ignored by the people of Judah in the same manner as it had been disregarded by the people of Israel in earlier times. According to Habakkuk, there was still hope for restoration, but the people were blinded by their sins, and seemed to enjoy their ungodly lives more than their relationship with God.

Life Application

Have you ever looked at the condition of this world and wondered where God is? When trials and tribulations come against you, do you cry out to God and wait impatiently for divine intervention to change your situation? The prophet Habakkuk lived in similar times and wondered where God was. The people of Israel had fallen away from God and their enemies were rapidly approaching the gates of Jerusalem. Habakkuk experienced inner turmoil as he wondered if God was truly with them. Yet, when Habakkuk regained his composure, he praised the LORD and proclaimed that the knowledge of the glory of the LORD was still covering the earth. Though he would be taken into exile, Habakkuk knew that wherever he went, there the LORD would be with him.

NT Scriptures

Romans 11:33–36; 15:14; 2 Corinthians 2:14; Colossians 1:9–12

Prayer

O LORD, raise up faithful and courageous prophets who will declare your message to our world. Make your voice resound in this earth and call us back to you, for we have turned away and we walk in darkness. Shed your light on our path and lead us back to you.

Personal Notes and Prayers

Habakkuk 3:3

אֱלוֹהַ מִתֵּימָן יָבוֹא וְקָדוֹשׁ מֵהַר־פָּארָן סֶלָה כִּסָּה שָׁמַיִם הוֹדוֹ
וּתְהִלָּתוֹ מָלְאָה הָאָרֶץ׃

God came from Teman, the Holy one from Mt Paran.
His glory covers the heavens and his praise fills the earth.

Biblical Context

TRYING TO NAVIGATE THE trouble in Judah, Habakkuk asks the LORD a series of straightforward questions: "*How long* must I call for help?" (1:2) "*Why* do you make me look at injustice and tolerate wrong?" (1:3) "*Why* do you tolerate the treacherous?" (1:13) "*Why* are you silent while the wicked swallow up the righteous?" (1:13) While the response to the first question may have shocked Habakkuk, for some reason God's responses to his other questions seems to have satisfied him. To the first question, God proclaims that he is raising up the Babylonians, that ruthless, impetuous, feared, violent, and dreaded people, to seize dwelling places not their own (including Judah). God accuses his own people of having mistreated foreign nations and consequently, they are now subject to the oppression of foreign nations. Habakkuk is obviously shaken as he responds: "Are you not from everlasting?" (1:12) "Since you are pure, how can you idly look at evil?" (1:13) Habakkuk begins to understand that God's people are meant to have a positive impact not only on their own little world, but on the global scene, so that God may be known throughout the earth. God is greater than his people and cares for all who are created in his image. Choosing to trust God in the midst of chaos, Habakkuk continues to proclaim God as the Holy One of Israel (1:12), as his Rock (1:12), as the everlasting God (1:12), as One who is pure (1:13), whose splendor and praise fill the heavens and the earth (3:3). And in the end, Habakkuk is satisfied with who God is and what God does, and breaks out in a spectacular song of joy and praise to the God of his salvation (3:17–19).

Life Application

Too often we are prone to look at God only in our own limited social context. We ask "Why?" "How long?" "When?" "Where?" and these questions are mostly about our personal lives. We forget that we serve a great, omniscient, omnipotent, omnipresent and loving God—the God of Abraham, Isaac and Jacob—who makes no mistakes. We forget that we serve the God of the multitudes who have come before us. We forget that we serve the same God they serve in Asia, Africa, South & North America, Australia, and the Middle East. Sometimes we just need, like Habakkuk, to be reminded of the greatness of our God who has a great plan for every human being and cares more about this world than we will ever know.

NT Scriptures

Matthew 5:14; 24:14; John 3:16; Colossians 3:15–20

Prayer

O LORD, there is darkness in the earth but there is light in your presence. Shine on us and show us your paths. Open our eyes that we may see the marvelous things you are doing all over the earth today. We want to see your works. We want to see you. We lift up our eyes and seek your face. Shine your light upon us O LORD.

Personal Notes and Prayers

Habakkuk 3:17–18

כִּֽי־תְאֵנָ֣ה לֹֽא־תִפְרָ֗ח וְאֵ֤ין יְבוּל֙ בַּגְּפָנִ֔ים כִּחֵשׁ֙ מַעֲשֵׂה־זַ֔יִת וּשְׁדֵמ֖וֹת לֹא־עָ֣שָׂה אֹ֑כֶל
גָּזַ֤ר מִמִּכְלָה֙ צֹ֔אן וְאֵ֥ין בָּקָ֖ר בָּרְפָתִֽים: וַאֲנִ֖י בַּיהוָ֣ה אֶעְל֑וֹזָה אָגִ֖ילָה בֵּאלֹהֵ֥י יִשְׁעִֽי:

Though the fig does not blossom and there is no fruit on the vine, though the yield of the olive fails and the fields do not produce food, though the flock is cut off and there are no cattle in the stalls, still I will exult in the LORD, I will rejoice in the God of my salvation.

Biblical Context

THE BOOK OF HABAKKUK was written in the late seventh or early sixth centuries BCE. By this time Israel (the Northern Kingdom) had fallen to the Assyrians and the Babylonian armies were a growing and approaching threat to Judah (the Southern Kingdom). Habakkuk questions why God would allow the wicked to prosper while allowing his own people to suffer hopelessly. Habakkuk knows that God is sufficiently powerful and can prevent calamity from devastating the people of Judah. It is incomprehensible to him that God would allow oppressors to continue marching unimpeded towards Judah. Surely God would stop them and protect his people, but God does not. Habakkuk earnestly pleads with God to come to the rescue of the Judahites, but God will not. Rather, God confirms Habakkuk's worst fears—the Israelites are going to experience divine judgment at the hand of the ruthless Babylonians. Habakkuk is understandably terrified. After pleading with God unsuccessfully for deliverance from the foreign enemies, Habakkuk resigns himself to submit to God's divine judgment. And rather than complain further, Habakkuk declares that even if God brings disaster on his people, he will continue to rejoice with pure joy, dancing, twirling and exulting the LORD, because no matter how bad things get, God is still his strength. The two verbs that appear in Habakkuk's final comments express joy and triumph. In verse eighteen, the verb אֶעְלוֹזָה means "I am willing to jump for joy" or "to exult, to triumph" while the verb אָגִילָה paints a glorious picture of twirling, spinning and rejoicing. Habakkuk knows that no matter what circumstances he faces, he can still rejoice because God is his strength and his salvation.

Life Application

It is believed that if Christians do everything right, God will answer every prayer with a "yes!" However, when bad things happen, we put a brave face on our suffering and wonder where God is during our times of sadness and pain. Habakkuk provides a tremendous example of trust in God in the midst of difficult circumstances. Like Habakkuk, we can affirm that God is our strength in the midst of trouble. Therefore, let us praise God, not based on our circumstances but because of who God is and who we are in Him. May we learn to dance, twirl, and rejoice as Habakkuk did, no matter what life brings our way.

NT Scriptures

Philippians 4:10–13; James 1:2–4

Prayer

O LORD, we want to celebrate you with all our hearts, all our minds and all our strength. Though we face difficult situations in life, we continue to celebrate you for you remain our God and Savior. You are our strength. You raise us up above life's circumstances and you celebrate with us. We will rejoice with you as you rejoice with us.

Personal Notes and Prayers

Habakkuk 3:17–18

כִּי־תְאֵנָה לֹא־תִפְרָח וְאֵין יְבוּל בַּגְּפָנִים כִּחֵשׁ מַעֲשֵׂה־זַיִת וּשְׁדֵמוֹת לֹא־עָשָׂה אֹכֶל

גָּזַר מִמִּכְלָה צֹאן וְאֵין בָּקָר בָּרְפָתִים: וַאֲנִי בַּיהוָה אֶעֱלוֹזָה אָגִילָה בֵּאלֹהֵי יִשְׁעִי:

Though the fig tree should not blossom, and there is no fruit on the vines, the produce of the olive fails, and the fields do not make food, from the fold the flock is divided, and there are no cattle in the stalls, yet I will rejoice in the LORD, I will exult in the God of my salvation.

Biblical Context

HABAKKUK PROPHESIED IN JUDAH during her invasion by the Babylonians. Before his very eyes, the prophet watches the final destruction of Jerusalem, the long-prophesied judgment for her disobedience, as well as the enslavement of God's people. Although a short book, Habakkuk wrestles with deep theological issues, namely how the LORD can allow his people to undergo such suffering. In the first two chapters, Habakkuk engages in a dialogue with the LORD, struggling to reconcile his love with his demand for justice. Habakkuk cries out to God as he watches the increasing chaos in Judah—iniquity, destruction, violence, evil, nakedness, drunkenness, strife and perversion are before him (1:2–4). While no specific words of comfort come, Habakkuk is finally able to pray the doxology found in chapter 3, recounting the power and sovereignty of the LORD. As he remembers who it is that he serves, he is able to respond with acceptance and worship. In the midst of the chaos that surrounds him, Habakkuk finds strength and joy in the LORD God.

Life Application

How do we cope when the unimaginable happens? What words of comfort can be given when our faith is shaken and our lives are broken? When asked to "give a reason for the hope that is within us" in the midst of suffering, what do we say? What is our reaction to the evil that surrounds us daily? Although Habakkuk wrestled with these issues, ultimately, he knew his hope must rest in the LORD of heaven and earth. Out of context, verses 17–18 can sound disingenuous or inauthentic: "All you need is trust!" However, placed within the larger context of the book of Habakkuk, they remind believers that the power of Almighty God is beyond any difficult life situation and dire circumstances. Like the prophet Habakkuk, we need to remind ourselves that God is mighty, loving, merciful, and seeks to bring salvation to those who trust in Him. God is in control of all things and longs to carry us to a place of joy and contentment, even in the midst of difficulties.

NT Scriptures

Matthew 5:11–12; John 16:22–24; Philippians 4:4–6

Prayer

O LORD, though judgment comes on the earth, we are not without hope. We stay silent before you and wait to hear from your comforting voice. We stand in awe of you and trust in your unfailing love. Though destruction is all around us, with great confidence we can declare, "The Lord is my strength. He makes my feet like the feet of a deer and enables me to go up on high places." O LORD, we trust in you.

Personal Notes and Prayers

Habakkuk 3:18

וַאֲנִי בַּיהוָה אֶעְלוֹזָה אָגִילָה בֵּאלֹהֵי יִשְׁעִי:

*I shall exalt in YHWH; I shall rejoice
in the God of my salvation.*

Biblical Context

THE PROPHET HABAKKUK HAS apparently foreseen the coming invasion of the Babylonian armies upon Judah (3:16). He realizes that this invasion is imminent and he feels helpless to prevent its coming. It is evident from the passage that this prophet is exceedingly troubled by what has been revealed to him by YHWH. He says, "in my place I tremble, because I must wait quietly for the day of distress, for the people to arise who will invade us." (1:16b). Habakkuk lists a few of the crop failures and livestock deaths sure to come, symbolic of the desperate situation which Judah will soon be thrust into, but concludes this list with the declaration, "yet I shall exalt in YHWH, I shall rejoice in the God of my deliverance!" For the prophet, YHWH is still sovereign, and whatever disaster befalls Judah, YHWH is no less worthy of praise.

Life Application

Some might describe this portion of Scripture as "fatalistic." What possible influence can simple believers have over challenging life circumstances? However difficult, circumstances of life do not change God's love, goodness, mercy and faithfulness towards us. The book of Hebrews describes how some men and women of faith saw great miracles and became powerful, while others equally faithful, experienced intense persecution and were forced into the wilderness. Yet the same God watched over all of them, rewarding them not with their circumstances but with the promise of new life to come. Freedom from the struggles of life is not always evident, however we can be assured, like Habakkuk, that what God has promised, God will do. He will deliver us from ALL our troubles. We can rejoice in all things because God is in control and He is our salvation.

NT Scriptures

Philippians 4:8-9, Hebrews 11; 1 Peter 1:6-7

Prayer

O LORD, our hope is in you. The circumstances of life are merciless and challenging, but you are far greater. You raise us up above the circumstances and give us hope. The world around us is dark and judgment is coming upon the earth, but in this we are confident: You are our refuge and strength. You are our help in times of trouble. You preserve our lives and renew our days. We are yours O LORD and we trust in you.

Personal Notes and Prayers

Habakkuk 3:18

וַאֲנִי בַּיהוָה אֶעְלוֹזָה אָגִילָה בֵּאלֹהֵי יִשְׁעִי׃

But in the LORD I will be exultant. I will rejoice in the God of my salvation.

Biblical Context

THE NATION OF JUDAH is corrupt, and Habakkuk begins his book by crying out and asking the LORD, "how long?" Nothing has been done about Judah's sin, so God answers that He is going to allow the Babylonians to come and judge them. This is not quite the answer Habakkuk wanted, because the Babylonians were much more evil than Judah. How could God use such an evil nation to judge Judah? God will use Babylon to judge, but in the midst of it all, the "righteous will live by faith" (2:4). Habakkuk is frightened of the future, of the judgment that is to come. But in chapter 3, he makes a choice. He decides to recount the things God has done. He decides to remind himself that God is good, no matter what. Although he trembles and decay enters his bones (3:16), he will exult in the LORD and rejoice in God. The Sovereign LORD is his strength, even in fear.

Life Application

Habakkuk is a great book because it is such a realistic explanation of the fears of life. Habakkuk wonders at God's justice. He questions *how* God could allow this type of judgment. But in the end, he *decides* to live by faith. He remembers the good character of his God, and he reminds himself that, because of the past, he has no reason not to trust God for the future. This is what gets us through day-to-day. We know who our God is, and we can trust that He will continue to provide for us in the good times and bad, in judgment and in peace. He is good and we will rejoice in the God who has saved us.

NT Scriptures

1 Peter 1:6–7; 5:6–7

Prayer

O LORD, how great is your faithfulness towards us. When we struggle, you are there. You refine us with fire and transform us into instruments of silver and gold, to be used for your glory and honor. Who is there in heaven but you, and on earth besides you. There is no other who sustains us, heals us, purifies us and transforms us from glory to glory into your image. How merciful you are to us. In our times of trials and difficulties, you walk with us and comfort us. You remind us that, "though the fig tree does not blossom and there is no fruit on the vines, though the olive crop fails and the fields produce no food though there are no sheep in the pen and no cattle in the stalls," you O LORD are our strength. You make our feet like those of deer and enable us to walk on mountain heights! Thank you LORD!

Personal Notes and Prayers

Zephaniah 2:3

בַּקְּשׁוּ אֶת־יְהוָה כָּל־עַנְוֵי הָאָרֶץ אֲשֶׁר מִשְׁפָּטוֹ פָּעָלוּ בַּקְּשׁוּ־צֶדֶק
בַּקְּשׁוּ עֲנָוָה אוּלַי תִּסָּתְרוּ בְּיוֹם אַף־יְהוָה:

Seek YHWH all you meek of the earth, who have upheld his justice. Seek righteousness, seek humility. Perhaps you will be hidden in the day of YHWH's anger.

Biblical Context

INTERESTINGLY, THE NAME ZEPHANIAH means "YHWH hides" or "YHWH has hidden" which is the exclamation point to this passage. The recurring theme in this prophecy is to "seek the LORD"—the phrase is repeated three times in this pericope. Why should one seek the LORD? Because only then can one be hidden in the LORD and protected from his wrath on the day of judgment. According to Zephaniah, those who did not seek the LORD and oppressed God's people—the Philistines, the Moabites, the Ammonites, the Cushites, the Assyrians—along with the rebellious inhabitants of Jerusalem, will suffer the wrath of God on the Day of the LORD. They have failed to seek the LORD. They have not turned to him and served him. The call to seek the LORD in Zephaniah is strong, serious, unwavering, and salvific. To seek the LORD is to seek righteousness and to seek humility, for God is righteous and humble. In the last chapter of Zephaniah, the outcome of a righteous life is unveiled. In that day, people will speak with a pure speech. They will call upon the name of the LORD and serve him in one accord. They will seek to act justly and speak the truth. They will lie down and not be afraid.

Life Application

In the New Testament, Paul reminds us that God did not appoint believers to wrath but to obtain peace, justice, righteousness, and salvation. In Revelation, the message of Zephaniah is echoed in these words: "Because you have kept My command to persevere, I will also keep you from the hour of trial which will come upon the whole earth." The invitation to seek the LORD and his righteousness has been extended to all, for it is good to continually seek the face of God. As the world slips into darker times, the LORD will protect those who seek him and live by his commandments.

NT Scriptures

Matthew 5:5; I Thessalonians 5:9; Revelation 3:10

Prayer

O LORD, you are so merciful to us. We cried out to you for forgiveness and you heard our cry. We repented of our sin and you cleansed us. We chose humility and you rewarded us with greatness. We endeavored to remain guiltless and you withheld your anger from us. Teach us to be faithful to you O LORD, and to live righteous lives in a world of unrighteousness. Teach us to keep your commands and observe your decrees. We are weak and we fall. You are strong and you raise us up to continue serving you with all our hearts. We are yours O LORD.

Personal Notes and Prayers

Zephaniah 3:17

יְהוָ֧ה אֱלֹהַ֛יִךְ בְּקִרְבֵּ֖ךְ גִּבּ֣וֹר יוֹשִׁ֑יעַ יָשִׂ֨ישׂ עָלַ֜יִךְ בְּשִׂמְחָ֗ה יַחֲרִישׁ֙
בְּאַ֣הֲבָת֔וֹ יָגִ֥יל עָלַ֖יִךְ בְּרִנָּֽה׃

The LORD your God is in your midst, a Mighty One who will save. He will rejoice over you with gladness. He will silence (you) by his love. He will dance joyfully over you with a ringing cry.

Biblical Context

GOD IS ANGRY. HE is ready to sweep away mankind from the face of the earth. Zephaniah announces the pending judgment against Judah. The inhabitants of Jerusalem have bowed down to the starry hosts and worshipped them. They have filled the temple with violence and deceit, and have replaced the LORD with their worthless idols. The people of Jerusalem have become complacent and drunk with wine. They are rich but their wealth is useless in the face of the upcoming judgment. The "Day of the LORD" is near declares Zephaniah, when sinners will be punished and those who commit violence will be destroyed. The Judahites will not be exempt because they have followed in the ways of foreign nations and have broken the covenant. In that day says the LORD, there will be cries, wails and devastation upon the earth. Distress, anguish, ruin and gloom will prevail and the stench of death will fill the air. But, once repentance has come and trust in God is restored, darkness will turn to light and sadness will turn to joy. God's wrath will come to an end and his anger will be silenced. His fury will be replaced with joy, gladness, dancing and a ringing cry. God will be the first to celebrate with shouts of joy and with dance.

Life Application

Imagine the most beautiful landscape painting you have seen. It is simply a reflection of the landscape God created. We can replicate it through art but we could never do justice to the original beauty of the scenery. Now imagine the most beautiful singing voice you have ever heard. God created that voice and gave it to one of his children. Now imagine the voice of the Creator. How would you describe the joyful sound that comes out of his mouth when He sings? God loves us so much and we give Him such joy that He breaks into song over us.

NT Scriptures

Luke 15:3–7; John 15:11; 16:16–24

Prayer

O LORD, dance and rejoice over us for we have repented from our sins and turned to you. Celebrate your power in us for we have humbled ourselves and now seek to obey your commands. We rejoice with you because we have received your mercy and have been saved by your outstretched hand. We now pursue righteousness and holiness. We join you at the table to feast on your delights. Keep us safe in your dwelling.

Personal Notes and Prayers

Zephaniah 3:17

יְהוָה אֱלֹהַיִךְ בְּקִרְבֵּךְ גִּבּוֹר יוֹשִׁיעַ יָשִׂישׂ עָלַיִךְ בְּשִׂמְחָה יַחֲרִישׁ
בְּאַהֲבָתוֹ יָגִיל עָלַיִךְ בְּרִנָּה:

The LORD your God is in your midst, a strong deliverer.
He will rejoice over you with gladness, he will cause you to
rest in his love, he will rejoice, twirling
over you with intense singing.

Biblical Context

OF THE THREE CHAPTERS in Zephaniah, all but the last few verses depict a graphic message of imminent judgment on Judah and her four surrounding nations: Philistia (west), Moab and Ammon (east), Cush (south) and Assyria (north). The expression, "the day of the LORD" is used more times in these chapters than by any other prophet emphasizing the impending wrath for the nation's rebellion, pride, and idolatry. Even Assyria, a boastful and threatening city is described abandoned and desolate. Through Zephaniah's language, all of the created order is depicted as overturned in judgment. Set against this picture of utter desolation for Judah and her neighboring nations is a picture of hope for a purified remnant. This promise of future blessing and restoration for God's people and the nations describes a glorious day of rejoicing filled with the LORD's presence. The near context of verse 17 stands in stark contrast to the message of judgment while boasting a beautiful and moving description of God's love and a future hope.

Life Application

Ever since Hillsong's *Mighty to Save* began to blare over Christian radio, I found myself raising my voice with the masses, entirely swept up in its catchy praise chorus. It was only later that I realized I had no idea what "mighty to save" even meant. I continually got hung up with the grammatical make up of the description of God, knowing it had to mean something beautiful, but unable to grasp the concept. Finally, the praise chorus took on new meaning set in the context of Zephaniah's endearing love poem. Here we see God's presence with us as a promise, his love as a message of hope, and his identity as a strong, just, hero, who is the first to lead his people into battle. The verse stands shouting a message of comfort following a dismal message of judgment. It points to a future restoration of the world when the LORD, the one who causes saving, will once again be in our midst. How meaningful and dynamic, then, is the beautiful threefold promise of his rejoicing over us, causing rest, and the opportunity to hear his voice singing, following the picture of our God as a strong deliverer, as mighty to save.

NT Scriptures

Matthew 28:20, John 14:16–17

Prayer

O LORD, how blessed we are to know that you rejoice over us, even when we fail to recognize you in our midst. We thank you for your love, your care, your Spirit, your Word, your encouragement, your healing, your protection and the hope you provide for an eternal future lived with you, in your kingdom. How we look forward to the day when we can experience fullness of joy in your presence.

Personal Notes and Prayers

Haggai 1:13

וַיֹּאמֶר חַגַּי מַלְאַךְ יְהוָה בְּמַלְאֲכוּת יְהוָה לָעָם לֵאמֹר אֲנִי אִתְּכֶם נְאֻם־יְהוָה:

Then Haggai the messenger of the LORD spoke with a message of the LORD to the people saying, "I am with you declares the LORD."

Biblical Context

THE JEWS WHO RETURNED from exile were faced with the task of rebuilding the Temple, the symbol that God dwelt with his people. Very early in the process, the people became discouraged. Their numbers were few and they could not build the Temple quickly and support themselves at the same time. In addition, their neighbors harassed them incessantly, so consequently, they stopped building. Then, God raised the prophet Haggai to rebuke his people for forsaking the rebuilding of the LORD's Temple and building their own homes. The people heeded the prophet's message and restarted their work on the Temple. The LORD spoke through Haggai again, and this time, the message was *"I am with you declares the LORD."* These were the words of assurance the struggling community of Jews needed to hear. Because they had decided to obey the word of the LORD and resume building the Temple, they were assured once again that the LORD was truly with them.

Life Application

When the LORD says *"I am with you"* it can mean a number of things. For the post-exilic Jews it meant that God was supporting the rebuilding of the Temple and the project would be a success. This is similar to the idea found in Paul's words in Romans 8:31, *"If God is for us who can stand against us?"* When God has identified the job He wants done, it will not fail. The Church is a great example of this. The LORD commissioned the twelve disciples to go into the world and make disciples of all nations.

He promised that He would be with them. Two thousand years later and that task is still being accomplished. There are countless stories of Christians who have overcome unbelievable obstacles to make disciples because the LORD was with them. It also means that He is literally "*with us*" (*Immanu-el*). One of the amazing promises that God has given to believers is that He resides with them in the person of the Holy Spirit. Not only does He reside with us, He resides in us. Our bodies are the temple of the LORD. Praise God for this truth!

NT Scriptures

Matthew 28:20; John 17:26; Romans 8:9–11, 31; Ephesians 2:22

Prayer

O LORD, you never leave us nor forsake us. What greater joy than to know that wherever we are, there you are also. You lead us and guide us. You reveal yourself to us and show us the way. What a privileged people we are!

Personal Notes and Prayers

Zechariah 1:3

וְאָמַרְתָּ אֲלֵהֶם כֹּה אָמַר יְהוָה צְבָאוֹת שׁוּבוּ אֵלַי נְאֻם יְהוָה צְבָאוֹת
וְאָשׁוּב אֲלֵיכֶם אָמַר יְהוָה צְבָאוֹת:

Say to them, "Thus says the LORD of Hosts: 'Return to me" says the LORD of Hosts, 'and I will return to you' says the LORD of Hosts."

Biblical Context

THREE TIMES IN THIS passage, we encounter the divine name יְהוָה צְבָאוֹת (*Adonai tsevaot*). In most English translations, this title is rendered "LORD of Hosts [of armies]" or "Almighty God." This divine name emphasizes God's power, especially his power over the gods of other nations. Decades before the prophet Zechariah came on the scene, Jerusalem fell to the Babylonians. Large groups of Jews were taken into exile to Babylon. When Zechariah spoke his prophetic message, his audience had been in exile for up to 85 years. Most of those to whom Zechariah spoke were likely born in Babylon (or later, Persia), never having personally known the blessings that God had bestowed upon his people in the Promised Land. To this generation, the Temple in Jerusalem was personally unfamiliar. Their forefathers had worshipped in the Temple, but their sins, violations of the covenant, and unwillingness to repent had invited God's judgment. And consequently, they had lost their Temple, their homes and their land. The new generation of Israelites who lived in exile knew they had been defeated and taken away from their ancestral land, and had no first-hand experience with the Temple in Jerusalem. The idea that their covenant God was "the LORD of Hosts [of Armies]" was only illusionary. How could their God be "the LORD of Hosts [of armies]" since their fathers had been defeated at the hand of foreign enemies. Yet, in God's eyes, it was not too late for the Israelites to return to the LORD. God was eager to forgive them and to renew his covenant with them. As Zechariah proclaimed, "If they chose to return to God, God would choose to return to them." This was great news for the exiled Israelites—finally, a message of hope.

Life Application

We may not relate to the exiled Israelites and we cannot claim that Zechariah is making this promise directly to us today. However, there are many similarities between us and those to whom he spoke. Most importantly, we worship the same God—יְהוָה צְבָאוֹת, the LORD of Hosts [of armies], the Almighty God. Like the Israelites, we are greatly influenced by our ancestors and by our own past. We tend to repeat the sins of our parents and commit our own sins again and again. And yet, it is never too late for us to receive God's forgiveness and be restored to Him. Just as God did then, God comes to us today and urges us to repent, even if we have lived in sin for years. And when we repent and return, God renews his power in our lives and restores us to himself. We are never too far from him, too deep into sin, and too lost for hope.

NT Scriptures

Matthew 3:2; Acts 3:19–21; 8:22

Prayer

O LORD, when we repent and turn to you, you remove our sins as far as the east is from the west. You bury them in the sea of forgetfulness. You never remind us of our past sins, for you have compassion on us and you cleanse us from all unrighteousness. O how we are blessed.

Personal Notes and Prayers

Zechariah 3:1

וַיַּרְאֵנִי אֶת־יְהוֹשֻׁעַ הַכֹּהֵן הַגָּדוֹל עֹמֵד לִפְנֵי מַלְאַךְ יְהוָה וְהַשָּׂטָן עֹמֵד
עַל־יְמִינוֹ לְשִׂטְנוֹ:

וַיֹּאמֶר יְהוָה אֶל־הַשָּׂטָן יִגְעַר יְהוָה בְּךָ הַשָּׂטָן וְיִגְעַר יְהוָה בְּךָ הַבֹּחֵר
בִּירוּשָׁלָםִ הֲלוֹא זֶה אוּד מֻצָּל מֵאֵשׁ:

*Then he showed me Joshua the High Priest standing before
the angel of the LORD, also the accuser standing at his
right side to accuse him. But the LORD said to the accuser,
"the LORD rebukes you accuser, the LORD, the One
who has chosen Jerusalem, rebukes you!"*

Biblical Context

AROUND 520 BCE, THE nation of Israel was returning to Jerusalem and rebuilding the city after being exiled for forsaking the LORD. When the prophet Zechariah came on the scene, the rebuilding of the temple had quickly tapered off because of apathy and discouragement. Zechariah was called to encourage the people and to remind them that the LORD was not done with his chosen nation. In a series of visions, the prophet Zechariah finds himself watching a scene from the heavenly courtroom. The accused was the representative of the nation of Israel, Joshua the High Priest, standing in filthy clothes. The prosecutor was הַשָּׂטָן "the accuser." The advocate was the Angel of the LORD and the judge was the LORD himself. The accuser had plenty of evidence in his favor to argue that God had rejected Israel. The fact that God's chosen nation had been conquered and exiled could be considered *prima facie* evidence. Perhaps the accuser was going to argue that Joshua was disqualified to be the High Priest, that he was somehow defiled by sin and therefore was unfit to function within the cultic system. The nature of the accusation will never be known because, before the accuser could speak a word, he is emphatically rebuked by the LORD himself. Then the Angel of the LORD removes Joshua's filthy clothes, signifying the removal of his sin, and clothes him in clean garments, making him fit for service. The event is a clear message of God's acceptance of the remnant of Israel.

Life Application

Not a single accusation was made! In spite of all the evidence the accuser was silenced simply because the LORD had chosen Jerusalem, and because He had chosen the nation of Israel to be his people. There is an unfathomable depth to God's forgiveness pictured in this scene. The LORD's forgiveness is not based on our merit. Like Joshua and Israel, we all stand before the LORD with a list of things that could be used to condemn us. But our "advocate is Jesus Christ the righteous," and based on his work on the cross, we can stand boldly before the throne of God. God will silence our accuser before he can even speak a word. Glory be to his glorious Name!

NT Scriptures

Romans 5:6–8; 8:1–2, 31–34; 1 John 2:1–2

Prayer

O LORD, because you defend us from the attacks of the enemy, we will not be moved. You preserve our life and maintain our cause. You set our feet on a solid rock to stay. You avenge us when we are targeted by the accuser. We are safe in you.

Personal Notes and Prayers

Zechariah 4:6

וַיַּעַן וַיֹּאמֶר אֵלַי לֵאמֹר זֶה דְּבַר־יְהוָה אֶל־זְרֻבָּבֶל לֵאמֹר לֹא בְחַיִל וְלֹא בְכֹחַ

כִּי אִם־בְּרוּחִי אָמַר יְהוָה צְבָאוֹת:

So he answered and said to me: "This is the word of YHWH to Zerubbabel: 'Not by might nor by power but by my Spirit,' says YHWH of Hosts."

Biblical Context

ONCE AGAIN, A PROPHET calls God's people to repentance. "Turn from your evil ways and your evil practices" says the LORD (1:4). In anger, God has withheld mercy from Jerusalem and from the towns of Judah because of their sins (1:12). But God is "jealous/zealous for Jerusalem and Zion" (1:14). He loves his people and out of mercy, He promises to return to Jerusalem, to bring prosperity to the towns of Judah, to comfort Zion and to watch over the rebuilding of his house (1:16–17). Jerusalem will be a city where the glory of God will be revealed, a city whose walls will be God himself. God will protect Jerusalem with his fire and will bring his people back from exile (2:5–6). He will live within the city with love and compassion for its inhabitants (2:10). In the third vision, the prophet Zechariah delivers a word concerning Zerubbabel who will rebuild the temple in Jerusalem. He will not do so in his own strength, but in the power of the Spirit, says the LORD. And as God said, so it was—by the power of his Spirit. God provided strength and ability to Zerubbabel for completing his task through his Spirit.

Life Application

It is clear that God wants us to rely on his Spirit instead of living life in our own limited human strength. God provides help and assistance through his Spirit for us to fulfill his will and establish his Kingdom on earth. God has made his supernatural power available to us, as he did to

Zerubbabel. We have not been left to our own devices. God is with us, in us, and works through us by the power of the Holy Spirit. And as long as we are on this earth, we can rely on this amazing gift from God—the Holy Spirit.

NT Scriptures

Matthew 12:18–21; John 14:26; Acts 2:17–18

Prayer

O LORD, we thank you for sending your Holy Spirit to teach us what to say, to counsel us, and to remind us of everything Jesus taught his disciples. We thank you for empowering us with your Holy Spirit to speak your word with boldness and to testify of your greatness. We thank you for filling us with your Holy Spirit who sanctifies us and cleanses us from all sins. You have made our bodies the temples of your Holy Spirit. May we not grieve the Holy Spirit who lives in us and renews us day by day.

Personal Notes and Prayers

Zechariah 9:9

גִּילִי מְאֹד בַּת־צִיּוֹן הָרִיעִי בַּת יְרוּשָׁלִַם הִנֵּה מַלְכֵּךְ יָבוֹא לָךְ צַדִּיק וְנוֹשָׁע הוּא

עָנִי וְרֹכֵב עַל־חֲמוֹר וְעַל־עַיִר בֶּן־אֲתֹנוֹת:

Spin for joy abundantly, O daughter of Zion! Cry out, O daughter of Jerusalem! Here your king comes to you, righteous and the one who saves, humble and riding on a donkey, on a colt, the foal of a donkey.

Biblical Context

THE ISRAELITES HAVE RETURNED from exile. They were punished by God for their unfaithfulness to him and are now restored and brought back to their land. Not only are they allowed to return but they are also promised a new temple, a restored community, the return of God's presence and protection through a king. After years and years of hopelessness, there is hope again. God is faithful and merciful to his people, as he brings them back and reaffirms his love for them. In this chapter the prophet is declaring judgment on Israel's enemies, and announcing that the people will return to their Land. This would have been something to hope in and something to look forward to in the hard times. This verse is declaring that the King will return and when He comes, the people will sing and dance for joy, for the LORD is faithful. He has fulfilled his promises to them. He has remembered them and been merciful to them despite their sinfulness and unfaithfulness. The King is righteous and he has come to save them and, therefore, all will praise the LORD.

Life Application

God has fulfilled his promise to his people through the sending of his son, the King, Jesus. This King was righteous and sinless, the perfect atoning sacrifice and the propitiation for our sin. This King was humble, even became a servant and washed the feet of those he was to rule over.

This King came into Jerusalem riding on the colt of a donkey. Not only are the people of Israel to "cry out" and "rejoice," but all the nations of the world are to rejoice with them. The word גִּיל literally means "to twirl with joy." In this text, it appears as an imperative—a command. The word הָרִיעִי which means to "cry out" or "shout" is also a command. Therefore, let us rejoice, spin for joy and to shout to the LORD so that all may hear that our King has come and He has brought hope and salvation to all.

NT Scriptures

Luke 19:28–40

Prayer

Thank you LORD for coming to earth to save us. We rejoice in you all day and every day. You have given us salvation and eternal life. We sing and dance and declare that you are the King of kings and the LORD of LORD who comes with salvation.

Personal Notes and Prayers

Zechariah 9:9

גִּילִי מְאֹד בַּת־צִיּוֹן הָרִיעִי בַּת יְרוּשָׁלַ͏ִם הִנֵּה מַלְכֵּךְ יָבוֹא לָךְ צַדִּיק
וְנוֹשָׁע הוּא
עָנִי וְרֹכֵב עַל־חֲמוֹר וְעַל־עַיִר בֶּן־אֲתֹנוֹת:

Rejoice exceedingly, O Daughter of Zion! Raise a shout, O Daughter of Jerusalem! Behold! Your King shall come to you! Righteous and having salvation is He! He is lowly and riding upon a donkey, upon a male donkey, a son of female donkeys.

Biblical Context

ZECHARIAH, A CONTEMPORARY OF Haggai (see Hag 1:1; Zech 1:1), was among those who returned from exile. He was instrumental in calling people to finish the rebuilding of the temple. Zechariah was given a message to proclaim the coming of the Messiah, a fact that is explicitly recognized by gospel writers (see Matt 21:1–5; John 12:14–15). Zechariah 9:9 includes an emphatic command to praise God with passion and excitement. גִּילִי "rejoice!" and הָרִיעִי "raise a shout!" are both imperatives. The coupling of these verbs—גִּילִי and הָרִיעִי—and the inclusion of the term מְאֹד "exceedingly" indicate heightened emphasis in the message of the prophet. The LORD *really* wants his people to praise. He commands *all* the inhabitants of Jerusalem *together* to praise Him. Though the people had returned from exile, they were still not "free." Jerusalem and the temple were being rebuilt but not to their former glory. So why the command to praise and rejoice? It was because *the King* was coming! By using the interjection הִנֵּה, and placing the subject "your king" before the verb "he shall come," the author highlights *the King* and not the act of his coming. *The King* himself was the reason for the praise and rejoicing. The author provides four descriptors for this coming *King*. First, He is righteous (צַדִּיק). Second, He brings salvation (וְנוֹשָׁע). The use of the participle implies ongoing action: He had, has, and will bring salvation! Third, though not expected, He is lowly, afflicted, and poor (עָנִי). Fourth,

He will be riding (וְרֹכֵב) on a donkey's colt. The description of the colt draws attention to its significance, as all four Gospels later record, recognizing Jesus as this King. This verse is an emphatic command to praise because of Israel's coming King.

Life Application

At times we find it difficult to praise, impossible to rejoice, and if we were to raise a shout it may not be joyous! Like many of the Israelites to whom Zechariah prophesied, our circumstances can discourage us, keep us from praise, and even turn us away from our God. Nevertheless, He commands us to rejoice exceedingly and raise a *joyful* shout! And we can do it! If our reason for praise is *not* our circumstances, but is rather our King Jesus, then we *can* praise in all circumstances. After all, our King *has* come and He is coming again. So let us rejoice exceedingly and raise a shout, for our *King* has come to us and He is coming again! Righteous and bringing salvation. He was lowly, but now He is highly exalted!

NT Scriptures

Matthew 21:1–11; Mark 11:1–11; Luke 19:28–40; John 12:12–16

Prayer

Heavenly Father, I rejoice and raise a shout knowing that my King has come and is coming again. I rejoice knowing that He is righteous, brings salvation, is humble, and though He came lowly and afflicted, He is now exalted! Help me praise You without ceasing because of Who You are, regardless of my circumstances. In Jesus's glorious name, I rejoice.

Personal Notes and Prayers

Malachi 2:7

כִּי־שִׂפְתֵי כֹהֵן יִשְׁמְרוּ־דַעַת וְתוֹרָה יְבַקְשׁוּ מִפִּיהוּ כִּי מַלְאַךְ יְהוָה־
צְבָאוֹת הוּא:

For the lips of a priest should preserve knowledge and from his mouth they should seek instruction for he is a messenger of the LORD of Hosts.

Biblical Context

IN THIS PASSAGE, GOD rebukes the priests of Malachi's day for offering defiled sacrifices on their altars and for leading the people astray with their words. According to the prophet, the priests of his day were not teaching and leading according to God's Word. Rather, they were misleading the people and causing them to stumble. Levi with whom God had established a covenant was to serve as a model of leadership for the priests perpetually. Levi had not led the people astray, rather "he revered me [God] and stood in awe of my [his] name. True instruction was in his mouth and nothing false was found on his lips" (2:6). Unfortunately, the priests who served during Malachi's day had "turned from the way and by your [their] teaching caused many to stumble" (2:5b-6, 8). The word שמר "preserve" found here has many nuances in English—"to keep, to watch over, to observe, to obey, and to devote oneself to." The priests were to seek the LORD and know his teachings so that they could properly instruct the people of God with divine knowledge. They were not to bring their own message to the assembly but rather they were to be "messengers of the LORD of Hosts." However, their lack of obedience not only brought about punishment, humiliation and a curse over them, but as a result of their false prophetic messages, the people were led astray away from the God of Abraham, Isaac and Jacob and suffered loss.

Life Application

Are you called to be in leadership in the church today? Are you a spiritual leader who is "preserving" the knowledge of God? Are you leading the flock of God in the path that leads to salvation or are you leading the flock astray? You may have studied Greek, Hebrew and/or Aramaic to better understand the Word of God. You may be digging deep into the meaning of the biblical text and seeking to exegete the text accurately. If so, are you doing it to be a better mouthpiece for God, a better instrument in his hands? As leaders in the Kingdom of God, we need to learn the Word of God in order to have an impact on the world. We need to preserve divine knowledge so that we can truly be the "messenger[s] of the LORD of Hosts" on this earth.

NT Scriptures

Matthew 23

Prayer

O LORD, we lift up our spiritual leaders to you. We pray that they be filled with your Holy Spirit and speak your word boldly. We pray that their hearts be filled with a love for you and that their minds be filled with the divine knowledge you reveal in your word. We pray that their feet would walk in your ways as they lead their flock in the paths of righteousness.

Personal Notes and Prayers

Malachi 3:6

כִּי אֲנִי יְהוָה לֹא שָׁנִיתִי וְאַתֶּם בְּנֵי־יַעֲקֹב לֹא כְלִיתֶם:

For I, the LORD, change not, so you sons of Jacob have not perished.

Biblical Context

IN THE PREVIOUS TWO chapters, Malachi outlines several ways in which Israel offended God. The priests were still going through the motions of offering sacrifice and honoring God. However, the things that they offered were unfit for sacrifice and their behavior toward the things of God and toward one another were completely unacceptable. God, through Malachi, threatens to throw the religious leaders out with the garbage. He laments that there is no one to shut the gates of the temple to prevent the priests from continuing their grotesque displays. In the midst of this litany of offenses, God affirms an amazing character trait that is far outside normal human experience: God does not change. Though their actions richly deserve destruction, they will not be utterly destroyed solely because God is faithful to his promises. God's covenant keeping is not at the mercy of the fickle human hearts. God himself does not change, though, it is implied, the sons of Jacob obviously do change. Also, it is the sons of Jacob, themselves, who are in danger of being destroyed not God. Their negligence however cannot change who God is. God is unchangeable. He loves those whom He has chosen even if they behave against his will. God is a redeemer who brings sinners back to his ways.

Life Application

How comforting to remember that, like his love toward Israel, God's love toward us does not change as a result of our erratic, selfish, sinful behavior. God did not tell Israel that they would not be punished for their behavior or that they would not suffer consequences. He tells them that He remains the same God who made a covenant with their fathers and that He will keep the covenant because and only because He is God and does not change. In our Christian walk, we sometimes stumble and fall. Sometimes we run headlong toward the very things that God has cautioned us against. We are sometimes disobedient. But we can cling to the knowledge that God, like a good parent, will continue to love us and will not leave us. This is not cheap grace (i.e., do whatever you want because God will forgive you) rather this is very costly grace. In the end, God remains faithful to us, He make us aware of the cost of our sins and He forgives us.

NT Scriptures

2 Timothy 2:13; Hebrews 10:23; 13:8

Prayer

O LORD, were it not for your love, we would be consumed. Were it not for your grace, we would be destroyed. Were it not for your faithfulness to us, we would surely have perished. Even in our weakness, you are there. You do not condemn us but rather, you strengthen us. You are the strength of our lives. We need you LORD.

Personal Notes and Prayers

Malachi 3:6

כִּ֛י אֲנִ֥י יְהוָ֖ה לֹ֣א שָׁנִ֑יתִי וְאַתֶּ֥ם בְּנֵֽי־יַעֲקֹ֖ב לֹ֥א כְלִיתֶֽם׃

For I am YHWH, I do not change; therefore you, sons of Jacob, are not consumed.

Biblical Context

THE MESSENGER IS COMING, God's purifier. The time for justice has come against the sons of Jacob. Like their forefathers, they have turned away and forsaken God's decrees (3:7). They have partnered with "sorcerers, adulterers and perjurers", defrauded laborers of their wages, oppressed the widows and the fatherless, and deprived the foreigners of justice (3:5). They have robbed God by keeping and eating the tithe (3:8). They have spoken arrogantly against him saying, "It is futile to serve God" (3:13). God who is like a "refiner's fire and a launderer's soap" announces judgment upon his people if they refuse to repent. He urges them to return to him and follow his decrees. Those who feared the LORD received the message of the prophet, consulted with each other and decided to return to him and honor his name. God heard their conversation and turned his judgement into compassion for his own "treasured possession" (3:17). In verse 5, God reminds his people of his unchanging nature. His ways are dependable and his justice and mercy can be relied upon, even when the ways of man have gone astray.

Life Application

The people I deal with day-to-day are certainly changeable. One minute they want this, the next, they want that. They make decisions only to reverse them the next day. Change is good. I am quite proud, for example, of my spiritual growth over the past, say, ten years. I would not want to view the world, God, and those who are in my life the way I viewed them ten years ago. Yet I am still conscious that my choices are often inconsistent, that I am wholeheartedly faithful to God one day and superficially the next. I suppose it is a rather predictable by-product of human nature that I feel as though I am failing on a regular basis. However, the words of the prophet remind me that God is faithful. He does not change, his promises are true, and He will not allow me to be consumed as I seek to live in his will. I trust in him.

NT Scriptures

1 Corinthians 1:9; 1 Thessalonians 5:23–24

Prayer

O LORD, you are faithful. You are patient and kind. You understand our frailty. You know our imperfections. You see us teeter and totter and yet, you remain faithful to us. Where would we be without the assurance that you love us and sustain us in our fragile state. Because of your goodness, we are not consumed. Thank you O LORD.

Personal Notes and Prayers

Malachi 3:24 [4:6]

וְהֵשִׁיב לֵב־אָבוֹת עַל־בָּנִים וְלֵב בָּנִים עַל־אֲבוֹתָם פֶּן־אָבוֹא וְהִכֵּיתִי
אֶת־הָאָרֶץ חֵרֶם׃

*He will turn the hearts of fathers towards their sons and
the hearts of sons towards their fathers lest I come
and strike the earth with destruction.*

Biblical Context

THE MESSAGE OF MALACHI is a rebuke to Israel for desecrating the Temple's sacrificial system. The LORD sees this as such a grievous sin that threats of judgment are spread throughout the book. The passage about Elijah's reconciling mission comes at the very end of the book. According to Malachi, Elijah will be sent to mend relationships between "fathers" and "sons." However, the passage ends with a sobering conclusion. Unless the mending of these relationships take place, God will send judgment upon the land.

Life Application

We could think of "fathers and sons" in general terms and see them as representing all human relationships. Peaceful and loving relationships between family members are surely what God wants for all people. As a man, I know the pain of a strained relationship with my father. It is nice to imagine that God could send someone with the specific purpose of mending that relationship. It would certainly produce deep spiritual healing for both of us. In churches I have attended, the congregants have been asked to pray that God would send the "spirit of Elijah" to mend the hurts that exist between Christian fathers and sons. These times of prayer usually become emotional times of reflection, repentance and reconciliation. According to the prophet Malachi, reconciliation is so important to God that judgment will be sent if reconciliation does not take place between fathers and sons. So, whether Elijah is an actual prophetic individual or a representation of the Messiah, the proper response to his visit is reconciliation. This passage makes me reflect on what I can do to mend the strained relationship with my father.

NT Scriptures

Matthew 22:37–39

Prayer

O Father in heaven, how thankful we are that you made it possible for us to come to you for healing, restoration and redemption. You know the chasm that separates us from others. You know the pain in our hearts. We ask you to show us how to restore the broken relationships in our lives. Jesus prayed that we would be one as you and your Son are one. Reveal this oneness to us and show us how to attain it. Forgive us for selfishly preserving our broken relationships and for ignoring the opportunities you provide for healing. Have mercy on us and heal us!

Personal Notes and Prayers

Psalm 8:2 [1]

יְהוָה אֲדֹנֵינוּ מָה־אַדִּיר שִׁמְךָ בְּכָל־הָאָרֶץ אֲשֶׁר תְּנָה הוֹדְךָ
עַל־הַשָּׁמָיִם׃

O LORD, our LORD, how magnificent is your name in all the earth! You have set your glory over the heavens.

Biblical Context

THIS VERSE OPENS A beautiful poem about the majesty of the name of God. The poem is a psalm of David, Israel's greatest king, with whom God established an enduring covenant. The poem is entirely devoted to praising God who is hailed for his greatness and majesty. First, the name of the LORD (יְהוָה) is highlighted for its magnificence. It is by this name that God revealed himself to his people (Exod 6:3). Second, God displayed his greatness by setting his glory over the heavens and creating mankind to rule over the earth. He positioned the stars in their place (8:3) and designed man as the crowning achievement of his creation (8:5–6). Next, the psalmist speaks of God's tender care for his people—babies worship him (8:2) and mankind is created "a little lower than God" to be in intimate fellowship with him. So significant is this verse about the magnificence of the name of the LORD that it is repeated at the conclusion of the psalm and forms an inclusio—a poetic feature that frames the poem and highlights an important theme.

Life Application

One of the biggest mental, emotional, and spiritual shifts we make during our spiritual growth is the realization that we are quite insignificant in comparison to our LORD. Although we were created in God's image and made only a little lower than God himself, we are still frail humans who need a great and magnificent God. Our complete dependence must be upon him who created us for his purposes. It is God who is great and magnificent; it is his name the world shall know, and it is his glory that fills the universe. He has certainly exalted humanity, and as a result, we are tasked with a great responsibility, but all that we are and all that we do is still infinitesimal in comparison to the LORD and his work in this world. May this verse encourage us in humility and warn us against pride, as we marvel at all that the Creator of the Universe has done and is doing in our lives and our world.

NT Scriptures

Romans 12:3; Ephesians 2:8–10

Prayer

O LORD, how majestic is your name in all the earth. How blessed we are to know you by name and to be invited into deep intimacy with you. Help us honor your name in everything we say and do. Do not let us desecrate your name and dim your glory in this earth. Thank you for placing your name in our mouths and on our lips. To you be the glory!

Personal Notes and Prayers

Psalm 12:4 [3]

יַכְרֵת יְהוָה כָּל־שִׂפְתֵי חֲלָקוֹת לָשׁוֹן מְדַבֶּרֶת גְּדֹלוֹת:

May the LORD cut off all divisive lips, (and) the tongue that boasts of great things.

Biblical Context

SCRIPTURE HAS MUCH TO say about the power of the tongue. When misused and left unbridled, the tongue can cause profound damage to the lives of its hearers: it oppresses the poor and needy (Ps 12:6), it brings destruction (Pro 10:14), it promotes violence (Pro 13:2), it invites ruin (Pro 17:20, 26:28), it spreads poison (Rom 3:13, Jas 3:8), it sows strife and discord (Pro 18:6, 21:9), and it even brings death (Pro 18:21). In other words, it affects its victims deeply and often irreparably. The righteous tongue on the other hand produces results that reflect the very nature of God. A tamed and instructed tongue reveals divine wisdom (Pro 10:31, 18:4), it brings health to the body (Pro 16:24), it interrupts strife and conflicts (Pro 26:20), it keeps its owner from trouble (Pro 21:23), it authenticates godly leadership (Mal 2:7), it confirms one's eternal salvation (Phil 2:11), it supports peace and unity (1 Pet 3:10–11), and it promotes life (Pro 15:4, 18:21, 1 Pet 3:10).

Life Application

What a powerful tool God has given each one of us. How we use this tool is left to our own discretion. We can choose to build or to tear down, to bless or to curse, to unite or to divide, and to heal or to hurt; the choice is ours. With the gift of speech comes great responsibility. Let us choose to imitate God and to create a world that is impacted powerfully and positively by the Word of God so that the Kingdom of God may be established in our midst.

NT Scriptures

Luke 6:44–45, Romans 10:8–10

Prayer

O LORD, how often we sin with our tongue. Please forgive us. Teach us to speak as you speak—bringing life, healing and redemption to all who would listen. Help us change this world for good one hearer at a time, with words that are fitly spoken and in due season. Have mercy on us for the wrong seeds we have sown in the past. Help us plant gardens of life with the words of our mouths.

Personal Notes and Prayers

Psalm 19:2 [1]

הַשָּׁמַיִם מְסַפְּרִים כְּבוֹד־אֵל וּמַעֲשֵׂה יָדָיו מַגִּיד הָרָקִיעַ׃

The heavens are retelling the glory of God; the firmament is declaring the work of his hands.

Biblical Context

ASTRONOMERS HAVE TRIED FOR millennia to understand the meaning of stars, their movements, composition, purpose, and exact location. The heavens are like an artist's canvas. From morning till night, they morph from one shade of blue to another. They display magnificent pink sunrises and end the day with glorious multicolor sunsets. The heavens speak to us unceasingly, from morning until night. Shortly after I became a believer, I had an experience that enabled me to appreciate the heavens in a new way. I remember walking out of my apartment building, and as I look up to the skies, I became acutely aware that God's eyes were looking down upon the earth. I walked several blocks, glancing at the skies after every few steps, and the realization that I could never escape God's eyes gripped my heart. It was as if I could read a huge G-O-D in the heavens. His presence was almost tangible. Since that incident, the skies have never looked the same to me.

Life Application

The two participles (מְסַפְּרִים "*are retelling*" and מַגִּיד "*is declaring*") suggest much drama and audible activity coming from above. These verbs imply continuous chatter, relentless communication, endless story telling, and persistent attempts to reveal to humans the glory of God and the majesty of his creation. God speaks to us in many ways. According to Scripture, God's heavens serve as agents of revelation and channels of communication. Are we listening? What is God saying to you?

NT Scriptures

Matthew 16:1–3; Acts 7:55–56

Prayer

Thank you LORD for revealing your majesty and your glory to your children. Help us see you, hear you and respond with grateful hearts and with overwhelming amazement at the works of your hands. Help us be aware of your constant presence with us. Indeed, you "never leave us nor forsake us." What an awesome God you are!

Personal Notes and Prayers

Psalm 19:8 [7]

תּוֹרַת יְהוָה תְּמִימָה מְשִׁיבַת נָפֶשׁ עֵדוּת יְהוָה נֶאֱמָנָה מַחְכִּימַת פֶּתִי׃

*The law of the LORD is perfect, restoring the soul.
The testimony of the LORD is trustworthy,
making wise the simple.*

Biblical Context

PSALM 19 IS DIVIDED into two parts. The first part (vv.1–7) focuses primarily on the glory of God proclaimed by the hosts of the heavens—sun, moon, stars—during the day and during the night. The second part (vv.8–15) highlights the significant merits of the Law of the LORD. As one quickly notes, the author uses several keywords to feature the main theme of the poem (i.e., the importance of God's Word in the life of his people). Keywords include "law" (תּוֹרָה), "testimony" (עֵדוּת), "precept" (פִּקּוּד), "ordinance" (מִשְׁפָּט), and "commandment" (מִצְוָה). According to the psalmist, the law, testimony, precepts, ordinances, and commandments of the LORD are perfect, life-giving, sure, wisdom-filled, right, joy-producing, pure, true, and righteous. They make wise anyone who seeks them more than fine gold and sweeten the life of the believer more than a honeycomb. Nothing can be compared to the power of the Word of God in the life of a worshipper.

Life Application

The law and testimony of the LORD are indeed perfect and trustworthy. They have been given to us freely to make us wise. However, we often fail to regard the Word of God as such. If we truly believed that God's law is without flaw, and utterly trustworthy, we would not cease to meditate on it. If we understood the wonderful promises that are attached to God's law, we would pursue it more than anything else in this world. His law *restores the soul*, and his testimony *makes wise the simple*. What human being does not long for these things or restoration and wisdom? They are truly more valuable than gold and silver, and sweeter than honey, as Psalm 19 will later describe. What is it then that keeps us from his word? Our prideful hearts have led us to believe a lie (i.e., that we are self-sufficient and in control). Maybe this is why Psalm 19 starts the way it does, with the heavens declaring their praise to God. No human, but Christ, is worthy of such praise! It is the Creator of all things whose words we trust and cherish. No other words compare to God's words. As believers, we must strive after the words from our precious Holy Scriptures, the words that change lives in power of the Spirit. We must surrender to them and allow them to transform our lives.

NT Scriptures

Matthew 24:35; Hebrews 4:12

Prayer

O LORD, teach our eyes to look deeply into your Word. Teach our ears to listen closely to your Word. Teach our lips to speak your Word. Transform our hearts and minds with the power of your Word. Purify us and sanctify us with your Word so that we may be fruitful instruments in your hands.

Personal Notes and Prayers

Psalm 19:13 [12]

שְׁגִיאוֹת מִי־יָבִין מִנִּסְתָּרוֹת נַקֵּנִי:

Who will discern errors? From errors that are hidden, hold me innocent!

Biblical Context

THIS PSALM IS FULL of praise and adoration. Interestingly, the psalmist's highest praise is sung not in regard to God's love, mercy, or power, but in reference to his speech, words, law, testimony, precepts, commandments, and rules. To describe them, the psalmist uses such adjectives as sure, right, pure, clean, true, and righteous. In fact, he says that the commandments of the LORD are more desired than gold and sweeter than honey. He notes that they have the power to revive the soul, to make the simpleminded wise, and to enlighten the eyes. In fact, he considers God's commands to be cause for the heart to rejoice. Initially, the psalmist's high regard for the law may seem a bit odd. Children do not often think too highly of their parents's rules, even if they come to appreciate them later. The psalmist has a positive view of the commands of God undoubtedly because he tested them and found freedom in living life God's way. In verse 12, the tone changes. It appears that in light of God's perfect law, the psalmist is keenly aware of his tendency to fall short. His humble prayer is inspiring. He knows that even when he is doing all he can to obey God's instructions, he still falls short in ways he may not even be aware of. Therefore, he asks for forgiveness for his *errors that are hidden*. He knows that while he may be blind to some of the sin in his life, God is not. He also knows that only God can declare him innocent from these charges.

Life Application

The psalmist asks a rhetorical question: *Who can discern errors?* His point is emphatically: "no one can." Like the psalmist, we should be wise enough to know that we have erred in ways that we are not even aware of. We may be blind to some of our sinful tendencies because they have been assimilated into our lives for so long. Perhaps this is due to our upbringing, socioeconomic status, church environment, or culture. After all, societal (and even Christian) norms that govern our "good" behavior do not always line up with God's prescription for righteousness. Lust, for example, is promoted as a marketing strategy in our world, but it is a grave sin in God's eyes. Let us therefore humble ourselves to acknowledge and seek forgiveness for those sins that are *hidden* from our own consciousness. Let us accept that, like a fish in water, we are swimming in a cultural sea of sin we do not even recognize. We truly need to depend on God's grace and mercy in order to glorify God in this life.

NT Scriptures

Romans 3:10–12, 23–26; Hebrews 9:24–28

Prayer

O LORD, indeed we are sinners. We sin consciously and we sin unintentionally. Our sins are both hidden and exposed. Open our eyes to see clearly the error of our ways. Keep our hearts from deception and dishonesty. Purify us with your word and make us usable instruments in your hands, for your glory.

Personal Notes and Prayers

Psalm 23

Biblical Context

A PERSON USUALLY TURNS to Psalm 23 to find comfort and reassurance in dark times, in the despair of a terminal illness, in the valley of deep depression, or at a funeral when we mourn the loss of a loved one. Many turn there while seeking to cultivate for themselves the kind of sweet relationship with the LORD that David enjoyed. This short devotion looks instead at Psalm 23 as a model to guide the work of pastors (1 Pet 5:2–4). Six verses provide an easy way to remember job description for all who lead the church on Jesus's behalf. In the first verse we see that we should *oversee* the work of the ministry in ways that inspire each church member to confidently say "I will not lack" (לֹא אֶחְסָר). Success means that no area needful for spiritual wellbeing suffers neglect. Second, in verse 2, our work must *create safe pastures*, spaces to live and grow with others while feeding on the Bible's truths (Jonah 21:15), in truth that produces contentment, tranquility, and rest without fear, in pastures (בִּנְאוֹת דֶּשֶׁא) as it were of new grass. The title "pastor" comes from the French word for pasture. We are pasture-ers. Third, in verse three, we *restore* the souls (נַפְשִׁי יְשׁוֹבֵב) of people from all forms of wickedness that the world system employs to seduce and lead astray. We turn souls back to the way of righteousness. We continually guide them in The Way for the sake of the Name! This guidance, in verse four, is no more keenly craved than when they ask us to simply *be present with them* (כִּי־אַתָּה עִמָּדִי) and walk with them through all the various calamities of life. In verse four, we see the proper use of pastoral authority with the rod (שִׁבְטְךָ). We must *wield it judiciously* and effectively against wild predators, against powerfully deceptive teachers (Acts 20:28–29). We must also *discipline* with the staff (מִשְׁעַנְתֶּךָ) whenever someone acts up in church in a way that disturbs the peace and well-being of others. Just as the LORD prepared King David's table for him at court, we should *celebrate life* by providing lavish recognition (תַּעֲרֹךְ לְפָנַי שֻׁלְחָן), helping each person succeed and *gain dominion* in whatever office God has called them to and champion their side against those who plot to bring them low. Lastly, we must remember to *lead by following*, letting each person live life fully, and blessing them with goodness and grace (טוֹב וָחֶסֶד) in the sure hope of *life after life* with the LORD forever.

Life Application

In doing all these things the good pastor *participates in the love of God* for his own. We (pastors, leaders) enjoy a privileged position: *working as one* with the One who is our Joy. We discover for ourselves the same sweetness that made Shepherd-King David sing this song. But we will only succeed at this when we start where David does, by *first* letting the LORD be our pastor. The LORD is *my* Shepherd (יְהוָה רֹעִי)! Amen.

NT Scriptures

John 10:11–18

Prayer

O LORD, what a privilege it is to serve you as a servant-leader, under your guidance, anointed by your Spirit, led by your truths, walking in your paths and growing to be imitators of Christ on this earth. Thank you for showing us the way to lead, to love and to live.

Personal Notes and Prayers

Psalm 24:3-4

מִי־יַעֲלֶה בְהַר־יְהוָה וּמִי־יָקוּם בִּמְקוֹם קָדְשׁוֹ:
נְקִי כַפַּיִם וּבַר־לֵבָב אֲשֶׁר לֹא־נָשָׂא לַשָּׁוְא נַפְשִׁי וְלֹא נִשְׁבַּע לְמִרְמָה:

Who can go up to the mountain of YHWH and who can stand in his sacred place? One who has clean hands and a pure heart, who does not lift up his soul to vanity and has not sworn treacherously.

Biblical Context

GOD CREATED THE WORLD and is the rightful owner of it and all that is within it. The Psalmist rightly asks: "Who can approach God and worship Him?" Scholars believe that Psalm 24 possibly originated during the return of the Ark of the Covenant to Jerusalem during the reign of David. The psalm was then used as a liturgy for those coming to the Temple. Scholars propose that verse three is a question asked by the pilgrims, while verse four reveals the priest's answer. The phrase "clean hands and pure heart" is a statement by the priest indicating that the pilgrims must live pure lives, inwardly and outwardly—God's ethical standards. Before the pilgrims could enter the divine realm in the Temple, they must first be morally pure. Verse 4b hints back at the Decalogue's prohibition against taking false oaths and worshipping idols. The word שָׁוְא (vanity) can refer to idol worship. To approach God, worshippers must be ethically righteous and avoid the sins of idolatry and swearing falsely. Though all have sinned, the pilgrims were expected to have a heart that desired to be perfectly righteous and to worship God, and then act accordingly.

Life Application

Psalm 24 shows us that God does not accept everyone's worship. Christians are called to represent God in the world. We are now the children of Abraham, called to bring God's blessing to the nations (Gal 3:29). The world looks to us and expects us to have a high moral standard. When we refuse to repent of sin, imitate Christ, and live a righteous life, we fail to be a light to the nations and God does not accept our worship. Christians must seek to have a heart that strongly desires to be Christlike. Sadly, the sins of idolatry and swearing treacherously are commonplace in the Church. Many Christians have put areas of their lives ahead of God. Others hatefully slander fellow Christians instead of seeking to build them up in love. And yet we are called to love our brothers and sisters in Christ. We do not have to be morally perfect. But we must desire moral perfection and allow God's Spirit to lead us to become more Christlike. Let us determine to show Christlike love to everyone, to surrender every area of our lives to God, and to follow the leading of God's Spirit, so that we will become more Christlike and so that God will accept our worship of Him.

NT Scriptures

Romans 12:1–2; James 3:7–18.

Prayer

Dear LORD, thank You for saving us through the blood of Your Son Jesus and for sending us Your Holy Spirit so that we can live our lives in accordance with Your will. Please forgive us for the times we have failed to follow Your guidance and continue to help us grow in Christlikeness and in love for all those created in Your image. In Your name we pray, Amen.

Personal Notes and Prayers

Psalm 24:7–8

שְׂאוּ שְׁעָרִים רָאשֵׁיכֶם וְהִנָּשְׂאוּ פִּתְחֵי עוֹלָם וְיָבוֹא מֶלֶךְ הַכָּבוֹד:

מִי זֶה מֶלֶךְ הַכָּבוֹד יְהוָה עִזּוּז וְגִבּוֹר יְהוָה גִּבּוֹר מִלְחָמָה:

Lift your heads O gates, and be lifted you ancient doors So that the King of Glory may come in! Who is this King of Glory? the LORD strong and mighty, the LORD mighty in battle!

Biblical Context

THE AUTHOR OF PSALM 24:7–10 reflects on the grand entrance of the "Ark of God" into the City of David (Jerusalem) from the home of Obed-Edom the Gittite who lived near Kiriath-Jearim (2 Sam 6:1–18; cf. 1 Chr 13). The author imagines the events of the glorious day when David led the procession up the hill into Jerusalem with dancing, shouts of joy and the sound of the shofar. What an amazing moment this must have been for all who witnessed David dancing with all his might before the LORD (the Ark) wearing only a linen ephod. The presence of the Ark of God in the midst of the people indicated that God—the LORD strong and mighty in battle—was with them to bless them and to give them victory in times of war.

Life Application

I have often prayed this section of the Psalm as an invitation for Jesus to return to our planet and to wrap all of history into his glorious kingdom, bringing with him the equity we all deserve. I cried out to all creatures of God to "lift up their heads," pleading and declaring to them, "He is coming back!" This study has deepened this prayer in my heart. I feel enriched, enlightened and more committed to God's sovereignty over the world than ever before. In my ministry, this study will forever encourage me to be more confident in God's strength and dominion over his creation. I hope to pass this knowledge on to others, encouraging them to trust God and to submit to Him. This idea of submission to God's sovereignty will probably be hard for some people, but hopefully, in the light of this Psalm, they will understand that the God who created and loves the world is not constrained and limited by human understanding. He is indeed the LORD of hosts, the King of kings, the Almighty, and his dominion is absolute.

NT Scriptures

Matthew 21:1-10; John 12:13

Prayer

O LORD, we lift up our heads and open our hearts to you so that you may come in and dwell in our thoughts, our heart and our emotions. We pray you find that the door of our heart is wide open every moment of the day as you seek to abide with us. We love you and we need you.

Personal Notes and Prayers

Psalm 27:1

יְהוָה ׀ אוֹרִי וְיִשְׁעִי מִמִּי אִירָא יְהוָה מָעוֹז־חַיַּי מִמִּי אֶפְחָד׃

The LORD is my light and my salvation, whom will I fear?
the LORD is the strength of my life,
from whom will I be afraid?

Biblical Context

THIS DAVIDIC PSALM SPEAKS of attacks that come against our lives, assaults of evildoers and adversaries who seek to defeat us. David faced many such enemies who wanted to destroy him. For example, twice Saul sought to kill him with his spear (1 Sam 18:11; 19:10). David was forced to flee from him and live among the Philistines (1 Sam 27:1). David was rejected by the Philistines (1 Sam 29:1–29). The descendants of Saul waged war against David for a long time (2 Sam 3:1). When David became King of Israel things did not necessarily get easier. David's reign was full of war and battles. Not to mention that within his family were the death of a child, rape, revenge, and murder, which led to a military coup by one of David's sons. Yet, David remained confident in and faithful to the LORD. In Psalm 27, we hear David declaring his strong confidence in the LORD, even in the midst of difficulties and personal tragedies. In a way, we can understand how David managed to get through the challenging times in his life. He saw God as the light that could lead him down the "straight path" (27:11). David dwelt in the presence of the LORD continually (27:4) and sought Him with all his heart (27:8). God did not simply lead and guide David, but He was his protector and deliverer. Evil men and his adversaries were always out to get him, but David did not worry for he knew that God would keep him safe (27:5).

Life Application

Life is not always "a walk in the park." There are times of confusion, distress, and desperation. There are times when we do not know which choice to make, which path to follow. Yet, God is our light. There are times when sickness overtakes us or one of our family members. Yet, God is our deliverer. Perhaps, you were laid off from your job and you do not know how you will provide for your family. Remember God is the protector of your life. You can trust in the LORD just like David did. You can trust that God will deliver you from our troubles, if you "seek his face" (27:8). God is faithful to his people. Even in the darkest times in our lives we can "seek Him" (27:4) and we can be confident that God will be our light and our salvation.

NT Scriptures

Matthew 6:25–34; Philippians 4:4–6

Prayer

O LORD, your word is a lamp to our feet and a light for our path. We thank you for sending Jesus, the light of the world, so that we may not be lost in the darkness but may have the light of life. You have made us lights to shine brightly into this world. Let us not hide our light under a bushel, but help us let our light shine brightly before men so that they may see our good works and praise our father in heaven.

Personal Notes and Prayers

Psalms 27:13–14

לוּלֵא הֶאֱמַנְתִּי לִרְאוֹת בְּטוּב־יְהוָה בְּאֶרֶץ חַיִּים׃

קַוֵּה אֶל־יְהוָה חֲזַק וְיַאֲמֵץ לִבֶּךָ וְקַוֵּה אֶל־יְהוָה׃

I believe I will yet see the goodness of the LORD in the land of the living. Wait for the LORD. Be strong and let your heart take courage. Wait for the LORD.

Biblical Context

IN THIS PSALM, DAVID expresses strong faith in the LORD while trouble is pressing in on him. Although David is a warrior with plenty of enemies to distract and attack him, he keeps his eyes on the LORD. He is concerned not simply to be delivered from the current crisis but to stay in fellowship with the LORD. David believes he will experience the goodness of God again, as he has many times before. Again, that deliverance is not simply deliverance or victory in the current battle but to live continually in the presence of the LORD. He may not see much good at this point in his life, but he hunkers down like a soldier to direct his attention and entrust his well-being to the LORD. As he does in many other Psalms (e.g., 20:7; 21:7; 22:8; 37:3; 42:5), David reminds himself and others to be strong and take heart, to trust in the LORD always. In this context, David shows us that even with all his military skills as a strong and successful warrior, he knows that fervent hope in God is the sure path to victory. Although hoping and waiting on the LORD seem too passive for a successful outcome, to wait on the LORD displays an act of faith in the one who ultimately brings the victory.

Life Application

In the face of despair and danger, we always have access to a supernatural hope, a hope that reaches into the heavens. Worldly hope depends on what we see and on a very limited list of what we think will make us happy. Godly hope however reaches far beyond what this world can offer.

It is not just an eschatological hope, but it is a strong assurance in the willingness of God to bless us now and forever. With this hope, we can taste of the goodness of the LORD every day, even in challenging and difficult times. When we hope with godly hope, we look to the One who has unimaginable and abundant resources. According to the apostle Paul, we can rely on "him who is able to do immeasurably more than all we ask or imagine, according to his power that is at work within us. To him be glory in the church and in Christ Jesus throughout all generations, for ever and ever! Amen." (Eph 3:20–21). God will surprise us with his unlimited resources in our times of need, if we wait upon the LORD.

NT Scriptures

Matthew 7:11; John 11:23–27; Romans 4:18–24

Prayer

O LORD, with you the best is yet to come. With you there is always hope. With you we soar like eagles. As the prophet Isaiah said, "those who hope in the Lord will renew their strength. They will soar on wings like eagles. They will run and not grow weary, they will walk and not faint" (Is 40:31). You raise us up higher than we could ever go in our own strength. Take us and surprise us with an increasing measure of your power. To you be the glory.

Personal Notes and Prayers

Psalm 29:2

הָב֣וּ לַֽ֭יהוָה כְּב֣וֹד שְׁמ֑וֹ הִשְׁתַּחֲו֥וּ לַ֝יהוָ֗ה בְּהַדְרַת־קֹֽדֶשׁ׃

Give to the LORD glory (honor) to his name, Worship (prostrate yourself) before the LORD in the glory of his holiness.

Biblical Context

PSALM 29 IS A song of praise and worship attributed to David. The psalmist summons the heavenly assembly to acknowledge that YHWH is to be elevated above all others and his glory is to be proclaimed by his created beings. In this verse, a direct command is given to acknowledge the honor and glory of YHWH's name. Unlike our modern context, names held great significance in the ANE. A name was holistically representative of a person's character. YHWH's name was so holy that it could not be spoken directly in the reading of Scripture. Additionally, scribes were to destroy their writing instruments once they had copied the holy name of YHWH. The Hebrew word for "glory" כָּבוֹד carries with it the idea of *heaviness*. According to the psalmist, YHWH is heavy with honor and glory. The weight of his glory demands our attention. The psalmist demands that the audience acknowledge the *weight* of his glory and prostrate himself or herself to the ground before one so holy. YHWH is not like any other Canaanite god. He is far superior; his name is holy and He is the only One worthy of worship by his creation.

Life Application

We worship an awesome and holy God. In the midst of challenging and trying situations, it is easy for us to lose sight of the One to whom we direct our prayers. We become unnecessarily overwhelmed with life's problems. We forget that our God is infinitely greater than any of our struggles. The psalmist reminds us that we should never lose sight of the One we honor and worship. We should glorify his *name* for his glory is found in his *name*. After the death and resurrection of Jesus, God exalted him and gave him a *name* that is above every other name. And it is to this *name* that every knee will bow and every tongue confess that Jesus is LORD. At the end of times, all creatures in heaven, on earth and under the earth will acknowledge the *name* of Jesus and bow down to worship Him only. Let us never forget the power, glory and honor due to the *name* of Jesus.

NT Scriptures

Acts 4:12; Philippians 2:9–10

Prayer

O LORD, thank you for allowing us to know you through your name, to worship you and to pray in your name. What amazing power you have placed in our hands when we invoke the name of Jesus. "I will tell of your name to my brothers and sisters; in the midst of the congregation, I will praise you" (Ps 22:22) and I will give glory and honor to your name Jesus.

Personal Notes and Prayers

Psalm 33:13–14

מִשָּׁמַיִם הִבִּיט יְהוָה רָאָה אֶת־כָּל־בְּנֵי הָאָדָם:
מִמְּכוֹן־שִׁבְתּוֹ הִשְׁגִּיחַ אֶל כָּל־יֹשְׁבֵי הָאָרֶץ:

From the heavens, the LORD looks down, he sees all human beings. From his established resting place, he gazes upon all the inhabitants of the earth.

Biblical Context

THE DESCRIPTION OF THE LORD's transcendence over all creation in this Psalm cannot be divorced from his intimate personal involvement on the earth. His act of creating (33:6–7, 9) was hardly a matter of detached aloofness. Even as his steadfast love is imbued in creation (33:5), it is more abundantly displayed in how he cares for those who fear him (33:18–19). This combination of sovereign rule and abundant love, provides ample justification for shouts of joy to him, as well as praises, thanksgiving, singing, and gladness (33:1–3, 22). That the LORD's eye is constantly gazing upon the works of his own mastery should come as no surprise. His gaze is no passive glance. From his dwelling place, he looks down upon ours, observes all people, and intervenes in the lives of all people . . . those who trust him, and those who do not (33:16–17). The combination of the double מִן ("from") preposition with the double כֹּל ("all") paints a clear picture in these verses. God may seem distant and inactive but, from where he sits, he is simultaneously able to see and interact with all things He created.

Life Application

The "all seeing eye" of the LORD, described by the psalmist, may seem both folkloric and oppressive to the one standing outside the community of faith. Why should God concern himself with so many trivial things? Why should we worry that there is always someone looking over our shoulders? Of course, any worry is unfounded for the believer. God does not peer into our lives because He is merely and minutely curious, but his gaze is one of righteousness and justice. His eye is on those who fear him, "in order to save their soul from death, and keep them alive in famine" (33:19). While there is a warning implied that secret sins do not go unnoticed, the explicit message is one of comfort. The one whose hope is in the LORD invites his generous and steadfast love (33:22). Even as we wait on the execution of his justice and righteousness, we do well to worship him in gladness, knowing well that he does not blindly regard the heart who trusts in his holy name.

NT Scriptures

Matthew 9:36; Hebrews 4:13

Prayer

O LORD, nothing in creation is hidden from your sight. Everything is naked and bare before your eyes. As we came into this world naked and vulnerable, teach us to live lives that are naked and transparent before you. Search the nooks and crannies of our hearts and free us from any hidden sin. Show us what we try to hide from you and help us release it into the open so that we may live free in your presence.

Personal Notes and Prayers

Psalm 39:5 [4]

הוֹדִיעֵנִי יְהוָה קִצִּי וּמִדַּת יָמַי מַה־הִיא אֵדְעָה מֶה־חָדֵל אָנִי׃

LORD, make me know my end and the measure of my days; Let me know how transient/lacking I am.

Biblical Context

PSALMS 37, 38, 39 and 40 are all psalms of David centered on the theme of waiting on the LORD and finding refuge in him. Each of these psalms expresses a desire for mercy and deliverance in the midst of trouble brought on as a consequence of personal sin. The troubles are real and significant, but despite them, the psalmist expresses an underlying confidence in the faithfulness of God. In Psalm 39, the psalmist attributes his suffering to God (39:9, 10), but acknowledges that it came as a result of his own personal sin (39:8, 11). He is in a posture of waiting silently on the LORD, hoping for mercy and deliverance. He breaks his silence to lament his situation and in the midst of his lament, he comments on the brevity of human life. He asks the LORD to make known to him the measure of his days (39:4, 5), and he concedes that each man's life is but a breath and his labor is in vain (39:6). But rather than issuing criticism on this reality, he seeks an appropriate perspective. He wants to grasp the fleeting nature of his life and the eternal security he has in the LORD.

Life Application

The perspective on the brevity and vanity of life in these verses is reminiscent of Ecclesiastes. Indeed, most of what we find ourselves pursuing is meaningless, a chasing after the wind (Eccl 2:18), and most of what we see as accomplishments is insubstantial in the grand scheme of things. However, the best perspective on life is hope, and not despair. Qohelet acknowledges that God is the appropriate context for any evaluation of our lives (Eccl 2:11–14), and here in Psalm 39, the psalmist declares that his hope is in the LORD (39:7). As we get older (and we are all getting older!), it would be wise to be mindful of these realities and put our hope not in the things of this world, but in the LORD.

NT Scriptures

Matthew 6:19–20; Hebrews 11:24–27

Prayer

O LORD, help us watch our ways, keep our tongue from sin, and put a muzzle on our mouth. Show us how valuable each day is with you. Teach us to number our days, for our life is but a breath. We only have a short time to accomplish your will. Do not let us waste the years, months, days, hours, and even minutes that remain in our lives. May our legacy honor you, and you only.

Personal Notes and Prayers

Psalm 39:7-8 [6-7]

אַךְ־בְּצֶ֤לֶם ׀ יִֽתְהַלֶּךְ־אִ֗ישׁ אַךְ־הֶ֥בֶל יֶהֱמָי֑וּן יִ֝צְבֹּ֗ר וְֽלֹא־יֵדַ֥ע מִי־אֹסְפָֽם׃

וְעַתָּ֣ה מַה־קִּוִּ֣יתִי אֲדֹנָ֑י תּ֝וֹחַלְתִּ֗י לְךָ֣ הִֽיא׃

Indeed, man goes about as but an image; indeed, they murmur nothingness; he heaps things up and does not know why he is gathering them. So now, what do I wait for, my LORD? My hope, it is with you.

Biblical Context

THE EXACT CIRCUMSTANCES OF this Psalm, as with many Psalms, are rather vague. At the opening of the Psalm, the psalmist lets us know that he has done his best to avoid sinning with his tongue. We then find out that his effort is ultimately futile (39:2-4). From there, he asks to be reminded of the brevity of his life (39:5-7). His ultimate hope is deliverance from God (39:8-14). He is suffering seemingly because of the sins he has committed. These verses appear in the transition from reflecting on the brevity of life to putting hope in God. These verses appear as the psalmist looks at life's brevity for comfort—"if I am not alive much longer I will not suffer much longer!"—but then realizes upon further reflection that God alone is the source of his comfort.

Life Application

While Qohelet notes the transience and emptiness of life, he truly experienced a lifetime of blessings, abundance, riches, and honor. In life, most people come to understand that the pursuit of material things leaves one wanting for more. And despite our hearts's deepest desires for comfort, renown, and approval, we know that having what we want will never put an end to the wanting. We are dependent creatures who must rely on God. Our existence could not have happened by itself. Our plans for the future can easily fall through. And what we have can be taken away suddenly. The realization of these truths—which we often ignore even though it is rather obvious to anyone who has lived for a while—is disheartening. But the psalmist does not stay in a state of lament. He looks elsewhere for hope to a God who is reliable, whose plans will never fail, and who cannot lose what he already has. This provides a wonderful model for handling the crushing reality of our own transience. Knowing how much we can lose drives us to put an even deeper trust in a God who holds everything in the unshakable grip of his unfailing love.

NT Scriptures

Matthew 6:34; James 4:13–17

Prayer

O LORD, you gave us everything we have. We have hoarded your blessings and set our eyes on them. We have allowed ourselves to be shackled by the material things of this world. Today, we surrender them back to you. We want to be free from the bondage of this world. Teach us to hold lightly the earthly blessings that pass through our hands and free us from the grip that holds of back. We want you to be at the center of our lives.

Personal Notes and Prayers

Psalm 46:11 [10]

הַרְפּוּ וּדְעוּ כִּי־אָנֹכִי אֱלֹהִים אָרוּם בַּגּוֹיִם אָרוּם בָּאָרֶץ׃

Relax and know that I am God! I will be exalted among the nations. I will be exalted in the earth.

Biblical Context

A FAMILIAR TRANSLATION OF this verse is, "Be still and know that I am God" (ESV, NIV, NKJV). This translation sends the reader into a posture of privacy with God where space is created for a time of intimacy between God and the worshipper. However, the meaning of Psalm 46:11[10] signifies far more than entering into isolated quiet meditation, stillness and prayer. Since the verbs "Relax!" (הַרְפּוּ) and "Know!" (דְעוּ) are plural imperatives, they are no doubt addressing the entire community involved in *public* worship and not the individual for *private* quiet times and silent listening. Verses 9–11 describe "the works of the LORD" as a power that causes "desolation on the earth," "makes wars cease," "breaks the bow and shatters the spear," and "burns the shields with fire." In context, the dramatic verbiage of the psalm requires an equally dramatic interpretation of this particular verse. The climax of the poem comes in verse 11, where the psalmist commands the community to "leave off (her own attempts)" (Gesenius) or "drop (the hands)" (BDB) from vain efforts to fight the nations in one's own strength. The psalmist's directives are an invitation to come with excitement to see the works of God and to discover the greatness of God. God will deal with the nations and display his power in order to draw his people to worship him publicly, together, with one voice.

Life Application

Psalm 46:11 exhorts us to cease from our own efforts to control all aspects of life and to cease from our attempts to determine our destiny. Rather than trying to direct life, we are to acknowledge that the LORD is God over all circumstances, in all his omnipotence, omniscience, and omnipresence. We are called to stop our activities and behold the awesome works of God. We are called to acknowledge Him together with boldness and courage, and to speak words of praise to Him in a posture of wonder and astonishment. God is our guide and our master. In this we can find strength, comfort and peace.

NT Scriptures

1 Timothy 3:16; 2 Peter 2:9; 1 John 1:5

Prayer

O LORD, in this culture, we fail to cease from our own striving. We want to succeed. We want to produce. We want to win at all cost. Teach us to slow down and experience rest. Teach us to wait upon you with patience and repose. Teach us to take a daily sabbath and remember your great and mighty deeds. Teach us how to live the way you live, with complete peace.

Personal Notes and Prayers

Psalm 46:11-12 [11-12]

הַרְפּוּ וּדְעוּ כִּי־אָנֹכִי אֱלֹהִים אָרוּם בַּגּוֹיִם אָרוּם בָּאָרֶץ׃
יְהוָה צְבָאוֹת עִמָּנוּ מִשְׂגָּב־לָנוּ אֱלֹהֵי יַעֲקֹב סֶלָה׃

Relax (be still) and know that I am God. I will be exalted among the nations, I will be exalted in the earth. the LORD Almighty is with us, the God of Jacob is our refuge.

Biblical Context

IN PSALM 46, GOD is portrayed as a refuge and strength in times of trouble. Though the psalmist identifies neither a specific threat nor its cause, it is possible that danger may be looming from impending war with surrounding nations. In verse 10, God breaks onto the scene like a triumphant warrior and orders his people to *relax and know* that He is God! He calls for all who hear Him to refrain from entering into military conflict and to trust him amid the threats of war. The psalmist calls his audience to *cease (from worry) and know* that the LORD is a strong refuge and a fortress for those who trust in Him. He reminds the Israelites that no enemy will be able to penetrate the divine fortification God provides for his people.

Life Application

Life is filled with all sorts of complexities: financial struggles, loss of a job, the death of a loved one, heartbreak, illnesses, hunger, exhaustion, and the list goes on. There is a wide spectrum of struggles and challenges one will experience during his or her lifetime. But there is a reality that is infinitely greater than any of the troubles of life: the LORD is faithful and will take care of his people. Just as the God of Jacob was the refuge and strength for Israel, He too is the refuge and strength for all who believe today. This truth has never changed. However, freedom only comes when the troubled and weak cease their efforts to overcome their trials by themselves, and rely on Almighty God. As the One who is exalted among the nations and the earth, God has ultimate control and power over all matters of life.

NT Scriptures

James 4:13–17; Matthew 6:25–34

Prayer

God of Jacob, I praise you for your faithfulness towards your people. Thank you for your mercy and grace that I receive daily. May I always remember who you are as the LORD Almighty and trust you instead of my own capabilities. Exalted over all creation, you are my steadfast refuge and strength. May you always be glorified when I face the trials of life. Amen.

Personal Notes and Prayers

Psalm 69:17 [16]

עֲנֵנִי יְהוָה כִּי־טוֹב חַסְדֶּךָ כְּרֹב רַחֲמֶיךָ פְּנֵה אֵלָי:

Answer me LORD, because your lovingkindness is good.
According to your abundant compassion turn towards me.

Biblical Context

THIS PSALM IS A personal lament (imprecatory psalm). David is crying out because things are not as they should be. Most likely, David wrote or first spoke these words in the midst of Absalom's rebellion. There are many similarities in language and themes between this psalm and 2 Samuel 15-19. This psalm is quoted seven times in the New Testament in reference to the life of Jesus (e.g., v.4 in John 15:25; v.8 in Matt 13:55; Mark 6:3; v.9 in John 2:17, Rom 15:3; v.11-12 in John 8:41; v. in; v.22-23 in Rom 11:9; v.25 in Acts 1:20). It is quite apparent in this psalm that David is suffering, and that he is in great distress. Yet, what is important is the fact that David is feeling this way due to his religious zeal to see God's righteousness prevail over the evils of the world in which he lived. The jealous emotions that David had for his house (which was falling apart due to the sin of Absalom) are paralleled by the deep feelings of grief that Christ was having as he watched his house, his people, and his city—Jerusalem—fall apart due to the sin. Jesus was heart broken by the realities of his world and grieved as he saw that his people rejected their God (Matt 23:37-39).

Life Application

Often times we think that we need to talk to God in a different way than the way that we would talk to others. Words that would seem out of place in an every day conversation somehow make their way into our daily prayers. In this passage, we find a clear example of David—a mere human—pouring out his heart and talking to God with deep passion and emotion. In his desperate address to God, David even commands God to *answer his prayers.* Then, a millennium or so later, Jesus himself uses the exact same language as David when He experiences severe persecution and rejection at the hand of his oppressors. When we speak to God in prayer, what matters most is that our words come from our heart, represent our own reality, and be genuine. There is no formula that can replace the power of an honest and real conversation with God in prayer.

NT Scriptures

Matthew 6:5–8; John 2:17

Prayer

O LORD, here we are mere humans, failing you and stumbling through life as drunken men who have lost their way. As we seek to serve you, we are oppressed on every side. We are ridiculed and rejected. Our words fall on deaf ears and echo silently in the chaos of this world. You understand rejection better than any of us. Help us remain faithful to you each day.

Personal Notes and Prayers

Psalm 91:1

יֹשֵׁב בְּסֵתֶר עֶלְיוֹן בְּצֵל שַׁדַּי יִתְלוֹנָן׃

He who dwells in the shelter of the Most High
will abide in the shadow of the Almighty.

Biblical Context

THIS PSALM HAS NO superscription, so the author's intent is not known. Nevertheless, the content of the psalm is so beautiful and universal that most readers draw great strength from it. Verse 1 speaks about the protection of the LORD—one of the most common themes in the book of Psalms. Several psalms refer to "the shadow of his wings" (צֵל כְּנָפֶיךָ), "the shelter" (מַחְסֶה), and "the hiding place" (מִסְתָּר) as God's protection (e.g., Pss 17:8; 27:5; 31:20; 32:7; 36:7). "The shelter" and "the shadow" indicate the continuous protection and covering of the LORD for the worshipper who dwells in his presence. The psalmist further describes God as a refuge, fortress, shield, buckler, deliverer, and rescuer. Victory is ensured for the one who abides in the presence of God, for God will deliver him from the snare of the fowler and from deadly pestilence (v.3). He will cover him with his wings (v.4), send his angels to guard him in all his ways (v.11), and speak to him in times of trouble (v.15). The reward of abiding in the presence of the LORD is great and secure. Though life is replete with obstacles and challenges, the worshipper need not fear for God is faithful to protect and deliver those who trust in him.

Life Application

I meditated on this verse this morning. Every morning I wrestle with myself to rise early and meet with my LORD. I used to be a night person, but I am trying to change my habits to become a morning person. I assume that if David was inspired to compose psalms, he would compose them in the morning, because the morning is the quietest and most meditative part of the day. In Psalm 59:16, David declared, "in the morning I will sing of your steadfast love, for your have been to me a fortress and a refuge in the day of my distress." If David could acknowledge the mighty deeds of the LORD and sing to him in the morning, then so will I. I will praise him early with all my heart, mind and soul. I will remember his deliverance and his help in times of trouble. And I will abide in the shadow of his wings to find rest and protection.

NT Scriptures

John 15:1–7; 2 Corinthians 1:8–10; 1 John 4:13–16

Prayer

O LORD, how beautiful is your dwelling place. It is the place where your glory dwells and your truth prevails. Show us O LORD the depths of Moses's words, "the eternal God is your dwelling place, and underneath are the everlasting arms" (Deut 33:27). How we long to be held in your loving arms for comfort, rest and strength. How we long to be secure in your everlasting arms. Wrap us up in your love and teach us to abide in you every day of our lives.

Personal Notes and Prayers

Psalm 103:11-12

כִּי כִגְבֹהַּ שָׁמַיִם עַל־הָאָרֶץ גָּבַר חַסְדּוֹ עַל־יְרֵאָיו׃

כִּרְחֹק מִזְרָח מִמַּעֲרָב הִרְחִיק מִמֶּנּוּ אֶת־פְּשָׁעֵינוּ׃

For as high as the heavens are above the earth, so his abundant love is upon those who fear him.
As far as the east is from the east is from the west, he distances our sins from us.

Biblical Context

THIS PSALM BEGINS AND ends with the psalmist telling his or her soul to praise the LORD (1, 22). The soul is also told not to forget all the benefits of the LORD (2). What follows is a beautiful list of the benefits the LORD offers to those who fear him, or those who hold him in right regard. Here the psalmist poetically reflects on the benefits of God's love and forgiveness. The love of God is as high as the heavens are above the earth. The Hebrew word חסד represents more than mere feelings of love. Rather, it involves tangible actions and faithfulness. In some instances, it can refer to going above and beyond relational obligation or expectation. This is wonderful in human relationships, but the חסד from God is so much bigger, its immensity cannot be measured! An ancient Israelite could *see* the heavens by looking at the stars, but could never *reach* it. The second benefit mentioned here is forgiveness. The LORD separates us from our sins as far as the east is from the west. These two ends are measured in terms of the sunrise and the sunset. In Denver, we refer to mountain towns as "the West," or in the U.S., we refer to either the West or East as geographic regions. But in this psalm they are not locations, but a direction that can be followed forever. We might be able to make it to Jefferson, CO or to New England, but we can never reach the point of the sunrise or the point of the sunset. Our sins are removed from us so far that we could not even reach them if we tried. God's immeasurably immense love is shown by separating us far from our sins—as far as the east is from the west.

Life Application

These verses do not just show us what we get from God. They show us who we are because of God. God loves us above and beyond what we would expect, and that love is measured to beyond human reach. Similarly, his love so powerfully and permanently removes from us our brokenness that we no longer can be identified with our sins. They are no longer ours to bear. God has taken them from us as far away as possible. This abundant love and this total forgiveness come for those who fear God. Rather than denoting that those who are afraid of God (as our English equivalent implies), this phrase suggests these benefits are for those who place God in the proper position over their lives. Additionally, this does not promote that fearing God requires perfect obedience to the law. If that were the case, there would be no forgiveness involved! Instead, acknowledging our own fallibility and recognizing God's power and goodness lies at the heart of relationship with God. As forgiven and loved people, we then have the ability to embody our identity in the world by responding to God's abundant love with the same חסד type of abundant love for our neighbors.

NT Scriptures

Romans 8:38–39; Ephesians 1:7; 1 John 1:9

Prayer

LORD, thank you for your immeasurable love and forgiveness. May we not forget these great benefits that come from you, and may we learn to embrace our identities as loved and forgiven beyond imagination. Help us to fear you by seeing your role and rule in the world and in our lives, and enable us to be agents of your kingdom in the world. Amen.

Personal Notes and Prayers

Psalm 111:2–3

גְּדֹלִים מַעֲשֵׂי יְהוָה דְּרוּשִׁים לְכָל־חֶפְצֵיהֶם:
הוֹד־וְהָדָר פָּעֳלוֹ וְצִדְקָתוֹ עֹמֶדֶת לָעַד:

Great are the works of YHWH, sought after by all who delight in them. Glorious and majestic are his deeds, and his righteousness endures forever.

Biblical Context

PSALM 111 IS A song of remembrance. The psalm is written in an acrostic format and yet, every verse moves toward the grand finale, when the psalmist declares, "The fear of the LORD is the beginning of wisdom; all who follow his precepts have good understanding. To him belongs eternal praise" (v.10—NIV). Psalm 111 speaks of God's covenant of grace, His mighty redemption, and the surety of his Word. Verses 2–3 remind the reader just how great God's works have been. The verb דרשׁ carries the idea of searching intently or studying rigorously. The natural response to knowing the mighty deeds of YHWH is reflection and pause. In fact, these deeds of splendor testify to God's enduring righteousness, a faithfulness to his covenant and character that will last for all time.

Life Application

The concept of remembering God's works appears throughout the Bible. Unlike many of the so-called gods in the world, the Triune God has invaded and participated in human history. He is not an abstract force or an unknowable something. He is the covenant God who interacts with his people. He creates; He redeems; and He sustains. His character is revealed in his deeds. Our hope is based in his work(s). Just think how Peter's sermon on Pentecost outlined God's working in history, culminating in Christ (Acts 2:14–21). His message was powerful, not simply because of mysterious flames of fire and the shocking utterances of many languages, but because Peter testified to how God had acted in history.

Likewise, Paul invited Timothy to cling to the Scriptures because it was in them that the testimony of God's saving work was made known (2 Tim. 3:14–17). But sometimes reading and remembering are not enough; sometimes the only proper response to God's actions is singing. Somehow in singing and psalmody, humans can express the deep emotions that spring from remembering the mighty God we serve! Songs allow us to praise, to remember, to reflect, and ultimately to bring glory to the Triune God.

NT Scriptures

Acts 2:14–41; Ephesians 2:11–12; 2 Timothy 3:14–17

Prayer

O LORD, you are alive, now, at this very moment. You seek to give us life as we have never known it before. Help us be revived by your testimony of your mighty deeds. You are beyond amazing and more than what our hearts and minds can fathom. What a privilege it is to know You!

Personal Notes and Prayers

Psalm 119:18

גַּל־עֵינַי וְאַבִּיטָה נִפְלָאוֹת מִתּוֹרָתֶךָ׃

Open my eyes that I may consider
wonderful things from your law.

Biblical Context

PSALM 119 IS A masterpiece of poetry. It is an acrostic, comprised of twenty-two stanzas of eight lines each. Each stanza begins with a successive letter of the Hebrew alphabet and each line within each stanza begins with the same Hebrew letter. It is really quite impressive, especially when viewed in the original language. Acrostics use both structure and content to express totality and completeness. Thus, Psalm 119 expresses the total and complete beauty of the law of God. The first verse of the psalm states its theme: "How blessed are those whose way is blameless, who walk in the law of the LORD" (119:1). The remaining verses expand on this idea that blamelessness is found in the lives of those who live by the law of God. Remarkably, all but four of the one hundred and seventy six verses contain a synonym for the law, extolling a special virtue about God's law. Verse 24 highlights several interesting aspects of the law. First, it emphasizes that God's law is full of wonderful, extraordinary things. Second, it underscores that the wonderful things contained in the law are to be revered by the believer. And third, it reminds us that the wonders of the law are accessible, but only as God opens our eyes to them.

Life Application

Many tend to look at the law as a set of restrictions on their freedom, but that is an unduly negative interpretation. The law should be viewed instead as an expression of the character of God. It provides principles of behavior that are still relevant for the Christian, even if the specific applications of those laws (and the punishment for noncompliance) are not. In these principles, we see character traits of God such as holiness, justice and righteousness. Instead of setting aside the law of God as an unnecessary burden negated by the grace of Jesus Christ, we should embrace the law as an expression of God's moral will and as a path to freedom. Certainly, the God of the universe who created us knows the kind of moral boundaries that fit our nature; and in his perfect law, wonderfully complemented by his grace and mercy, we find true freedom.

NT Scriptures

2 Corinthians 3:17; Galatians 5:1; James 1:25

Prayer

O LORD, we thank you for giving us your Word. It is our life. It transforms us and instructs us. It reveals to us who you are and what you do. It is perfect, pure and beautiful. It is delicious and good. You invited us to "taste and see" that you are good. Jesus reminded us that we are not to "live by bread alone, but by every word that comes from the mouth of God" (Matt 4:4). What a feast you have serve for us. Let us meet at your table.

Personal Notes and Prayers

Psalm 121:3-4

אַל־יִתֵּן לַמּוֹט רַגְלֶךָ אַל־יָנוּם שֹׁמְרֶךָ׃ הִנֵּה לֹא־יָנוּם וְלֹא יִישָׁן שׁוֹמֵר יִשְׂרָאֵל׃

May He not permit your foot to slip; may He not sleep, the One who keeps you. Indeed, He will not sleep, and He will not slumber, the One who keeps Israel.

Biblical Context

PSALM 121 IS PART of the collection of the Songs of Ascent (Ps 120–34) that constitute a major portion of the Great Hallel psalms (Ps 118–36). The Songs of Ascent are identified by the use of the root עלה ("to go up, ascend") in the title. These songs may have been used as pilgrim songs when Israelites journeyed up to Jerusalem for annual feasts (Ps 122:4). A Jewish tradition from the Mishna suggests that the Levites recited or sang these songs on the southern steps to the temple in Jerusalem while making their way up to the Temple: "On the fifteen steps which led into the women's court, corresponding with the fifteen songs of degrees, stood the Levites, with their musical instruments, and sang" (*m. Sukkah* 5:4–5). Those who sang Psalm 121 were convinced that God never removed his eyes from them. They were persuaded that God never slept nor slumbered and remained on permanent watch over his people. In contrast, Canaanite gods were not as alert and were thought to sleep during the winter months to be renewed with the birth of spring.

Life Application

As savvy Christians, we likely do not consciously think of the LORD as "asleep on the job." But perhaps we secretly worry that he is too busy or too important to be bothered with the mundane details of our lives. Do we allow the anxiety and concerns of life to drown out the powerful truth that the LORD, the God of heaven and earth, watchfully guards our steps? It is easy to understand how this secret worry could find a foothold in our hearts. We unconsciously fear that He is asleep or too busy for us, causing us to doubt his power in our daily lives. However, let us remember the context of this psalm. If any people had reason to doubt the power of the LORD, it would have been the Israelites. They could have lost hope in God during their difficult journey in the wilderness, during their challenging entry into the land of Canaan, and during the time of the ungodly judges. Yet, the entire collection of "Songs of Ascent" is filled with hope, encouragement, and firm belief that the God of Abraham, Isaac and Jacob is ever present with his people. Rather than focus on life's challenges, we should remember that the One who promised to be with us, to keep us from falling, and to manifest himself in the lives of those whom He loves, is indeed omnipresent and cares more than we will ever know.

NT Scriptures

2 Thessalonians 3:3; Hebrews 13:5–6

Prayer

O LORD, forgive our slumber and inattentiveness to the matters of your Kingdom. Rouse us, energize us and stir us to be incessantly effective for you. Make us the dynamic instruments through whom you wish to establish your Kingdom on earth. To you be the glory!

Personal Notes and Prayers

Psalm 121:5

יְהוָ֥ה שֹׁמְרֶ֑ךָ יְהוָ֥ה צִ֝לְּךָ֗ עַל־יַ֥ד יְמִינֶֽךָ׃

The LORD is your keeper; the LORD is the shade at your right hand.

Biblical Context

THE SECOND PSALM OF Ascent voices the cry of a person who gazes up to the LORD for protection. The worshipper lifts us his eyes to the hills, to the place where divine help is accessible, and declares with confidence, "my help comes from the Lord, the Maker of heaven and earth" (v.2). This cry is answered swiftly by the LORD as the psalmist recalls the sovereignty of God over all, and his care and protection in times of trouble. The psalmist reassures the worshipper and reminds him that God is the "keeper" of Israel, that He never slumbers nor sleeps. The Hebrew root for "keeping" or "guarding" (שמר) is repeated six times in the psalm, highlighting its importance as the main theme of the poem. In verses 5, 7, and 8, the "keeper" of Israel is none other than the LORD himself. As "keeper," the LORD preserves and protects and is "the shade" or "the shadow" at the right hand of his people. The word "shade" suggests refreshing, sustaining protection from literal and figurative heat. And "at your right hand" indicates the proximity of the LORD. He is as close as He can be, right beside the worshipper, forever connected to him.

Life Application

In our complex world, anxiety can be a constant companion. We worry about our safety in troubled neighborhoods. We worry about the well-being of our family and children. We worry about our level of productivity at work, our reputation in the world, our financial situation, and our future. The list of areas in which we feel anxiety may seem overwhelming and rob us of the abundant life to which God has called us. However, in Psalm 121:5, the LORD reminds us that he is closer to us than anyone or anything else in this world. He is closer than our own shadow, therefore we can never run away from him since we can never separate ourselves from our shadow. He reminds us that, if we put ourselves in his hands, in his care and under his protection, we can experience safety, refreshment and nourishment under his mighty wings. The LORD is our keeper, and he is our shade. When we feel anxious, we can lift our gaze to the LORD in prayer like the psalmist so that he might point us to the reality that we truly are safe in his hands.

NT Scriptures

Jude 20–25; Revelation 3:10–13

Prayer

O LORD, make us aware of your continual presence in our lives. Forgive us for forgetting that you are near us, ready to lead us in the paths of righteousness. As Paul reminds us, "Do not say in your heart, "Who will ascend into heaven?" (that is to bring Christ down) or "Who will descend into the deep?" (that is, to bring Christ up from the dead). But what does it say? "The word is near you; it is in your mouth and in your heart" (Rom 10:7–8).

Personal Notes and Prayers

Psalm 124:7

נַפְשֵׁנוּ כְּצִפּוֹר נִמְלְטָה מִפַּח יוֹקְשִׁים הַפַּח נִשְׁבָּר וַאֲנַחְנוּ נִמְלָטְנוּ:

Our soul, like a bird, escaped from the net of those laying snares, The net broke and we escaped.

Biblical Context

THIS SONG OF ASCENT calls for responsive praise due to God's deliverance of Israel. In verses 1–5, the psalmist explains what could have happened to Israel if God had not intervened. The psalmist uses the same negative conditional particle to begin the parallel colons of 1a and 2a (לוּלֵי), thereby assuring the listener outright that God had intervened for Israel against her enemy. Using images of fire and flood in verses 3–5, the psalmist then explains the potential dramatic fate of Israel, had God not intervened. Particularly in verses 4–5, the psalmist uses parallel intensification within an AB-B'A' chiastic structure to draw attention to the complete destruction Israel would have undergone without God's help. The psalm transitions to thanksgiving and praise in verses 6–8, as the psalmist calls for Israel to praise the LORD for delivering them. Situated within the concluding doxology lies the highlighted verse 7 in which the psalmist figuratively declares God's historic act of deliverance for Israel. First, the psalmist compares Israel's being to that of a bird caught in a trap, signifying the fragility and vulnerability of its life. Then, using three verbs, he explains that though the enemy had trapped Israel, God had provided for her escape by breaking the trap.

Life Application

Can you recall a time in your life when you felt caught and vulnerable—perhaps in an unhealthy relationship or a sin or within the grip of a physical enemy—and then God made a way out for you? In my late 20's, during a particularly difficult season at work and in life, I started dealing with my stress by controlling my eating and exercise habits in an unhealthy way.

Through a condition related to my deafness, the LORD literally broke me out of this destructive trap and brought me to a healthier, freer place. We all experience times when our lives feel fragile and vulnerable—like small birds caught in a trap. We face assaults from physical and spiritual enemies, but the psalmist and our own life experiences remind us that God is faithful to his people. He delivers us not only from various earthly circumstances, but ultimately from sin and death (and our fear of it) through our Savior, Jesus Christ. The psalmist exhorts us to declare God's historic acts of deliverance in our individual and corporate lives in order that we might rightly respond in worship.

NT Scriptures

2 Timothy 2:22–26; Hebrews 2:1–4; 2 Peter 1:3–4

Prayer

O LORD, from you comes our deliverance. You protect us from trouble and deliver us from the snares of life. You are our refuge and strength, a very present help in time of trouble. You open doors and surprise our enemies. You put to shame those who try to entice us and lead us in paths of destruction. Thank you for being there, always, forever and ever.

Personal Notes and Prayers

Psalm 139:11-12

וָאֹמַר אַךְ־חֹשֶׁךְ יְשׁוּפֵנִי וְלַיְלָה אוֹר בַּעֲדֵנִי:

גַּם־חֹשֶׁךְ לֹא־יַחְשִׁיךְ מִמֶּךָ וְלַיְלָה כַּיּוֹם יָאִיר כַּחֲשֵׁיכָה כָּאוֹרָה:

I said, "Surely darkness will cover me; the night will be light for me." Even the darkness will not be dark to you; the night will shine like the day, for the darkness is as light.

Biblical Context

HERE IS ANOTHER OF the many psalms לְדָוִד (to/for/of David). In it we find a beautiful picture of God's complete knowledge of and love for us. "Before a word is on my tongue, you know it completely, O LORD," (v. 4), "Even there your hand will guide me, your right hand will hold me fast," (v. 10), "For you created my inmost being; you knit me together in my mother's womb," (v. 13). Where can any of us go that is too far away for God to reach us? The psalmist answers this concretely: nowhere. Even while the wicked and bloodthirsty speak against God (vv. 19–20), the psalmist lifts up the LORD and acknowledges his omniscience and devotion to us.

Life Application

This psalm is one nearly every Christian has heard in a sermon, as a word of encouragement, or as lyrics in a song, and it is one that is dear to my heart. There have been many periods in my life since I became a Christian when I have felt completely alone. I was sure I was unworthy of God's notice and outside of his loving care. Even though I called for him, I did not hear a response. At other times I have purposefully tried to run from God. The shame of past or present sins had made me fearful of the consequences of those sins. Sometimes it was a desire to continue sinning without God finding out about it. But the truth is as plain as the words in this psalm: "O LORD, you have searched me, and you know me," (v. 1). Even when trying to hide in the darkness, God knows where I am. Even when trapped in the darkness and trying to escape it, God knows where I am. Verse 11 consists of two parallel phrases: *darkness will cover me*, and *night will be light for me*. Verse 12 consists of three parallel phrases, indicating an x+1 poetic device: *darkness will not be dark, night will shine like the day*, and *darkness is as light*. The repetition three times is stronger that the repetition twice, indicating God's ability to see us clearly, even in the dark. Additionally, the pair, dark (חֹשֶׁךְ) and light (אוֹר), occurs three times together in three different forms: first as masculine nouns, then as verbs in the Hiphil stem, and again as feminine nouns. This suggests the strong contrast between the dark and light and, consequently, God's power to overcome the dark. It is clear that there is no hiding from God. No matter where, and no matter how dark, God knows us and sees us. This can be a frightening thought if not coupled with the truth that God also loves us.

NT Scriptures

John 2:24–25; Romans 8:35–39

Prayer

O LORD, "I love [you] not as the conductor of a distant orchestra that makes of the universe a band shell and space an acoustic device but God who takes me by the wrist firmly and points ahead." ("Maestro" in *Thumbprint in the Clay: Divine Marks of Beauty, Order and Grace* by Luci Shaw, 114)

Personal Notes and Prayers

Psalm 145:1–2

בְּכָל־יוֹם אֲבָרֲכֶךָּ וַאֲהַלְלָה שִׁמְךָ לְעוֹלָם וָעֶד: אֲרוֹמִמְךָ אֱלוֹהַי הַמֶּלֶךְ
וַאֲבָרֲכָה שִׁמְךָ לְעוֹלָם וָעֶד:

I will exalt you, my God the king, and I will bless your
name forever and ever, Every day I will bless you,
and my desire is to praise your name forever and ever.

Biblical Context

THIS PSALM, SET AS an acrostic and beginning each line with a different letter of the Hebrew alphabet, focuses on the exaltation of God as king and the reasons why such praise is warranted. In the ancient Near East, it was the king's responsibility to provide safe haven for his subjects to live. Later in the psalm, we see the psalmist declare that God, as king over all creation, does indeed provide for his subjects—not just in Israel, but for "every living thing" (Ps 145:6). Such provision merits the high praise of the psalmist. The verbs in the second halves of vv. 1–2 appear in the cohortative, indicating that the praise is an act of volition: the psalmist willingly desires to praise God on behalf of all that he has done. This worship takes place within the context of two different time references. The first is the time frame of one's entire life span ("for ever and ever")—and indeed, even surpassing one's own lifetime and passing into the generations beyond (Ps 145:4). There is so much praise to be ascribed to God that it simply cannot be contained within a single life span; it must go on and on as long as earthly creatures have breath (Ps 150:6). The second time reference views worship from the opposite end of the temporal spectrum and complements the first: worship takes place "every day." Praising God is the psalmist's daily habit, recognizing God's goodness in the everyday moments of life.

Life Application

The words "worship" and "praise" tend to bring to mind images of singing in a Sunday morning service. While this is absolutely an appropriate and good setting for worshipping God, we cannot limit our worship to a few hours of our week. Worship must be a daily practice, acknowledging the goodness of God's gifts that we receive moment to moment. Moreover, true worship requires more than our words; it demands our hearts and minds as well. Love is not simply an emotion, but a willful choice of commitment towards another. Like the psalmist, we must choose, day in and day out, to praise God for all that he has done. One of the best ways to practice this habit of worship is, like the psalmist, to recall and proclaim God's works to the next generation. Remembering God's work in the past will provide us all the more with reasons to praise God in the present and trust him in the future.

NT Scriptures

Luke 24:53; Romans 11:33–36; Ephesians 3:20–21; Revelation 5:9–13

Prayer

Our God the king, we praise you for every good and perfect gift that you provide for us. Help us to see more clearly the ways in which you are at work in our midst so that we might proclaim your mighty deeds all the more. May our worship be both a lifelong and daily commitment to acknowledge your praiseworthy character. Mold our hearts so that they might be more inclined toward worshipping you. And help us to proclaim your works to the next generation so that they, too, might recognize you as God and king.

Personal Notes and Prayers

Proverbs 9:17-18

מַיִם־גְּנוּבִים יִמְתָּקוּ וְלֶחֶם סְתָרִים יִנְעָם׃

וְלֹא־יָדַע כִּי־רְפָאִים שָׁם בְּעִמְקֵי שְׁאוֹל קְרֻאֶיהָ׃

Stolen water is sweet, and secret food is delightful, but he does not know that the shades are there, in the depths of Sheol are her invited guests.

Biblical Context

PROVERBS 9 PRESENTS A story of two hostesses and two banquets. In vv. 1–12, Lady Wisdom invites all "who are simple" (מִי־פֶתִי, v. 4) to come and partake of a lavish feast of wine, meat and bread. This feast represents the acquisition of knowledge and an abundant life that is open to anyone willing to pursue wisdom (beginning with a fear of YHWH and a knowledge of Him, v. 10). Then in vv.13–18, a second hostess—the Foolish Woman—makes her own call to those "who are simple" (מִי־פֶתִי, v.16). But her deception should be seen as a sham, for her supposed feast is marked only by a meal appealing to base instincts and bodily pleasures. Not only that, but the two words she uses to describe the meal ("stolen . . . secret") maliciously propose that there is an added enjoyment to a meal that must be hidden or gained through immoral behavior ("water" may also suggest sexual delights; cf. Pr. 5:15–20). And yet, anyone with a keen eye will see that the meal itself pales in comparison to the luxuriant meal of meat, wine, and bread in the decorative home of Lady Wisdom. The final verse (v. 18) reveals that all such people who dine with the Foolish Woman end in the depths of Sheol. Additionally, the use of "shades of the underworld" (רְפָאִים, v. 18) may indicate that even before death, there is a shallowness and emptiness to life for all who abandon Wisdom for Folly.

Life Application

The pleasures of sin are fleeting (Heb 10:25), but the depth of joy available to those who pursue God and his wisdom is unfathomable (1 Pet.

1:8). Only the naïve can be won over by the pathetic substitutes pandered by the Foolish Woman or Satan. All too often, however, we succumb to these base temptations. One way to say "no" to temptation and "yes" to wisdom is to saturate ourselves with God's Word *and* then to obey it. Faithfulness to God requires an experiential knowledge that his Word is true and that (only!) his path brings life.

NT Scriptures

Luke 12:15–21; Ephesians 5:17; Titus 3:3

Prayer

O LORD, how quickly we follow the foolish things of this world. LORD forgive us! Teach us to seek after divine wisdom and to walk in your ways all the days of our lives. Help us respond to your call to listen to your words and to apply your instructions to our lives. We give you all the glory!

Personal Notes and Prayers

Proverbs 12:18

יֵשׁ בּוֹטֶה כְּמַדְקְרוֹת חָרֶב וּלְשׁוֹן חֲכָמִים מַרְפֵּא׃

There is one who speaks thoughtlessly like the piercings of a sword But the tongue of those who are wise brings healing.

Biblical Context

THE BOOK OF PROVERBS is a collection of short, memorable sayings gleaned from observation of everyday life. This specific proverb is an antithetical proverb, contrasting one type of individual or situation against another. The antithetical proverb "attempts to commend wise conduct highly and make foolishness completely unappealing." In this case, the destruction wrought by the person who speaks carelessly is compared to the wise person whose words bring life and healing. The word "to speak thoughtlessly," indicates that this heedless discourse is not just a one-time occurrence. Instead, it indicates a character trait, an ongoing pattern of behavior. Using a simile, the author equates this thoughtless speech to the repeated stabbing of a sword. The violence of this comparison startles the reader, emphasizing the powerful significance of one's words. In contrast to this destruction, the tongue of the wise person brings healing.

Life Application

This proverb provides graphic imagery illustrating the result of the words we speak both for harm and for good. Thoughtless words brutally destroy the one to whom they are addressed. When one grasps the cruelty of this image, it serves as motivation to avoid this type of behavior. The chiastic structure of the proverb draws one's attention immediately forward to the next line. It is here that the poet emphasizes the preferred alternative. The tongue of the wise person delivers healing. While thoughtless words may tear down, the alternative is a character of wisdom out of which flow words that bring healing, and ultimately life, to the receiver. Are we, as believers, called to limit thoughtless words? Most definitely! Even more so, we are called to develop character such that the words that come out of our mouths offer healing and bring life to those around us. It is clear from this contrast that the reader is to shun thoughtless speech and seek to develop wisdom and practice the healing power of words.

NT Scriptures

James 3:3–11; 1 Peter 3:10

Prayer

O that our words would be filled with wisdom and righteousness. O that our lips would release healing and power. O that our mouths would be filled with your praise all day long, that we may draw men and women to your presence. Heal our lips LORD. Clean our mouth LORD. Make our tongue an instrument in your hands to speak of your glory on the earth.

Personal Notes and Prayers:

Proverbs 12:25

דְּאָגָה בְלֶב־אִישׁ יַשְׁחֶנָּה וְדָבָר טוֹב יְשַׂמְּחֶנָּה׃

Anxiety in a man's heart subdues it, but a good word makes it glad.

Biblical Context

CHAPTER 12 OF THE book of Proverbs continues a section of wise sayings that is attributed to Solomon. Unlike chapters 1 to 10, chapters 11 through 29 are not centered on any one central theme. Rather, each proverb may be taken as a stand-alone-saying. Nonetheless, words and the use of the tongue are a frequent topic throughout Proverbs.

Proverbs 12:25 can be classified as an antithetical proverb, in which the first clause is contrasted by the second clause. The Hebrew word for "anxiety" (דְּאָגָה) occurs only sparsely throughout the Hebrew Bible. The proverb brings to mind the scene in Joshua, in which the Reubenites, the Gadites, and the half-tribe of Manasseh build an altar at the edge of the Jordan out of "anxiety" that their sons would be excluded from the sons of the other tribes of Israel. In Joshua, the leaders of the ten tribes are concerned about the punishment that the transjordanian tribes could bring on the community. Interestingly, community is the solution that Proverbs 12 suggests in response to anxiety. For it is only in community that one finds encouragement.

Life Application

Anxiety weighs on people from every culture, gender and age, but recent sociological studies show that the average American suffers from anxiety much more frequently than those of other backgrounds. I am convinced that this is not only a result of the fast-paced environment that the American culture produces. Rather, the severe anxiety in North America should also be viewed as a result of the individualistic lifestyle that most Americans operate in. Whether anxiety stems from circumstances, relationships, or inward struggles, the solution is to find other people with whom you can truly share your life. Only then will you find the encouragement that you need.

NT Scriptures

Matthew 6:31; Luke 12:29; Romans 15:5

Prayer

O LORD, you came to show us the true meaning of "shalom" and to teach us our need for one another. Forgive us for living self-centered lives and for trying to manage our anxieties in our own human strength. How foolish we are to depend on ourselves when the Creator of Heaven and Earth seeks relentlessly to show us his power, strength and wisdom. LORD, have mercy on us!

Personal Notes and Prayers

Proverbs 16:9

לֵב אָדָם יְחַשֵּׁב דַּרְכּוֹ וַיהוָה יָכִין צַעֲדוֹ׃

*The heart of a man devises his own way,
but the LORD establishes his steps.*

Biblical Context

THE BOOK OF PROVERBS contains much wisdom for living in a fallen world, where the path is not always clear and the road is often filled with obstacles. Advice ranges from speaking only what edifies (Prov 25:11) to avoiding sins that lead to death (Prov 2:18). Believers are instructed to seek wisdom in order to know how to live a life that is righteous, just (Prov 1:2), and filled with knowledge and the fear of the LORD (Prov 1:7). The book of Proverbs teaches believers how to experience happiness, avoid disasters, trust God in all things, and live successfully in ways that please God in all spheres of life. Furthermore, the proverbs contrast the futility of human plans with the fruitfulness of divine strategies, and encourage readers to trust in a living God rather than trusting in human resources.

Life Application

As believers, we readily affirm the sovereignty of God. However, our trust in him is often tested with situations that are troubling, tragic and confusing. Roadblocks, relationship problems—personal and/or work related—tragedies and unexpected challenges often send us into states of anxiety and imbalance, as if success and failure in life were dependent solely upon us. This anxiety creates doubts in our minds and causes us to fear that we have stepped outside of God's will for our lives. Looking to God's sovereignty and trusting in his love is guaranteed to remove any fear and apprehension we may have during our times of trouble. Despite the confusion that results from our wrong choices, we can trust that God is in fact guiding our steps and will do so until we meet him face-to-face in heaven (Ps 48:14).

NT Scriptures

1 Corinthians 3:11–15; James 4:13–17

Prayer

O LORD, you have not left us without a road map. You have provided guidance, instruction, commandments through your Word. You open our eyes day after day to the path that you set before us. Help us trust in you every step of the way. Help us not rely on our own resources, but rather, may we trust in your unfailing provisions for the journey. Help us keep our eyes on you, our faithful Guide, our generous Provider, and our Everlasting God.

Personal Notes and Prayers

Proverbs 27:1

אַל־תִּתְהַלֵּל בְּיוֹם מָחָר כִּי לֹא־תֵדַע מַה־יֵּלֶד יוֹם׃

Do not boast about tomorrow,
for you do not know what a day may bring forth.

Biblical Context

A MAJOR THEME ADDRESSED in Scripture is that of humility. God hears the prayers of those who humble themselves, pray and seek his face (2 Chron 7:14). He crowns the humble with salvation (Ps 18:17; 149:4). He guides the humble in the way of righteousness (Ps 25:9) and sustains them in times of trouble (Ps 147:6). The prophet Micah speaks of what God requires of his people—that they act justly and love mercy and walk humbly with their God (Mic 6:8). However, we know that as sinful human beings, we struggle to remain humble. Our sinful nature causes us to boast of great things, to aggrandize ourselves, and to seek accolades from others. Pride is always there, ready to pounce and gain a foothold in our lives. The dangers of pride, hubris, and boasting are highlighted in almost every book of the Bible, and the consequences of arrogant behavior are severe. In Exodus 10:3, Pharaoh refused to humble himself before the God of Israel. Consequently, the plagues continued to afflict his people and even led to the death of the Egyptian households's firstborn. In Isaiah 10:12, God promises to punish the Assyrians for the pride of their hearts and the haughty looks in their eyes. God's people—Israel and Judah—did not escape divine judgment for their pride and arrogance. The Israelites deceived themselves, thinking that they were invicible because the Temple of the Lord was in their midst (Jer 7:4). They were convinced that their tomorrow was safe.

Life Application

Our self-confidence is often built on pride. We think we can run our lives on our own terms, and decide what tomorrow will bring. We are encouraged to strategize, and trust that our plans will succeed, but we must remember that God is the one who orchestrates our lives. God determines if there will be a tomorrow. God gives us the breath we need for each day. We should rise up every day, in awe that we are still alive, with another opportunity to serve the Lord. Our tomorrows belong to the Lord. They are gifts from God.

NT Scriptures

Matthew 6:34; James 4:13–14

Prayer

O Lord, help us put our trust in you, for each day, hour, minute and second belongs to you. Deliver us from our arrogance and pride, and restore us to a place of humility where we can commune with you. This day is a gift from you, and so is tomorrow. Have your own way in us.

Personal Notes and Prayers

Proverbs 28:13

מְכַסֶּה פְשָׁעָיו לֹא יַצְלִיחַ וּמוֹדֶה וְעֹזֵב יְרֻחָם:

The one who covers over his transgressions does not prosper, but the one who confesses and forsakes them receives compassion.

Biblical Context

IN THIS CHAPTER, ANTITHETICAL parallelism (the contrast of two opposite elements) predominates. Positive behaviors and their negative alternatives are laid out for the reader, whose responsibility it is to choose the path that leads to life. In verse thirteen, the contrast is clear. The failure of *one who covers his sins* is compared to the compassion and forgiveness received by *one who confesses and forsakes his transgressions*. The opposite of *covering* (מְכַסֶּה, "hiding, concealing") sin is not only *confessing* (מוֹדֶה "acknowledge") the transgression, but it requires the act of *forsaking* (עֹזֵב "abandoning, leaving"). The verbs *to confess* and *to forsake* form a hendiadys (one idea expressed with two words). The verbs highlight two important steps to freedom from sin: (1) acknowledgement of the transgression through confession, and (2) active and tangible movement away from iniquity through the abandoning of the sinful behavior. Without these two steps, sin continues to lurk in the shadow and continues to haunt the life of the sinner. Divine prosperity and compassion only accompany those who are willing to turn away from sin in word (מוֹדֶה *confess*) and in abandon their evil deeds (עֹזֵב *forsake*).

Life Application

As believers, we tend to fail at confession and we do even worse at repentance. In a culture of positive thinking and self-help, the concept of sin is an unpopular one. Yet in the biblical text, confessing and turning away from sin is life-giving. Humanity has been trying to hide from God since the garden of Eden, and yet, God extends to us an invitation to bring into the light willingly what he already knows, so that he may forgive and restore us. As the author of Hebrews states: *"No creature is hidden from his sight, but all are naked and exposed to the eyes of him to whom we must give account"* (Heb 4:13). God calls his people to a level of holiness beyond a passing "oops" response to sin. He want us to confess (literally "make known") our sin and then love him so much that we completely forsake it. May he give us the courage to stop hiding and run to the only One who can truly give life.

NT Scriptures

Ephesians 5:8–11; 1 John 1:9

Prayer

O LORD, how great is your mercy so freely given to us, sinners. We displease you, we sin against you, we transgress your covenant, and yet, you call us to repentance and forgive us our transgressions. Help us turn from our wicked ways and gaze into your face, without wavering and without shame. Purify our hearts, our minds, our lips and our hands. You desire for us to be holy as you are holy. Help us be quick to repent and to forsake our sinful ways. Infuse a deep desire in us to live holy lives, naked and open before you

Personal Notes and Prayers

Job 2:9–10

וַתֹּאמֶר לוֹ אִשְׁתּוֹ עֹדְךָ מַחֲזִיק בְּתֻמָּתֶךָ בָּרֵךְ אֱלֹהִים וָמֻת: וַיֹּאמֶר אֵלֶיהָ כְּדַבֵּר אַחַת הַנְּבָלוֹת תְּדַבֵּרִי גַּם אֶת־הַטּוֹב נְקַבֵּל מֵאֵת הָאֱלֹהִים וְאֶת־הָרָע לֹא נְקַבֵּל בְּכָל־זֹאת לֹא־חָטָא אִיּוֹב בִּשְׂפָתָיו:

Then his wife said to him, "How long will you keep hold of your integrity? Curse God and die!" But he said to her, "You speak like the foolish women do. Moreover, shall we receive only good from God but not receive the bad?" In all this, Job did not sin with his lips.

Biblical Context

SATAN MADE A WAGER with God to test Job's faith. He believed that if Job was stripped of everything—family, wealth, and health—he would turn away from God and even curse him. God allowed Satan to take Job's possessions, children and health. Afflicted, Job sat among the ashes of his life, grieving his loss and scraping his sores and boils with potsherd. His wife lost faith however and found no reason to remain faithful to a God who allowed calamity to come to her God-fearing husband. But Job remained loyal to God, convinced that there was a good reason for the disastrous events of his life. His three closest friends—Eliphaz the Temanite, Bildad the Shuhite and Zophar the Naamathite—came and tried to convince him that he must surely have done something wrong to incur this sort of misfortune. But Job remained firm that he had not sinned and in spite of his suffering, he remained obedient and faithful to God.

Life Application

Somehow, we seem to think that followers of Christ who read the Bible faithfully, pray regularly, and go to church weekly, should not be subjected to suffering. We should be blessed with abundance and live free from emotional and physical pain. However, nowhere in Scripture is this confirmed. Suffering is evident throughout the biblical text—OT & NT. Faithful servants of God mourned loved ones (Abraham, Gen 23:2; Bathsheba, 2 Sam 11:26; Mary & Martha, John 11:18-19), suffered injuries (Mephibosheth, 2 Sam 4:4; Jeremiah, Jer 10:19), experienced defeat (Joshua 7:6-7) and struggled emotionally (Elijah, 1 Kgs 19:3-4). According to Peter and James, suffering is beneficial for believers. Trials test our faith and tested faith develops perseverance and spiritual growth (Jas 1:2; 1 Pet 1:6-7). During challenging times, God wants us to be dependent on Him alone. Job suffered more than many of us. He lost all of his children in a single day. The death of one child is a major tragedy, so the death of ten children is enough to undo almost anyone forever. Job grieved, he cursed the day of his birth (Job 3:1-12), he mourned his loss, he wept over the foolishness of his friends, however, he remained faithful to God. He accepted that under a sovereign God, there had to be a reason for his suffering. His behavior should serve as a model for us: grieve and mourn, but ultimately keep your eyes on the LORD and wait on Him for in the grand narrative of life, there is a purpose for all things.

NT Scriptures

James 1:12; 5:11; 2 Thessalonians 1:3-4; 1 Peter 1:6-7

Prayer

O LORD, thank you for showing us that you are present in our times of suffering. As you were with Job, so are you with us. You walk with us when we hurt. You pick us up when we fall. You set us back on the path when we deviate. You remain with us in every situation of life. Thank you for remaining faithful to us in good times and in bad times.

Personal Notes and Prayers

Job 28:28

וַיֹּאמֶר לָאָדָם הֵן יִרְאַת אֲדֹנָי הִיא חָכְמָה וְסוּר מֵרָע בִּינָה:

Then he said to man, "See, the fear of the LORD, that is wisdom, and to turn aside from evil is understanding."

Biblical Context

JOB, A MAN OF integrity, uprightness, and one who feared God, has been struck with the worst of the worst. His family is dead, his land is destroyed, and he has fallen ill, yet, he does not charge God with his hatred. Even when his friends try to tell him that there must be something wayward and sinful in him, he knows that he has been blameless and upright. So why is this his story? What should he believe in the face of what seems to be a counter action of God? To help us understand, we get a strange interjection in the book of Job, a poem about wisdom. Job speaks about the ways in which people go looking for it as they would precious gems. Twice he asks where it shall be found, and twice it is said to be hidden. Yet, the end of chapter 28 gives us an answer that, instead, affirms Job. It is not so hard for wisdom to be found since God has revealed it to man. It is simply this–to fear God and turn aside from evil, both of which have already been used to describe Job in 1:1. Therefore, if Job already has these virtues, then this can only stand to teach us something about God. It teaches us that God knows what is happening in our lives and he can be trusted, we are purely responsible for remembering that and then acting in accordance with truth.

Life Application

The beauty of Job is that throughout all of his questions to God, he never once actually sinned against God. This means that we can approach God with our curiosities about our circumstances, although this would prove foolish because even if he answered, we cannot understand what God understands. Job's story also proves that we can pursue life and faith in full obedience and still come up against suffering and hardship. Yet, the joy is this, that in the dark, unfathomable moments, we can turn to a God who does know what is happening and because he loves us, he will work toward our good. We are only responsible for trusting him in both our faith and actions. It is wisdom, in our trials, to not give up following him even when life has become too hard and we perceive he has gone away. It is also wisdom to continue in obedience, the way we always have, because we know that he alone can restore us. If we do this, if we practice both wisdom and understanding as Job, we will come up with the most precious gem of all-hope.

NT Scriptures

James 3:13–18

Prayer

God of all creation, only you understand the ways of your world. We rely on you to make sense of our circumstances, whether or not we will understand them ourselves. Yet, we can have hope that you are good and that you have marked out all the paths for us to walk in. Help us to trust you, to have wisdom even when life is bleak and the battle has been hard-fought. Remind us of your goodness and teach us to continue in obedience. We love you, we need you. Amen.

Personal Notes and Prayers:

Job 31:15

הֲלֹא־בַבֶּטֶן עֹשֵׂנִי עָשָׂהוּ וַיְכֻנֶנּוּ בָּרֶחֶם אֶחָד׃

Did not the one who made me in the womb make him,
And the one who formed [both of] us in the womb?

Biblical Context

EARLY IN THE STORY of Job, Job loses his children, his land, and his property. The more Job seems to endure, the more difficult situations occur! His friends become convinced that Job has done something wicked, and all these terrible things are punishment for his crimes. Even his wife suggests that Job should curse God and be over with all this madness. But Job remains a righteous man. Chapter 31 is part of one of Job's many defenses of his righteousness against the examination of his friends. In the earlier part of the discourse, Job laments the loss of his position and the change of how he is perceived in the eyes of others—and with no reason! And so in an emotional appeal, he goes through an impressive list of his ethical credentials. He claims that he has maintained sexual integrity and economic integrity by calling curses upon himself if indeed he has acted outside of his high ethical paradigm. This verse comes in the context of how he has treated his household servants. Job wonders what he would be able to say to God if he had neglected the requests or complaints of his household servants. As a further appeal to his righteousness, he shows his reason for taking care of his servants. In this verse he asks rhetorically, whether or not the same one who made Job also made his servant? The answer is an emphatic yes! Job argues that treating even those under his supervision have been created totally equal, since the same God made both him and his servant.

Life Application

Today slavery is rightfully seen as a negative institution. While this passage regards Job's ethical actions toward his servants, he appeals to the same truth that underlies the emancipation movement. That is, God is the one who has made each one of us. We are essentially no different. There is a great equalizing principle here! Even in a context where some form of slavery was allowed, Job recognizes that in the most basic sense, humans in different positions are no different from each other. This applies to almost any situation of interpersonal interaction! We may have different cultural values, religious beliefs, political views, economic status, skin complexion, or any number of differences big and small. The core of our conflict is often our perceived differences. But at our core our similarities are more important than our differences. God gave us all life, and we all need him. Recognizing this minimizes even the most significant differences, and shows us that any dividing wall can be crossed. At the same time, this God who made us also knows the problems in the world are far greater than we could solve on our own. So he sent a savior to be like one of us. Jesus also was formed in the womb, just like you and me, and all of our neighbors and enemies. In taking on humanity, he began the work of breaking down the great barrier that separated us from relationship with God.

NT Scriptures

Matthew 22:39; Ephesians 6:9; James 2:1

Prayer

LORD, how easy it is to make our differences the most important thing about us. But you have shown us that you form us all. Help us remember who we are as we live in this world. Help us remember that we are all human beings made in your image. And teach us what it means that Jesus also took on the same flesh as the one we all wear.

Personal Notes and Prayers

Job 42:2

יָדַעְתָּ כִּי־כֹל תּוּכָל וְלֹא־יִבָּצֵר מִמְּךָ מְזִמָּה:
*You know that you are able to do everything
and no plan of yours can be thwarted.*

Biblical Context

JOB LIVED A RIGHTEOUS and blessed life for many years. In the prime of his life however, he experienced a series of disasters that robbed him of almost everything—property, children, friends, health. Disheartened by these major tragedies, his wife pled with him to curse God and die. His close friends—Eliphaz the Temanite, Bildad the Shuhite and Zophar the Naamathite—tried to comfort him and to prompt him to confess his sins so that his fortunes may be restored but Job could think of nothing evil he had done to deserve God's unjust affliction (Job 34:5). He countered the arguments of his comforters with strong theological statements (Job 12:13; 19:25–26; 21:22), and eventually blamed God for his misery (Job 24:1; 27:2; 30:11a, 20–23). In his anguish and frustration, Job talks as though God were not listening (Job 23:2–3, 8–9). His focus has turned completely away from God and is directed on himself. In his mind, he is right and God is wrong (Job 32:2). Having been falsely accused, God confronts Job in a long speech replete with rhetorical questions about creation, seasons, nature, astronomy, life, animals, justice, and humans. Confronted with this powerful divine discourse, Job acknowledges that he is just a frail human with limited wisdom and understanding. Job is truly humbled by God's rebuke. In Job 42, we can hear his repentant heart as he remembers that it is the Almighty God, the Creator of heaven and earth, whom he is addressing.

Life Application

Sometimes we live as though God is not really present in our midst, as though He cannot hear our complaints and conversations. Like Job, we speak as if God left the world unattended. We feel that we have to fend for ourselves and have to find a way to survive the challenges that we face on our own. Our faith, wisdom and understanding is limited. We make small plans and ask for small things because we believe that some things are too hard for God. We are fearful to follow God when He is leading us beyond our own human resources. God knows how to shake us from our small-minded mentality and remind us that He spoke the universe into being and is in full control of it. Our needs can undeniably never be too great for Him. We can think big, ask big and expect big things from life because our God is great and mighty.

NT Scriptures

Mark 10:27; Luke 1:37

Prayer

O LORD, yes you are great and mighty. Forgive us for limiting your power in our lives. Help us see your power and majesty. You are above all things. You do marvelous wonders we cannot understand. You surprise us with newness of life every day. You hold the world together. How we need you. How we long to trust you more for you alone are God. There is none like you.

Personal Notes and Prayers

Job 42:6

עַל־כֵּן אֶמְאַס וְנִחַמְתִּי עַל־עָפָר וָאֵפֶר׃

Therefore, I despise myself and repent in dust and ashes.

Biblical Context

AT THE CONCLUSION OF the book, Job repents of his hidden sin—pride—and declares "I despise myself and repent in dust and ashes." According to Job's friends, Job must have sinned and must deserve this divine retribution. Throughout his speeches, Job's ego rears its ugly head in full-blown hubris. He considers himself innocent, undeserving of God's punishment and concludes that it was God who was unjust. It may have been his overly pious and successful lifestyle that led to his arrogance and to the self-assured conviction that he was innocent in all things. God confronts Job with his ignorance and lack of knowledge. If Job cannot understand how God oversees nature, how could he even begin to understand how he maintains human affairs? With no direct answer to his pressing question, *why am I suffering*, Job repents in utmost humiliation.

Life Application

The book of Job is about theology; it is about God and not about Job. Job did not have the full picture of his circumstances, and his friends had it completely wrong. In the end, there was a sacrifice for Job's friends, because of what they said about God. Thinking wrongly about God can be sinful. In our western world of systematic theologies, we ought to learn from the book of Job that God is a lot bigger than our nice little heavenly god. In our world of quick answers, maybe we ought to allow God to provide his wise counsel on all matters, instead of filling in blanks with our own inadequate understanding of him. If science has revealed anything, it has revealed how little we know about God and his creation. If we cannot understand the natural world in which we live, how are we to understand God and eternity? Ultimately, we are left in Job's position.

We must trust God even if we do not understand life events, suffering, and injustice. We may not have all the answers and we may struggle with God, but in the end, we must choose to trust that he is a good God, and that his ways are perfect.

NT Scriptures

1 Corinthians 2:1–5; James 1:2–8; 3:13–18

Prayer

O LORD, teach us to seek you in all matters of life. Teach us to seek your wisdom and humility. Do not let us be corrupted by pride and arrogance, for we know that pride comes before destruction and a haughty spirit before a fall (Prov 16:18). Help us consult with you at all times and surrender to your will whatever it may be. Help us especially when the road is not clear and your voice is muffled. Help us trust in you at all times.

Personal Notes and Prayers

Song of Songs 8:6

שִׂימֵנִי כַחוֹתָם עַל־לִבֶּךָ כַּחוֹתָם עַל־זְרוֹעֶךָ כִּי־עַזָּה כַמָּוֶת אַהֲבָה
קָשָׁה כִשְׁאוֹל קִנְאָה רְשָׁפֶיהָ רִשְׁפֵּי אֵשׁ שַׁלְהֶבֶתְיָה:

Put me like a signet on your heart, like a seal on your arm,
for love is as mighty as death, Jealousy is fierce as Sheol;
its sparks are sparks of fire, a raging flame.

Biblical Context

THE LOVER AND HER Beloved have thoroughly recounted what comes of the individual found under the influence of true love. Now, the Lover calls upon her Beloved to make her a *seal* or a *signet* (חוֹתָם) on his heart. In biblical times, a *seal* was a cylindrical device worn around the neck or an engraved signet ring worn on the finger. It was as good as one's own signature. The stamp from a personal *seal* was equivalent to a person's own presence. The Lover's longing to be a *seal* around her Beloved's neck speaks of her strong desire to be one with him, to share his life, to partake of his pain and comfort, and to join in his victories and defeats. The simile that follows likens the Lover's yearning to two of the most powerful forces known to humans—love and jealousy. Neither of these can be avoided. The love spoken of in this text implies irrevocability. Just as the grave—personified by Sheol—does not relent to hold onto the deceased, neither are the mighty flames of true love capable of being quenched. These are flames that transcend all earthly passions, having their origin in the Creator himself.

Life Application

Such words cannot but evoke passion in the reader. But in a culture that has little assurance of anything but in the reality of death, the hope of transcendent love that conquers all remains a fairytale that few ever realize. Even if one has the fortune to find such love, the cruelties of life and the corruption of humanity will often distort it until it is unrecognizable.

It is in this hopeless context that the Creator of love declares that true love is not only as strong as death. It is so much more. It has conquered death. Only one who holds the hope of eternal life through Jesus Christ can take delight in this truth that true love is so much more than romance. It is a burning fire and a raging flame from God that consumes both the Lover and the Beloved. And death will never be able to quench it.

NT Scriptures

Romans 5:8; 8:35–39; 1 John 3:14–20

Prayer

O LORD, to love and be loved with such passion. Oh, if only we believed that love is the strongest force in the universe. You have proven it. You have loved us more than anyone ever could. You have conquered death for us through your love. Teach us LORD to love with such powerful love.

Personal Notes and Prayers

Ruth 1:16–17

וַתֹּאמֶר רוּת אַל־תִּפְגְּעִי־בִי לְעָזְבֵךְ לָשׁוּב מֵאַחֲרָיִךְ כִּי אֶל־אֲשֶׁר
תֵּלְכִי אֵלֵךְ וּבַאֲשֶׁר תָּלִינִי אָלִין עַמֵּךְ עַמִּי
וֵאלֹהַיִךְ אֱלֹהָי: בַּאֲשֶׁר תָּמוּתִי אָמוּת וְשָׁם אֶקָּבֵר כֹּה יַעֲשֶׂה יְהוָה לִי
וְכֹה יֹסִיף כִּי הַמָּוֶת יַפְרִיד בֵּינִי וּבֵינֵךְ:

*Then Ruth said, "Do not plead with me to abandon you, to
return from going after you for where you go I will go and
where you stay I will stay. Your people are my people and
your God is my God. Where you die I will die and I will be
buried. Thus may YHWH do to me and more
for only death will separate you and me.*

Biblical Context

AFTER MOVING TO MOAB with her family to flee a famine in Israel, Naomi's husband and two sons died. Naomi found herself alone, away from home, in the lowly state of widowhood. When she heard that the famine in Canaan had ended, she decided to return to her ancestral home in Bethlehem. Her two daughters-in-law—Orpah and Ruth—followed along but, aware that she could not provide for them, Naomi insisted they return to their families of origin. Orpah and Ruth refused and cried, "*No! We will go with you.*" Eventually, Naomi persuaded Orpah to take the seemingly wise course and return home to her family. However, Ruth, passionately repeated her decision to stay with Naomi, almost to the point of breaching the bounds of propriety. She tells Naomi "*Please, stop pressing me to abandon you*" (1:16, אַל־תִּפְגְּעִי־בִי לְעָזְבֵךְ). The verb "to press" or "to plead with" appears as a negative command, making it a strong appeal to Naomi. Ruth's passionate declaration of loyalty to Naomi is expressed with three sets of statements. The first set—"*I will go*" & "*I will stay*"—and the last set—"*I will die*" & "*I will be buried*"—are statements of determination regarding Ruth's future. Embedded in this series of statements is a phrase that indicates her emphatic intention—"*your people are my people and your God is my God."* Ruth ends her plea to Naomi with an oath to remain with Naomi until death.

Life Application

Out of love, Ruth cast her lot with Naomi. Her commitment was not one that she would break easily. As promised, she would follow Naomi whether or not Naomi was willing to agree with her. The question of giving up all that she had to follow Naomi had already been decided when she first chose to give her love and loyalty to Naomi and her son. Verse 18 indicates that Naomi stopped trying to convince Ruth after she heard her strong declaration. Naomi then embraced Ruth's friendship and loyalty. However, Naomi was a bitter old woman at this point. She may well have simply ignored Ruth but undoubtedly, Ruth would have continued to follow her, bound by her loyalty to her husband's family. In the NT, Jesus did not consider equality with God something to grasp, but out of love, gave up everything for those He was committed to save. Then, before He died he admonished the disciples to love one another in that same manner, to be committed to one another's welfare without abandoning or giving up on those whom the LORD placed in their lives. The type of covenantal love shown by Jesus is to be emulated by his followers. It is unconditional, without boundaries and never ending.

NT Scriptures

John 15:12–17; Philippians 2:1–11; 1 John 5:16–17

Prayer

O LORD, teach us to love as you love us. Empty us of selfishness and help us be true imitators of Christ. As our LORD gave his life for us, may we learn to sacrifice ourselves for the sake of others and may we seek to follow in his footsteps wherever He leads.

Personal Notes and Prayers

Ruth 3:10–11

וַיֹּאמֶר בְּרוּכָה אַתְּ לַיהוָה בִּתִּי הֵיטַבְתְּ חַסְדֵּךְ הָאַחֲרוֹן מִן־הָרִאשׁוֹן לְבִלְתִּי־לֶכֶת אַחֲרֵי הַבַּחוּרִים אִם־דַּל וְאִם־עָשִׁיר:
וְעַתָּה בִּתִּי אַל־תִּירְאִי כֹּל אֲשֶׁר־תֹּאמְרִי אֶעֱשֶׂה־לָּךְ כִּי יוֹדֵעַ כָּל־שַׁעַר עַמִּי כִּי אֵשֶׁת חַיִל אָתְּ:

Blessed are you by YHWH, my daughter! You have done well; the latter kindness is kinder than the first, not going after the young men, either poor or rich. And now, my daughter, do not be afraid; all that you say I will do for you, for all my people's elders know that you are a heroic woman.

Biblical Context

BOAZ TOOK NOTICE OF Ruth's faithfulness toward her mother-in-law. Ruth was an impoverished widow and foreigner, and very likely did not see herself as a hero. However, Boaz and the town elders certainly did. They respected her strength of character so as to liken her to earlier and contemporary military heroes who were powerfully and highly regarded. Boaz had observed Ruth's assiduous work ethic and her quiet faith (see chapter 2). Modern translations identify her (אֵשֶׁת חַיִל; cf. Prov 31:10) as "a woman of excellence" (NASB), "a woman of noble character" (NIV), "a worthy woman" (NRSV, ASV), and "a virtuous woman" (NKJV). Used by itself, the word חַיִל is often refers to an army (e.g., 2 Sam 8:9; 2 Kgs 6:15; 25:1). In reference to Boaz (Ruth 2:1), the expression אִישׁ גִּבּוֹר חַיִל is translated "a worthy man" (ESV), "a man of great wealth" (NASB, NKJV), "a man of standing" (NIV), "a prominent rich man" (NRSV), and "a mighty man of wealth" (ASV). Even if Ruth was a powerless in her own eyes, completely dependent on Naomi, God transformed her into a woman of great valor, one who is compared to military men and to prominent and affluent biblical characters.

Life Application

Stories make us stronger. When my parents left me at home alone for the first time and I was afraid, I crawled into my bedroom closet and pretended to be Jeremiah in the cistern. His example gave me courage. Ruth's faithfulness is a powerful example for us. Simply by loving her mother-in-law and by doing what was necessary to survive, she became a paradigm of valor and strength for her contemporaries and for us. Her story of bravery and faithfulness can shape our imagination and help us develop the courage necessary to become a model of strength and valor for our contemporaries.

NT Scriptures

Hebrews 11; Romans 15:4; 2 Timothy 1:5; Titus 2

Prayer

LORD, thank You for Your grace in making the feeble strong, and for giving us examples to follow when we need courage. Help us to be such examples for others.

Personal Notes and Prayers

Lamentations 3:22–23

חַסְדֵי יְהוָה כִּי לֹא־תָמְנוּ כִּי לֹא־כָלוּ רַחֲמָיו: חֲדָשִׁים לַבְּקָרִים רַבָּה
אֱמוּנָתֶךָ:

*God's steadfast love does not end (and) his compassionate
deeds are never exhausted. They are new every morning.
Your faithfulness is great.*

Biblical Context

JERUSALEM IS LAID WASTE. Her brightest youth are in exile. Those left behind are starving. All cultic practices and social norms are swept away by war. The poet writes an extended acrostic poem, lamenting how his once great home is stripped bare of her glory and made into a mockery. He acknowledges that her sin has brought her these consequences. Although Babylon is more evil than Judah, God used her to bring holy retribution upon his own people. For sixty-five verses, the poet details the destruction and despair of his people. Then, suddenly, a ray of resolute hope shines through. *"The steadfast love of the LORD never ceases. His compassion is new every morning."* The poet remembers his theology. We cannot tell what prompted this particular stubborn assertion, that the brightness of the morning follows the darkness of night, but we thank him for remembering the character of God. For in these few verses, all of God's suffering people, in every generation and everywhere, are told they can hope in the most difficult of circumstances. After all, it is the LORD himself who is our portion, our light, and our salvation.

Life Application

How difficult would it be to redefine our Christianity if our faith were taken away from us? Maybe our reputation would be ruined—whether or not we deserved it. Perhaps we would come to a crisis of faith where we would have to redefine our very life's foundation. Are we determined, like the poet of old, to lift up our eyes to God daily and confess that his mercies never fail? In the hours of darkness, do we look for the sun to rise in the morning? With God, there is always hope. He will bring us through the most dire of circumstances and restore us. He will never leave us nor forsake us, whether in darkness or in the light. We can trust in him.

NT Scriptures

Matthew 14:25–27; Romans 8:18–27

Prayer

O LORD, we thank you for giving us hope in our times of lament and mourning. You hold us, protect us and preserve us. You infuse strength in us and lift us up when we fall down. You encourage us by your Spirit and renew us daily. We depend on you. We trust in you, even when your presence seems far away. We know that you are there for you are faithful.

Personal Notes and Prayers

Ecclesiastes 7:21–22

גַּם לְכָל־הַדְּבָרִים אֲשֶׁר יְדַבֵּרוּ אַל־תִּתֵּן לִבֶּךָ אֲשֶׁר לֹא־תִשְׁמַע אֶת־עַבְדְּךָ מְקַלְלֶךָ׃

כִּי גַּם־פְּעָמִים רַבּוֹת יָדַע לִבֶּךָ אֲשֶׁר גַּם־אַתְּ קִלַּלְתָּ אֲחֵרִים׃

Do not pay attention to all the words people might say, lest you hear your servant cursing you. For your heart knows that you have cursed others many times yourself.

Biblical Context

IN THIS GENERAL SECTION of wisdom sayings, Qohelet poses the picture of a man who has his illusion burst. Imperious and oblivious, the man moves through his day with serenity until he is arrested by the unguarded words of a servant. To have servants one must have wealth or social prominence. Maybe this is a landowner or queen or nomadic chieftain. This person is accustomed to deference from others. He has power, but words have power too, even the chance complaints of a servant. To this attitude Qohelet admonishes humility. We might have expected a call to simply have a "thick skin". He could have left it at this: "You are in a position of authority so get used to the fact that not everyone is going to respect or love you all the time." God has a better way. Qohelet's counsel goes deeper by appealing to the heart to recognize the weakness of his own humanity. "Let a little air out of your inflated view of yourself and recall your own indiscretions with words", he suggests. By deflating his pride and reflecting on his own lapses, he can free himself to extend some grace to a frustrated person.

Life Application

Words are important expressions of our attitudes and none of us is perfect in what we say. Often in hearing the words of others we act self-righteously and scandalized. "I cannot believe he said that to me!" "How dare she bring that up!" I think we can afford to get off our high horses and join the rest of humanity. By humbly recalling our own careless words, we can more easily cut others slack when their private words get back to us. This is particularly helpful for those of us in leadership. It is easy to mistake the habitual outward deference of others for real acceptance of all our policies and personalities. Show a little grace when you hear potshots and grumbling from the disappointed and disillusioned. Remember, we sometimes express our disappointment and disillusionment in the same way.

NT Scriptures

Ephesians 4:29–32; James 3:2

Prayer

O LORD, keep us humble and meek. Help us forget about ourselves and concentrate on those you place on our paths. Teach us to respond to the needs of our neighbors and friends. Keep us from becoming judgmental and disrespectful. Help us be a witness for you in all we say and do.

Personal Notes and Prayers

Esther 4:14

כִּי אִם־הַחֲרֵשׁ תַּחֲרִישִׁי בָּעֵת הַזֹּאת רֶוַח וְהַצָּלָה יַעֲמוֹד לַיְּהוּדִים מִמָּקוֹם אַחֵר וְאַתְּ וּבֵית־אָבִיךְ תֹּאבֵדוּ וּמִי יוֹדֵעַ אִם־לְעֵת כָּזֹאת הִגַּעַתְּ לַמַּלְכוּת׃

For if you remain completely silent at this time, relief and deliverance will arise for the Jews from another place but you and your father's house will perish. Who knows if for a time such as this you have come to the kingdom?

Biblical Context

THE BOOK OF ESTHER may include one of the best examples of God's intervention in human affairs. In the Esther story, the Jewish people were threatened with annihilation as a result of Haman's deep anti-Semitic sentiments and a conspiracy he orchestrated against the Jews of Persia. Without God averting this slaughter, extermination would certainly come to the Jews on the thirteenth day of the month of Adar (Esth 3:13). Esther, who had become King Ahasuerus's wife, served as Queen at a pivotal point in Jewish history. Following the decree of Haman against the Jews, she was presented with the opportunity to change the course of events and prevent the annihilation of her own people. Mordecai, Esther's uncle, realized that Esther's true destiny was to be instrumental in the salvation of her own people and said to her "Who knows if for a time such as this you have come to the kingdom?" Mordecai challenged Queen Esther to intervene before the king on behalf of the Jews in order to save them from Haman's sinister plot. It was an extremely risky plan but Esther accepted the challenge. She showed tremendous courage and came into the presence of the king uninvited. Fully aware of the possible consequences, she said: "If I perish, I perish" (Esth 4:16). What a great sacrifice she was willing to make, to lay down her life for the salvation of her own people!

Life Application

What is your purpose and destiny as a believer in the LORD? Have you been called to be an instrument in God's hands for such a time as this? How would you respond if you were asked to lay down your life for your brothers and sisters? Would you understand the importance of the calling on your life and act accordingly? You may not be a king or a queen with power to change the course of history, but you have been empowered by the Holy Spirit to establish the kingdom of God on this earth. There is no greater calling in life but to do the will of the Father wherever he leads. God has not given us a spirit of fear but of power, of love and of a sound mind (2 Tim 1:7). What an honor it is to serve God in the world today and to obey his will with courage and purpose. There is no greater calling!

NT Scriptures

Luke 19:40; 1 Corinthians 16:13; Philippians 1:20

Prayer

O LORD, you have empowered us to serve you and to do great things on this earth. You have not left us alone but you sent your Holy Spirit to lead us, teach us, reveal your will to us and enable us to do your will. Help us focus on you and you alone. Help us decrease so that you may increase in us. Give us the courage to follow you to the ends of the earth and to fulfill your will.

Personal Notes and Prayers

1 Chronicles 16:34

הוֹדוּ לַיהוָה כִּי טוֹב כִּי לְעוֹלָם חַסְדּוֹ׃

*Oh, give thanks to YHWH for He is good,
for his mercy endures forever.*

Biblical Context

THE POEM FOUND IN this chapter (also found in Ps 105:1–15) was sung or recited in response to the installation of the Ark of the LORD in the City of David (Jerusalem). This event was so significant in David's life (see 2 Sam 6:12–23) that David bellowed in ecstatic delight a poem honoring the God of Israel. David cried out, "Sing praises to the LORD. Tell of his wonders. Give glory to his holy name. Tell of his salvation and declare his glory among the nations. Give thanks to the LORD for he is good and his steadfast love endures forever. And bless the LORD from everlasting to everlasting!" (1 Chr 16:8–36). David understood that the Ark of the LORD represented the tangible presence of God in the midst of his people. He understood that without the presence of God in the City of David, there would be no protection from surrounding enemies. David knew God. He knew that God was good and merciful. He knew that he could rely on God's goodness and mercy, and for this, he was extremely thankful. Therefore, he begins his public declaration of praise with these truths—that God is good and merciful—themes that are repeated throughout Scripture, more specifically in Psalms 106:1, 107:1, 118:1, 29, and 136:1. David was deeply aware that God's goodness and mercy could be relied upon at all times by those who love him.

Life Application

It seems appropriate to highlight this verse since it appears so many times in Scripture, both in the psalter and elsewhere. This short phrase is simple but it highlights two major aspects of God's attributes. First, God is intrinsically good and second, he is eternally merciful. If you stop to reflect on the implications of these two divine characteristics—goodness and mercy—it is hard to think of more important divine qualities. If God is not good, then what could we reasonably expect of him? Would he exercise perfect justice with us and be truly concerned about us? If God is not good, our sense of security is severely damaged. As for his mercy, what would he be like if he were not merciful to us? Would we be able to stand under his judgment if God were not truly forgiving and loving? If we fail to recognize God's goodness and mercy towards us, how can we find any comfort or assurance in this life or in the one to come?

NT Scriptures

Ephesians 2:4–7; 1 Peter 1:3–5

Prayer

O LORD, you are our Shepherd, we shall not want. You make us to lie in green pastures and lead us beside quiet waters. You restore our soul and guide us in paths of righteousness for your name's sake. Even though we walk through difficult times, we fear no evil for you are with us. Your rod and staff comfort us. You provide for us in the presence of our enemies. You anoint our head with oil and our cups overflow. And most of all, your goodness and your mercy follow us all the days of our lives and because of this, we will dwell in your house forever.

Personal Notes and Prayers

1 Chronicles 22:18a–19a

הֲלֹא יְהוָה אֱלֹהֵיכֶם עִמָּכֶם וְהֵנִיחַ לָכֶם מִסָּבִיב ... עַתָּה תְּנוּ
לְבַבְכֶם וְנַפְשְׁכֶם לִדְרוֹשׁ לַיהוָה אֱלֹהֵיכֶם

*Has not the LORD your God been with you and granted
you rest from surrounding (foes) . . . Now, set your heart
and your soul to seek the LORD your God.*

Biblical Context

DAVID DESIRED TO BUILD the Temple for the LORD in Jerusalem, but since he had shed much blood during his reign as king, God chooses his son Solomon to accomplish the noble task. Since David was advanced in years, he could have retired from active duty and watched his son do the work. But instead, he chooses to remain fully engaged and prepares the way for Solomon to build the Temple. He secures the location in Jerusalem and orders the leaders of Israel to help his son. David charges them to seek the LORD with all their heart and soul first, and then to begin to build the sanctuary. This was a time of relative political tranquility with the neighboring states and the work of maintaining the Ark of the Covenant had been reduced since it was safely in the hands of the Israelites. Now was the perfect time for David to step back, retire, relax and let his son fulfill this important task. David understood that his mission would only be fully accomplished on earth when his day would come to join his forefathers in death.

Life Application

Retirement is viewed by the secular world as a period of well deserved rest and a time to live-it-up, free from work. It is natural for seasoned individuals who have labored for decades to want to retreat to a restful pasture for a season after spending decades in the workforce. But for believers, there is always more work to do and the yoke must be carried until the end. Jesus speaks of a special yoke uniquely designed for those who believe in Him. Jesus says, "Come to me, all you who are weary and burdened, and I will give you rest. Take my yoke upon you and learn from me, for I am gentle and humble in heart, and you will find rest for your souls. For my yoke is easy and my burden is light" (Matt 11:28–30 NIV). The secular world would suggest that the elderly should lay down their yoke, but as believers, we are admonished to pick up the yoke of Christ, the only one under which we find true rest.

NT Scriptures

Hebrews 4:8–9

Prayer

O LORD, how often we feel overwhelmed by the work at hand and the demands of this life. We strive to do more work and fail to keep Sabbath. We do our daily labor and fail to engage you in the process. We work tirelessly in our own strength. Forgive us and help us look to you for the divine rest that soothes the soul.

Personal Notes and Prayers

1 Chronicles 29:14

וְכִי מִי אֲנִי וּמִי עַמִּי כִּי־נַעְצֹר כֹּחַ לְהִתְנַדֵּב כָּזֹאת כִּי־מִמְּךָ הַכֹּל וּמִיָּדְךָ נָתַנּוּ לָךְ:

Yet who am I and who are my people that we are able to freely offer so much? For everything is from you; from your hand we have given to you.

Biblical Context

GOD CALLED SOLOMON TO build a Temple for his name's sake. Although David had desired to be the one to manage the building of God's sanctuary, God did not want someone whose career had been soaked in blood to handle the task. Yet despite not being granted what he wanted, David was astonished that God had extended grace to him and had chosen his family to lead Israel. With a spirit of humility, thankfulness, and gratitude, David commissioned his son Solomon to oversee the construction of the Temple in Jerusalem. United under Solomon's leadership, all Israel vowed to make the Temple great and to honor God with their possessions. David gave gold, iron, silver, and bronze from his personal treasury. Israel followed suit and donated giant quantities of gold, silver, bronze, and iron for the construction of the Temple. Everyone who had precious stones donated them to the Temple's treasury. After the leaders had gathered to present their gifts to the LORD, David offered a prayer of consecration before the assembly. The first half of the prayer honors God for his splendor; the second half recognizes that Israel's success—from her escape out of Egypt to these recent events—would have been impossible without the blessings of the LORD. God provided all that was needed and more.

Life Application

Everything we have is a gift from God. This includes talents and abilities, the qualities about us that seem to make us able to do good for the Kingdom of God. As God uses who we are—our vocations, our personalities, our relationships, our material resources, our abilities—we easily forget that the good things we do are rooted in the fact that we are a reflection of his goodness, possessing positive attributes insofar as God has given them to us. Sometimes we forget that our gifts are for not for ourselves but for God's glory. Oftentimes we forget that our gifts are from God. We are inadequate in ourselves to please God and fulfill his will. God provides the power and wisdom we need to accomplish his tasks. He alone is worthy of the complete devotion of our talents and resources. He alone is the source of our talents and resources. For from Him and through Him and to Him are all things. What abilities has God given you? Have you surrendered them to God? Ask God to show you the special gifts He has given you and use them for his glory.

NT Scriptures

Romans 11:33–36; 1 Corinthians 3:5–17

Prayer

O LORD, to Israel you gave covenants (e.g., Exod 20; 2 Sam 7; Jer 31:31), land (e.g., Gen 28:4; 35:12; Josh 24:13; Judg 6:9), riches (e.g., Deut 8:18; 1 Kgs 3:13; 10:23), wisdom (e.g., Gen 41:39; Deut 34:9; 1 Kgs 4:29), favor (e.g., Gen 39:21; Exod 3:21; Ps 30:5), and health (e.g., Prov 4:22; Isa 38:16; Jer 30:17). You are the Giver of life. We owe all things to you, even our very breath. We thank you LORD for extending your hand to us so generously. Teach us to be generous towards those who are around us.

Personal Notes and Prayers

2 Chronicles 5:14

וְלֹא־יָכְלוּ הַכֹּהֲנִים לַעֲמוֹד לְשָׁרֵת מִפְּנֵי הֶעָנָן כִּי־מָלֵא כְבוֹד־יְהוָה אֶת־בֵּית הָאֱלֹהִים:

The priests were not able to stand to minister before the cloud because the glory of the LORD had filled the house of God.

Biblical Context

SOLOMON HAD JUST FINISHED building the Temple, furnishing it with all the implements needed for priestly duties. The culminating event of that day was bringing the Ark of the Covenant from the tent in the City of David to the Most Holy Place in the Temple. After such a long time of not having a permanent place for the Ark, and the Ark traveling from place to place for centuries, God allowed Solomon to complete his father's vision and mandated him to build the Temple as a dwelling place for his name. At this point in her history, Israel was united with her religious and political center in Jerusalem. This place was significant for her national identity until this point, but now that the sanctuary was ready, communal life would be richer and even more meaningful. On the day of the dedication service, a great miracle happened. Summoned by king Solomon, the elders of Israel gathered at the Temple and as the Levitical singers's voices resounded in praise to God, God's presence became so intense that the priests were not even able to stand, for the "glory of the LORD filled the house" (5:14). This was a sign that the Israelites would experience God in a new way, in a way they had never experienced God before.

Life Application

As believers, we seek to do the LORD's work everyday. However, sometimes we feel like slowing down and even quitting. It is at such times that we should be quiet and listen to the voice of the LORD for it is possible that God simply wants to manifest himself miraculously to us to show us that all of our efforts are worthless without him. Solomon completed the work of the Temple, and the irony is that the priests could not even do what they were called to do in the Temple that day because God manifested himself in a way that was far beyond what they expected. Simply by being in the presence of God, they experienced God in a new and powerful way. God had taken over the Temple and even prevented the priests from performing their task. It goes to show that sometimes, being in the presence of God is more important than doing the LORD's work. If we do not pause from time to time to experience God, our work will be in vain, even if we are doing the work of the sanctuary.

NT Scriptures

John 15:5–8; Acts 2:1–4; 10:1–4, 30–31

Prayer

O LORD, give us strength for the task as we serve you faithfully in this world. Walk with us as we labor to establish your Kingdom. Show us the day of rejoicing that is before us. Give us hope that we will see you face-to-face in the fullness of your glory. How we yearn for the great day of rejoicing when we finally enter into your complete manifest presence in heaven.

Personal Notes and Prayers

2 Chronicles 20:17a

לֹא לָכֶם לְהִלָּחֵם בָּזֹאת הִתְיַצְּבוּ עִמְדוּ וּרְאוּ אֶת־יְשׁוּעַת יְהוָה
עִמָּכֶם יְהוּדָה וִירוּשָׁלַם

*This battle is not for you to fight. Take your positions
and stand still; and see the deliverance of the LORD
on your behalf, O Judah and Jerusalem.*

Biblical Context

KING JEHOSHAPHAT AND THE people of Judah were threatened by a great multitude of Moabites, Ammonites and warriors from Edom and Aram. When Jehoshaphat was informed of the threat, the enemy had already reached Ein-Gedi on the Dead Sea. The king's initial response was to fear however, he quickly declared a fast throughout Judah and turned to God in prayer. He stood before all the people and declare aloud, "You rule over all the kingdoms of the nations. Power and might are in your hand and no one can stand against you" (vv.6–7). He further proclaimed: "We will stand before this House and before you for your name is in this house, and cry to you in our distress and you will hear and deliver us" (v.9). In like posture, all of Judah—with their infants, their wives and their children—stood before the LORD and worshipped. Then the priest Jahaziel proclaimed: "Do not be afraid or be dismayed because of this great multitude, for the battle is not yours, but God's" (v.15). Echoing the words of Moses when trapped at the edge of the Sea of Reeds (Exod 14:13), Hazael added, "You will not fight this battle. Take your stance, stand up and see the salvation of the LORD" (v.17). In this passage, the directive is intensified with the use of both הִתְיַצְּבוּ "take a stand" and עִמְדוּ "stand." Why so much standing? Based on Jehosaphat's declarations, we know they did not stand in defiance or arrogance. Instead, they stood before their LORD of Hosts in humility and reverence. They did not stand to hear the LORD's signal to attack, rather, they were to stand and watch as *He* did the fighting and as *He* brought them salvation.

Life Application

We often face circumstances out of our control. In Judah's plight, the LORD provided יְשׁוּעָה ("salvation"). In the face of danger, temptation, or dire circumstances, we can also trust in the יְשׁוּעָה ("salvation") of the LORD and respond in worship and prayer as King Jehoshaphat and the Judahites did. As directed by the LORD, we need to take our stand and equip ourselves with the weapons of warfare listed in Ephesians 6—the belt of truth, the breastplate of righteousness, the gospel of peace, the shield of faith, the helmet of salvation, and the sword of the Spirit which is the Word of God—so that, when the day of evil comes, we may be able to stand our ground against the enemy of our soul.

NT Scriptures

Ephesians 6:10–17

Prayer

O LORD, you are our shield and buckler, our refuge and strength, our fortress and the rock of our salvation. You are a very present help in time of trouble. You go before us and protect us. You surround us on every side with your presence. You give us victory against our enemies and you set our feet on a solid rock.

Personal Notes and Prayers

2 Chronicles 25:9

וַיֹּאמֶר אֲמַצְיָהוּ לְאִישׁ הָאֱלֹהִים וּמַה־לַּעֲשׂוֹת לִמְאַת הַכִּכָּר אֲשֶׁר נָתַתִּי לִגְדוּד יִשְׂרָאֵל

וַיֹּאמֶר אִישׁ הָאֱלֹהִים יֵשׁ לַיהוָה לָתֶת לְךָ הַרְבֵּה מִזֶּה׃

Amaziah said to the man of God, "But what do I do about the one hundred talents that I have paid for the Israelite troops?" The man of God replied, "the LORD can give you more than that."

Biblical Context

AMAZIAH HAD INVESTED AN exorbitant amount of money (nearly four tons of silver) in order to ensure Judah's victory against Esau's descendants (the Edomites) by purchasing one hundred thousand warriors from Israel to add to his army of three hundred thousand. What seemed to be a logical and strategic investment of power, was instead a seal of certain defeat. The man of *God* (אִישׁ הָאֱלֹהִים) warned Amaziah that because God was not with Israel, He would not be with any army consisting of Israelites: "Even if you go and fight courageously in battle, God will overthrow you before the enemy, for God has the power to help or to overthrow." In order to receive God's help, Amaziah had to let go of one hundred thousand men and one hundred talents of silver. Because Amaziah obeyed the man of God, dismissed the Israelite warriors, and marched boldly into battle despite his reduced resources, God gave him victory. However, Amaziah, of the line of David and coming Messiah, foolishly brought home the *gods* (הָאֱלֹהִים) of the defeated Edomites and worshipped them.

Life Application

None of our efforts, strategies, or investments matter if God is not in them. Amaziah was asked to let go of what he thought he needed in order to survive and win the battle. He did so, but he quickly returned to foreign resources (*the gods of other people*) in order to ensure future victories. What about us? Are we ready to let go of our own resources and fulfill God's plan with only the resources He provides? If so, are we willing to let go of our own strategies and walk in the light of the LORD, without resorting to foreign resources? God's provisions are more than we will ever need to accomplish his work.

NT Scriptures

Philippians 3:7–11

Prayer

O LORD, help us rely on You only—on your resources, your timing, your promptings, your Spirit and nothing else. Help us let go of our own human strategies and help us establish our lives on your Word only. Should we deviate from the path, we ask for your forgiveness and restoration. Please keep foreign gods far from us and fill the screens of our lives with your presence.

Personal Notes and Prayers

List of Scriptures for Devotionals:

Genesis 1:3, 26–27; 5:24; 11:4–5, 31; 15:1, 8; 16:13; 19:22; 22:12 (2x); 24:58; 26:4–5; 32:29, 30; 37:10: 38:1–26; 45:8a; 49:10; 50:17, 20

Exodus 1:15, 17; 3:5, 7; 4:12–13, 31; 5:22–23; 12:23, 48; 14:13–14, 27b; 15:3; 19:5–6; 20:20; 31:12–13; 33:15–16, 17; 34:1

Leviticus 16:30; 20:7; 23:3

Numbers 6:24–26; 11:12–13, 14; 12:7–8; 14:24; 18:20; 22:28

Deuteronomy 4:7, 37; 6:4–5, 13; 7:21; 8:7, 11; 9:5–6; 10:12–13; 15:15a; 23:25–26; 32:10–11

Joshua 1:5; 3:4; 5:9; 7:10–11a; 10:14; 20:2–4; 23:14; 24:15

Judges 2:11; 3:15a; 7:7; 13:18

1 Samuel 3:10; 7:3, 12; 12:10, 24; 14:6; 17:33; 20:14–15a

2 Samuel 6:20–21; 9:13; 12:23 22:47; 23:16; 24:10

1 Kings 15:4–5; 18:21 (2x), 27; 21:29

2 Kings 5:2b, 11; 6:16–17; 10:2–3; 19:14, 19

Isaiah 2:5; 9:5; 28:9–10; 30:15; 40:11, 15–17; 41:10; 42:8; 43:19; 49:6; 53:3; 55:1; 61:3

Jeremiah 1:7–8; 9:23–24; 20:8–9

Ezekiel 18:31–32; 34:2b

Hosea 2:16 [14];

Joel 2:16

Amos 4:12

Jonah 1:16; 2:9 [8]; 4:10–11

Micah 6:8

Nahum 1:3, 7 (2x)

Habakkuk 1:2–4, 11; 2:4, 14; 3:3, 17–18 (2x), 18 (2x)

Zephaniah 2:3; 3:17 (2x)

Haggai 1:13

Zechariah 1:3; 3:1–2; 4:6; 9:9 (2x)

Malachi 2:7; 3:6 (2x), 24 [4:6]

Psalms 8:2; 12:4; 19:2, 8, 13; 23; 24:3–4, 7–8; 27:1, 13–14; 29:2; 33:13–14; 39:5, 7–8; 46:11 [10], 11–12; 69:17; 91:1; 103:11–12; 111:2–3; 119:18; 121:3–4, 5, 7; 139:11–12; 145:1–2

Proverbs 9:17–18; 12:18, 25; 16:9; 27:1; 28:13

Job 2:9–10; 28:28; 31:15; 42:2, 6

Song of Songs 8:6

Ruth 1:16–17; 3:10–11, 22–23

Lamentation 3:22

Ecclesiastes 7:21–22

Esther 4:14

1 Chronicles 16:34; 22:18a-19a; 29:14

2 Chronicles 5:14 20:17a; 25:9

www.ingramcontent.com/pod-product-compliance
Lightning Source LLC
Chambersburg PA
CBHW071311150426
43191CB00007B/579